MANAGEMENT ACCOUNTING

Dr. R. JAYACHANDRAN

Asst. Professor,
Dept. of Commerce,
Govt. Arts College,
Udhagamandalam.

Himalaya Publishing House

MUMBAI • NEW DELHI • NAGPUR • BENGALURU • HYDERABAD • CHENNAI • PUNE • LUCKNOW • AHMEDABAD • ERNAKULAM • BHUBANESWAR • INDOSRE • KOLKATA

First Edition : 2011

Published by : Mrs. Meena Pandey
for **HIMALAYA PUBLISHING HOUSE PVT. LTD.,**
"Ramdoot", Dr. Bhalerao Marg, Girgaon, **Mumbai - 400 004.**
Phone: 022-2386 01 70/2386 38 63, Fax: 022-2387 71 78
Email: himpub@vsnl.com
Website: www.himpub.com

Branch Offices:

New Delhi : "Pooja Apartments", 4-B, Murari Lal Street, Ansari Road, Darya Ganj, New Delhi - 110 002. Phone: 23270392, 23278631, Fax: 011-23256286

Nagpur : Kundanlal Chandak Industrial Estate, Ghat Road, Nagpur - 440 018. Phone: 0712-2738731, 3296733, Telefax : 0712-2721215

Bengaluru : No. 16/1 (Old 12/1), 1st Floor, Next to Hotel Highlands, Madhava Nagar, Race Course Road, Bengaluru - 560 001. Phone: 080-22281541, 22385461, Telefax: 080-22286611

Hyderabad : No. 3-4-184, Lingampally, Besides Raghavendra Swamy Matham, Kachiguda, Hydrabad - 500 027. Phone: 040-27560041, 27550139, Mobile: 09848130433

Chennai : No. 85/50, Bazullah Road, T. Nagar, Chennai - 600 017. Phone: 044-28144004,28144005

Pune : First Floor, "Laksha" Apartment, No. 527, Mehunpura, Shaniwar peth, (Near Prabhat Theatre), Pune - 411 030. Phone: 020-24496323/24496333

Lucknow : Jai Baha Bhavan Church Road, Near Manas Complex and Dr, Awasthi Clinic Aliganj, Lucknow - 226 024 Phone: 0522-2339329, 4068914, Mobile: 09305302158, 09415349385, 09389593752

Ahmedabad : 114, "SHAIL", 1st Floor, Opp. Madhu Sudan House, C.G.Road, Navrang Pura, Ahmedabad – 380 009. Phone: 079-26560126, Mobile: 09327324149, 09314679413

Ernakulam : 39/104 A, Lakshmi Apartment, Karikkamuri Cross Rd., Ernakulam, Cochin – 622011, Kerala. Phone: 0484-2378012, 2378016, Mobile: 09344199799

Bhubaneswar : 5 Station Square, Bhubaneswar (Odisha) - 751 001. Mobile: 09861046007, E-mail: orissa@himpub.com

Indore : Kesardeep Avenue Extension, 73, Narayan Bagh.Flat No. 302, IIIrd Floor, Near Humpty Dumpty School, Narayan Bagh, Indore (M.P.) 452 007 Mobile: 09301386468

Kolkata : 108/4, Beliaghata Main Road, Near ID Hospital. Opp. SBI Bank, Kolkata – 700 010, Mobile: 09910440956

DTP by : **HPH, Editorial Office, Bhandup (Shubhangi)**
Printed by : **Bengaluru**

PREFACE

The need of accounting knowledge is getting importance since there is a stiff competition among business concern. Sufficient knowledge and strength is required to face the competition at National and International level. This can be developed and improved by increasing the accounting knowledge. Management accounting that emerged as an independent branch of study about half a century ago has experienced phenomenal changes in the theoretical content as well as in the tools being used for financial decisions and their implementation. The aim of this book is to acquaint professionals and students of business studies, which will make them more conversant with the conceptual foundation. The concepts and tools are presented in a lucid language and simple sentence. To have a better grasp of the subject, a large number of objective type questions and test problems have been given at the end of each chapter.

The present text-book is experienced to serve better towards the interest of the readers who are not well versed in the terminology of business studies.

The unparalleled features of this book are:

- The subject is presented in a self-explanatory manner, so that even self-taught students may not feel difficult in understanding it.
- Objective type questions and numerical problems are provided at the end of each chapter.
- The present text is reader-friendly.
- All possible patterns of questions and problems of major universities are included in this book.
- This text is based on the Syllabus of B.Com., B.Com. (CA), B.Com. (IT), B.Com (e-commerce) of Bharathiar University.

I would like to express my sincere gratitude to the members of the Himalaya Publishing House especially ***Mr.Niraj Pandey***, whose in-depth knowledge of publishing have been invaluable in the development of the text. I also thank ***Mr.Yaswanth Rao,*** Chennai Branch Manager, Himalaya Publications and ***Mr. A. Anandaraj,*** Area Sales Executive for their wholehearted support and co-operation in bringing out this book elegantly and in time.

Critical comments and constructive suggestions for improving the content of this book will be greatly appreciated.

DR. R. JAYACHANDRAN

SYLLABUS

B.Com. B.Com. (IT) / B.COM. (CA)

Bharathiar University, Management Accounting, Semester IV

UNIT I

Management Accounting – Meaning, Objectives and Scope – Relational between Management Accounting, Cost Accounting and Financial Accounting – Need and Significance of Management Accounting.

UNIT II

Analysis and Interpretation of Financial Statements – Ratio Analysis – Significance of Ratios and Long-term Financial Position – Profitability – Uses and Limitations of Ratios.

UNIT III

Working Capital – Concepts, Kinds, Importance of Working Capital – Working Capital Requirements and their Computation – Sources of Working Capital – Fund Flow and Cash Flow Analysis.

UNIT IV

Cost-Volume – Profit Analysis – Marginal Costing and Break-even Analysis – Managerial Applications of Marginal Costing – Significance and Limitations of Marginal Costing.

UNIT V

Budgeting and Budgetary Control – Definition, Importance, Essentials, Classifications of Budget – Master Budget, Preparation of Different Budget – Steps in Budgetary Control.

(**Note :** 40% mark theory and 60% mark for problem.)

CONTENTS

CHAPTER 1

MANAGEMENT ACCOUNTING

MANAGEMENT ACCOUNTING

Accounting involves the collection, recording, classification and presentation of financial data for the benefit of management and outside agencies such as shareholders, creditors, bankers and the government. Accounting is the recording of the business transactions with the purpose of managing the concern in a better way and also reporting the true financial position of business operations.

Definition of Accounting

Eri L. Kohlen defines accounting as, "the procedure of analysing, classifying and recording transactions in accordance with a preconceived plan for the benefit of – (a) providing a means by which an enterprise can be conducted in orderly fashion, and (b) establishing a basis for reporting the financial condition of enterprise and the results of its operations".

Classification of Accounting

Accounting can be broadly classified into three categories as mentioned below:

1. Financial accounting
2. Cost accounting, and
3. Management accounting.

Meaning of Financial Accounting

Financial accounting may be defined as-the science and art of recording and classifying business transactions and preparing summsaries of the same for determining year end profit or loss and the financial position of the concern. It is that part of accounting which is employed to communicate the financial information of a business unit.

The object of financial accounting is to find out the profitability and to provide information about the financial position of a concern.

MANAGEMENT ACCOUNTING

Management accounting is a system of accounting concerned with the internal reporting or information to the management for planning and controlling operations, decision-making on special matters and formulating long range plans. Management accounting involves collecting, classifying, analysing, interpreting and presenting all accounting informations which are useful to the management.

Definition of Management Accounting

H.M. Treasury: In the words of H.M. Treasury, management accounting refers to, "The application of accounting knowledge to the purpose of producing and of interpreting accounting and statistical informations designed to assist management in its functions of promoting maximum efficiency and in formulating and co-ordinating future plans and subsequently in measuring their execution".

The Institute of Charted Accountants of India: The view of the institute is, "Such of its techniques and procedures by which accounting mainly seeks to aid the management collectively have come to be known as management accounting".

The Institute of Cost and Works Accountants of India: Defines management accounting as, "a system of collection and presentation of relevant economic information relating to an enterprise for planning, controlling and decision-making".

The American Accounting Association: According to the American Accounting Association, "Management accounting includes the methods and concepts necessary for effective planning, for choosing among alternative business actions and for control through the evaluation and interpretation of performances".

Characteristics of Management Accounting

The following are the main characteristics of management accounting :

1. **Providing Accounting Information:** Management accounting involves the presentation of information in a way it suits the managerial needs. Management accounting is a service function and it provides necessary information to different levels of management.
2. **Taking Corrective Actions:** The recording of actual performance and comparing it with targeted figures will give an idea of the management about the performance of various departments. In case there are deviations between the standard set and actual performance of various departments, corrective measures can be taken at once.
3. **Use of Special Techniques and Concepts:** The techniques usually used include financial planning and analysis, standard costing, budgetary control, marginal costing, project appraisal, control accounting etc. The type of technique to be used will be determined according to the situation and necessity.
4. **Taking Important Decisions:** Management accounting helps in taking various important decisions.The implications of various alternative decisions are also taken into account while taking important decisions.

5. **No Fixed Norms Followed:** No specific rules are followed in management accounting as in the case of financial accounting. So, every concern has its own rules and by-rules for analysing the data.
6. **Increase in Efficiency:** The performance appraisal will enable the management of pinpoint efficient and inefficient spots. An effort is made to take corrective measures to that efficiency is improved at all levels.
7. **Supplies Information and not Decision:** The management accounting supplies information to the management. The decisions are taken by the top level management.
8. **Concerned with Forecasting:** The management accounting is concerned with the future. It helps the management is planning and forecasting.
9. **Internal Use:** The information provided by management accounting is exclusively for the use of management for internal purposes only.
10. **Flexibility in Presentation of Information:** In management accounting there are no prescribed formats for presentation of information to the management. Hence, there is high flexibility.

Scope of Management Accounting

The following facts of management accounting are of great significance and form the scope of this subject.

1. **Financial Accounting:** Financial accounting deals with the historical data. The recorded facts about an organisation are useful for planning the future course of action. Though planning is always for the future but still it has to be based on the past and present data. So, management accounting is closely related to financial accounting
2. **Cost Accounting:** Cost accounting provides various techniques for determining the cost of manufacturing products or the cost of providing services. Cost accounting also helps in finding out economical and non-economical fields of production. So, cost accounting is an essential part of management accounting.
3. **Financial Management:** Financial management is concerned with the planning and controlling of the financial resources of the firm. It deals with rising of funds and their effective utilisation. Its main aim is to use business funds in such a way that the earnings are maximised. Finance has become so much important for every business undertaking that all managerial activities are connected with it. Thus, financial management has become an important task of management accounting.
4. **Budgeting and Forecasting:** Budgeting means expressing the plans, policies and goals of the enterprise for a definite period in future. The targets are set for different departments responsibility is fixed for achieving these targets. Forecasting is a prediction of what will happen as a result of a given set of circumstances. Both budgeting and forecasting are useful for management accounting in planning various activities.
5. **Inventory Control:** The control of inventory will help in controlling the cost of products. The management will need effective inventory control for controlling stock. The management

accountant will guide the management as to when and from where to purchase and how much to purchase. So, the study of inventory control will be helpful for taking managerial decision.

6. **Reporting to Management:** One of the functions of management accountant is to keep the management informed of various activities of the concern so as to assist in controlling the enterprise. The reports are presented in the form of graphs, diagrams, index numbers or other statistical techniques so as to make them easily understandable. The reports may be monthly, quarterly, and half-yearly. The reports may cover profit and loss statement, cash and fund flow statement, stock reports, absentee reports and reports on orders in hand, etc.

7. **Interpretation of Data:** The management accountant interprets various financial statements to the management. These statements give an idea about the financial and earning position of the concern. These statements may be studied in comparison to the statements of earlier periods or in comparison with the statements of similar other concerns.

8. **Control Procedures and Methods:** Control procedures and methods are needed to use various factors of production in a most economical way.The studies about cost, relationship of costs and profits are useful for using economic resources efficiently and economically.

9. **Internal Audit:** An internal audit system is necessary to judge the performance of every department. The actual performance of every department and individual is compared with the predetermined standards. The internal audit helps the management in fixing responsibility of different individuals.

10. **Tax Accounting:** The management is informed about the tax burden from Central Government, state government and local authorities.Various tax returns are to be filed with different departments and tax payments are to be made in time. Tax accounting comes under the purview of management accountant's duties.

11 **Office Service:** The management accountant will be expected to deal with office services like data processing, filing, copying, duplicating, communicating, etc.

12. **Management Information System:** In a large scale organisational information is preserved and supplied to the management with the help of computers. This information which is usually recorded and supplied by the accountants manually, is processed and communicated with the help of computers.

Objectives of Management Accounting

The functions of management accounting are given hereunder:

(i) **Planning and Forecasting:** One of the important functions of the management accounting is to help the management in planning for short-term and long-term periods and also in making forecasts for the future. Management accountants use various techniques such as budgeting, standard costing, marginal costing, fund flow statements, probability and trend ratios, etc., for fixing targets. These techniques are used in various activities.

(ii) **Modification of Data:** Management accounting helps in modifying the accounting data. The information is modified in such a way that it becomes useful for the management. If production figures are needed, these can be classified according to product, quality, time taken by the manufacturing process, rate of production, etc. The management accountant classifies and modifies information according to the requirements of the management.

(iii) Financial Analysis and Interpretation: The management accountant analyses and interprets financial data in a simple way and present it in a non-technical language. He gives facts and figures about various policies and evaluates them in monetary terms. He gives his opinion about various alternative courses of action so that it becomes easy for the management to take a final decision.

(iv) Facilitates Managerial Control: The standards of various departments and individuals are set up. The actual performance is recorded and deviations are calculated. It enables the management to access the performance of everyone in the organisation and thus facilitates effective management control.

(v) Communication: Management accounting establishes communication within the organisation and also with the outside world. The management accountant prepares reports for the benefits of different levels of management and employees. The activities of the concern are communicated to outsiders such as bankers, investors, creditors, government agencies, etc., who are the stakeholders.

(vi) Use of Qualitative Information: Management accountant collects and uses qualitative information also. While preparing a production budget the management accountant may not only use past production figures, but also he may relay on the assessment of persons dealing with production, productivity reports, consumer surveys and many other business documents.

(vii) Co-ordinating: The management accountant acts as a co-ordinator among different financial departments through budgeting and financial reports.

(viii) Helpful in Taking Strategic Decisions: Management accounting supplies analytical information regarding various alternatives and the choice of management is made easy. These decisions may be regarding stoppage of production, replacement decisions, expansion or diversification of works, etc.

(ix) Supplying Information to Various Levels of Management: The management accountant feds information to different levels of management, so that further decisions are taken. The supply of adequate information at the proper time will increase the efficiency of the management.

(x) Helpful in Organisation: Every management is concerned with the establishment of cost centres, preparation of budgets, and preparation of cost accounts and fixing of responsibilities for different functions. All these aspects are helpful in setting up an effective and efficient organisational framework.

(xi) Helpful in Tax Administration: Management accounting helps in accessing various tax liabilities and depositing the correct amount of taxes with the concerned authorities. Tax administration is carried on with the advice and guidance of the management accountant.

Differences Between Management Accounting and Financial Accounting

Basis	*Management Accounting*	*Financial Accounting*
Object	Management accounting is essential to help the management in formulating policies.	The object of financial accounting is to record various transactions with the purpose of maintaining accounts and to know the financial position and to find out the profit or loss at the end of the financial year.
Nature of Data Used	In management accounting projected or estimated figures are used.	In financial accounting actual figures are used.
Subject Matter	Management accounting deals separately with different units, departments and cost centres.	It is concerned with assessing the results of the whole business.
Compulsion	The management is free to use or not to use management accounting.	The preparation of financial accounts is compulsory in certain undertakings, while these are a necessity in others.
Precision	In management accounting, no emphasis is given to actual figures. The approximate figures are considered more useful than the exact figures.	In financial accounting, only actual figures are recorded and there is no room for using approximate figures.
Reporting	Management accounting reports are meant for internal use only. These are prepared for the benefit of different levels of management.	Financial accounts are prepared to find out the profitability and financial position of the concern. These reports are used for the outsiders like bankers, investors, shareholders, government agencies, etc.
Description	Management accounting uses both monetary and non-monetary events. The competition in the market, impact of political changes, a situation of trade cycles and such other factors are also considered in management accounting, though these cannot be measured in monetary terms.	Only those things which can be measured in monetary terms are recorded in financial accounting. Anything which cannot be recorded in figures is outside the scope of financial accounting.
Quickness	Reporting of management accounting is very quick. Management is fed with reports at regular intervals.	Reporting of financial accounting is slow and time-consuming. Profit and loss accounts and balance sheet are prepared at the end of the financial year. The management is able to know the profitability and financial position only after the preparation of the final accounts.

Accounting Principles.	No standard principles are followed in management accounting.	Financial accounts are strictly governed by the generally accepted principles and conventions.
Period	The management accountant supplies information from time-to-time during the whole year. There are no specific period for which the management accounts are prepared.	Financial accounts are prepared for a particular period. Profit and loss account is generally for one year.
Publication	Management accounting statements are prepared for the benefit of the management only and these are not published.	Financial accounts like profit and loss account and balance sheet are published for the benefit of the public. Under the Companies Act, every registered company is supposed to supply a copy of profit and loss account and balance sheet to the Registrar of Companies at the end of the financial year.
Audit	Management accounts cannot be audited. They are not based on the actual figures and projected data are also used in management accounting. So, it is not possible to get management accounts audited.	Financial accounts can be got audited. Under the company law, auditing of financial account is compulsory.

Cost Accounting vs. Management Accounting

Basis	*Cost Accounting*	*Management Accounting*
Object	The object is to record the cost of producing a product or providing a service.	The purpose is to provide information to the management for planning and co-ordinating the activities of the business.
Scope	Cost accounting deals primarily with cost ascertainment.	The scope of management account is very wide.
Nature	Cost accounting uses both past and present figures.	Management accounting is generally concerned with the projection of figures for future.
Data used	Only quantitative aspects are used in cost accounting.	Management accounting uses both quantitative and qualitative information.
Development	The development of cost accounting is related to industrial revolution.	The management accounting has been developed only in last 30 years.

Advantages of Management Accounting

The following are the advantages of management accounting:

1. **Measurement of Efficiency:** The targets of different department are fixed in advance and achievement of these goals is used as a tool for measuring their efficiency.

2. **Proper Planning:** Budgets are prepared department-wise and then a master budget is prepared for the whole organisation. The workload of every individual is fixed in advance. The activities of the concern are thus planned in a systematic manner.

3. **Measurement of Performance:** In standard costing, standards are determined and then the actual cost is compared with the standard cost. It enables the managements to find out deviations between the standard cost and the actual cost. The performance will be good if the actual cost does not exceed the standard cost. Budgetary control system too helps in measuring the efficiency of all employees.

4. **Maximising Profitability:** The thrust of various management technique is to control cost of production and increase the efficiency of each and every individual in the organisation. The steps for controlling cost are able to reduce the cost of production. The profits of the enterprise are maximised with the help of management accounting system.

5. **Improves Service to Customers:** The cost control devices employed in the management accounting enable the reduction of prices. The quality of products becomes good because quality standards are predetermined. The customers are supplied with goods at reasonable prices.

6. **Effective Management Control:** The tool and techniques of management accounting are helpful to the management in planning, co-ordinating and controlling activities of the concern. The setting of standard and assessing actual performance regularly enables the management to have "management by exception".

7. **Helps in Decision-making:** The management accounting helps in decision-making such as pricing, making or buy, acceptance of additional orders, selection of suitable mix, etc.

8. **Facilitates Communication:** The management accountant prepares reports for the benefits of different levels of management and employees. The activities of the concern, are communicated to outsiders such as bankers, investors, creditors, government agencies, etc.

Limitations of Management Accounting

1. **Based on Accounting Information:** The management accounting is based on data supplied by the financial and cost accounting. If financial data is not reliable, then management accounting will not provide correct analysis.

2. **Lack of Knowledge:** Every management should be conversant with accounting principles, statistics, economics, principles of management, etc., and only then management accounting can be effectively utilised. Deficiency in knowledge of any of these subjects limits the use of management accounting.

3. **Intuitive Decision:** Sometimes, management may avoid a lengthy course of deciding things and may take an easy course of arriving at decisions using intuition. Intuitive decision limits the usefulness of management accounting.

4. **Not an Alternative to Administration:** It does not provide an alternative to administration. The tools and technique of management accounting provide only information and not decisions.

5. **High Cost:** Introduction of management accounting system is a costly affair and can be used by big concerns only. Smaller units cannot afford to use this system because of the heavy cost.

6. **Evolutionary Stage:** Management accounting is only in a development stage and it has not yet reached a final stage. This creates doubts about the utility of management accounting.

7. **Personal Bias:** There is every likelihood of personal bias of analysis and interpretation. Personal prejudice and bias affect the objectivity of decisions.

8. **Resistance from Staff:** The installation of management accounting involves basic changes in organisational set up. New rules and regulations are also required to be framed which affect a number of personnel and hence there is a possibility of resistance from employees.

TEST YOUR KNOWLEDGE

Choose the Best Answer

1. Financial accounting deals with

   (a) Determination of cash

   (b) Determination of profits

   (c) Determination of prices

2. Financial accounts record only

   (a)Actual figures (b) budgeted figures (c) standard figures

3. The term management accountancy was first used in

   (a)1910 (b) 1939 (c) 1950

4. The use of management accounting is

   (a) Compulsory (b) optional (c) obligatory

5. Management accounting relates to

   (a) Recording of accounting data

   (b) Recording of costing data

   (c) presentation of accounting data

Short Answer Questions

1. Define management accounting.
2. What are the limitations of financial accounting?
3. Mention various functions of management accounting.
4. What is the scope of management accounting?
5. Enumerate the functions of management accounting.

Essay Type Questions

1. In what way management accounting is differ from financial accounting?
2. What are the advantages of management accounting?
3. What are the limitations of management accounting?
4. In what way management accounting is differ from cost accounting?
5. Explain management accounting and state the objectives of management accounting.
6. Explain the nature and scope of management accounting.

☆☆☆

CHAPTER 2

FINANCIAL STATEMENT AND RATIO ANALYSIS

MEANING AND CONCEPT OF FINANCIAL ANALYSIS

Financial Statements are the results of the accounting process which begins with recording of transactions. The accounting process involves recording, classifying and summarising business transactions in a systematic way. Financial statements relate to the third process, viz., summarising.

The term 'Financial Analysis' is also known as analysis and interpretation of financial statements. It refers to the process of determining the financial strengths and weaknesses of a firm by establishing strategic relationship between the items of the balance sheet, profit and loss account and other operative data.

DEFINITION

According to **Metcalf and Titard**, "It is a process of evaluating the relationship between component parts of a financial statement to obtain a better understanding of a firm's position and performance".

Objectives

- To estimate the earning capacity of a firm
- To estimate the financial position and financial performance of a firm
- To determine the long-term liquidity as well as solvency of a firm
- To determine the debt capacity of a business
- To decide about the future prospects of a firm.

METHODS OR DEVICES OF FINANCIAL ANALYSIS

A number of methods or devices are used to study the relationship between different statements. The following methods of analysis are generally used :

- Comparative statements
- Trend analysis
- Common-size statements
- Fund flow analysis
- Cash flow analysis
- Ratio analysis
- Cost-volume-profit analysis

Comparative Statements

The comparative financial statements are statements which show the financial position of a firm at different periods or time. The elements of financial position are shown in a comparative form so as to give an idea or the financial position at two or more periods. Any statement prepared in a comparative form will be covered in comparative statements. Generally, two financial statements are prepared in a comparative form for financial analysis purposes. They are :

(1) Comparative Income Statement, and (2) Comparative Balance Sheet

(1) **Comparative Income Statement:** This statement gives an idea of the progress of a business over a period of time. The changes in absolute data in money values and percentages can be determined to analyse the profitability of the business.

***Illustration 1*:** From the following profit and loss accounts of Soundarya Ltd., for the years ended 31st December, 2008 and 2009, you are required to prepare to a comparative income statement for the years 2008 and 2009.

Profit and Loss Account

Particulars	*2008 (Rs.)*	*2009 (Rs.)*	*Particulars*	*2008 (Rs.)*	*2009 (Rs.)*
To cost of goods sold	600	750	By Net Sales	800	1,000
To adm. exp.	20	20			
To selling expenses	30	40			
To Net Profit	150	190			
	800	**1,000**		**800**	**1,000**

Solution:

Comparative Income Statement

For the years ended 31st December, 2008 and 2009

Particulars	*2008 (Rs.)*	*2009 (Rs.)*	*Increases/ Decreases of amount*	*Increases/ Decreases of (%)*
Net Sales	800	1,000	+200	+25
Less: Cost of goods sold	600	750	+150	+25
Gross Profit	200	250	+50	+25
Less: Operating Expenses				
Administrative	20	20	-	-
Selling	30	40	+10	33.3
Total Operating Expenses	50	60	+10	+20
Operating Profit	**150**	**190**	**+40**	**+20.7**

The above statement shows that though the sales have gone up in 2008, the rate of gross profit remains at 25%. The cost of goods sold and its percentage remain at 75%. Administrative expenses remain the same, but selling expenses have been increased. This is due to the increases in sales. The rate of operating profit has also increased. On the whole the profitability of the firm is good.

(2) Comparative Balance Sheet: The comparative balance sheet analysis is the study of the trend of the same items, group of items and computed items in two or more balance sheets of the same business enterprise on different dates. The changes in periodic balance sheet items reflect the conduct of a business. The changes can be observed by a comparison of the balance sheet at the beginning and at the end of a period and these changes can help in forming an opinion about the progress of an enterprise.

***Illustration 2*:** The following are the balance sheets of a concern for the years 2008 and 2009. Prepare a comparative balance sheet and study the financial position of the concern.

Balance Sheet as on 31st December **Rs.'000**

Liabilities	*2008 (Rs.)*	*2009 (Rs.)*	*Assets*	*2008 (Rs.)*	*2009 (Rs.)*
Equity Share Capital	600	800	Land and Building	370	270
Reserve and Surplus	330	222	Plant and Machinery	400	600
Debentures	200	300	Furniture	20	25
Long-term loans on mortgage	150	200	Other fixed assets	25	30
			Cash	20	80
Bills Payable	50	45	Bills Receivable	150	90
Creditors	100	120	Debtors	200	250
Other Current Liabilities	5	10	Stock	250	350
			Prepaid Expenses	-	2
	1,435	**1,697**		**1,435**	**1,697**

Solution:

Comparative Balance Sheets for the years ending 31/12 /2008 and 2009.

Particulars	*31.12.2008 (Rs.)*	*31.12.2009 (Rs.)*	*Increases/ Decreases of amount*	*Increases/ Decreases of (%)*
Assets:				
Current Assets				
Cash	20,000	80,000	+60,000	+300
Bills receivable	1,50,000	90,000	-60,000	-40
Sundry Debtors	2,00,000	2,50,000	+50,000	+25
Stock	2,50,000	3,50,000	+10,000	+40
Prepaid expenses	-	2,000	+2,000	-
Total current assets	**6,20,000**	**7,72,000**	**+1,52,000**	**+24.52**
Fixed Assets:				
Land and Buildings	3,70,000	2,70,000	-1,00,000	-27.03
Plant and Machinery	4,00,000	6,00,000	+2,00,000	+50
Furniture and Fixtures	20,000	25,000	+5,000	+25
Other fixed assets	25,000	30,000	+5,000	+20
Total fixed assets	**8,15,000**	**9,25,000**	**+1,10,000**	**+13.49**
Total assets	**14,35,000**	**16,97,000**	**+2,62,000**	**+18.26**
Current liabilities				
Bills payable	50,000	45,000	-50,000	-10
Sundry Creditors	1,00,000	1,20,000	+20,000	+20
Other current liabilities	5,000	10,000	+5,000	+100
Total Current Liabilities	**1,55,000**	**1,75,000**	**+20,000**	**+12.9**
Long-term liabilities				
Debentures	2,00,000	3,00,000	+1,00,000	+50
Long-term loans on mortgage	1,50,000	2,00,000	+50,000	+33
Total Current and Long-term liabilities	**5,05,000**	**6,75,000**	**+1,70,000**	**+33.66**
Equity Share Capital	6,00,000	8,00,000	+2,00,000	+33,.33
Reserve and Surplus	3,30,000	2,22,000	-1,08,000	-32.73
Total liabilities	**14,35,000**	**16,97,000**	**+2,62,000**	**+18.26**

Common Size Statements

In the common size statements, balance sheet and income statements are shown in analytical percentages. The figures are shown as percentages of total assets, total liabilities and total sales. The total assets are taken as 100 and different assets are expressed as a percentage of that total. Similarly, various liabilities are taken as a part of total liabilities. These statements are also known as component percentage or 100 per cent statement because every individual item is stated as a percentage of the total 100.

There are two common-size statements. They are : (i) Common-size income statement, and (ii) Common-size balance sheet.

(i) **Common-size Income Statement:** Common-size income statement can be shown as percentages of sales to show the relation of each item to sales. A significance relationship can be established between the items of income statements and volume of sales. The increase in sales will certainly increase selling expenses and not administrative or financial expenses. In case the volume of the sales increases to a considerable extent, administrative and financial expenses may go up. In case the sales are declining, the selling expenses should be reduced at once. So, a relationship is established between the sales and other items in income statement and this relationship is helpful in evaluating operational activities and operational efficiency of a concern.

***Illustration 3*:** Following are the income statements of a company for the year ending Dec 31st, 2008 and 2009:

Particulars	*2008 (Rs. in lakhs)*	*2009 (Rs. in lakhs)*
Sales	1,000	1,400
Miscellaneous Income	40	30
	1,040	**1,430**
Expenses:		
Cost of sales	650	1,020
Office expenses	40	50
Selling expenses	60	90
Interest	50	60
	800	**1,220**
Net profit	240	210
	1,040	**1,430**

Solution:

Common Size Income Statement for the year ending 31st Dec., 2008 and 2009

Particulars	*2008 (Rs.in lakhs)*	*%.*	*2009 (Rs. In lakhs)*	*%*
Sales	1,000	100.00	1,400	100.00
Less: Cost of sales	650	65.00	1,020	72.86
Gross profit	**350**	**35.00**	**380**	**27.14**
Operating Expenses:				
Office expenses	40	4.00	50	3.58
Selling expenses	60	6.00	90	6.42
Total operating expenses	**100**	**10.00**	**140**	**10.00**
Operating profit	250	25.00	240	17.14
Miscellaneous income	40	4.00	30	2.14
Total Income	**290**	**29.00**	**270**	**19.28**
Less: Non-operating exp:				
Interest	50	5.00	60	4.28
Total Non-operating expenses	**240**	**24.00**	**210**	**15.00**

Interpretation

1. The sales and gross profit have increased in 2009 as compared to 2008 but the percentage of gross profit to sales has gone down from 35% to 27.14%.
2. The increases in cost of sales as a percentage of sales has brought down the profitability from 35% to 27.14%
3. The net profit has decreased both in figures as well as in percentage in 2005 as compared to 2008.

It means that, the company should take immediate steps to control its cost of sales to increase the profitability of the concern. Otherwise the company will be in trouble.

Common-size Balance Sheet: A statement in which the balance sheet items are expressed as the ratio of each asset to total assets and the ratio of each liability total liabilities is called, 'Common-size Balance Sheet'.

For example, following assets are shown in a Common size Balance Sheet:

Assets	*Rs.*	*Percentage*
Cash in hand	15,000	6.00
Inventory	10,000	4.00
Land and Buildings	1,00,000	40.00
Plant and Machinery	1,25,000	50.00
Total Assets	**2,50,000**	**100.00**

RATIO ANALYSIS

Meaning of Ratio

A ratio is simple arithmetical expression of the relationship of one number to another. The ratio analysis is one of the most powerful tools of financial analysis. It is the process of establishing and interpreting various ratios. It is with the help of ratios that the financial statements can be analysed more clearly.

For example, if the current assets of a firm on a given date are Rs. 7,50,000 and the current liabilities are Rs. 5,00,000 then the ratio of current assets to current liabilities will workout to be 7,50,000/5,00,000 = 1.5

Definition

According to Accountant's Handbook by **Wixon, Kell and Bedford**, a ratio "is an expression of the quantitative relationship between two numbers".

OBJECTIVES OF RATIO ANALYSIS

- Ratio analysis is very helpful in financial forecasting.
- With the help of ratio analysis ideal ratios can be composed and they can used for comparison of a particular firm's progress and performance.
- Ratios are a very useful for measuring the performance and very useful in cost control.
- Different financial ratios communicate the strength and financial standing of the firm both internal and external parties.
- Financial ratios are very helpful in the diagnosis and financial health of a firm.

USES OF RATIO ANALYSIS

- Ratio analysis helps in making decisions from the information provided in the financial statements.
- Ratio analysis helps in forecasting and planning.
- The financial strength and weakness of a firm are communicated in a more easy and understandable manner by the use of ratios.
- Ratio analysis even helps in making effective control of the business.
- Comparison of ratios of same firm over a period of years can be made.
- It helps to know the improvements in financial performance over a period of years.
- Ratios of a firm can be compared with the ratios of similar nature of firms.

LIMITATIONS OF RATIO ANALYSIS

1. **Limited Use of a Single Ratio:** A single ratio does not convey much of a sense. To make a better interpretation a number of ratios have to be calculated which is likely to confuse the analyst.
2. **Lack of Adequate Standards:** There are no well accepted standards or rules of thumb for all ratios which can be accepted as norms. It renders interpretation of the ratios difficult.
3. **Inherent Limitations of Accounting:** Ratios of the past are not necessarily true indicators of the future.
4. **Change of Accounting Procedure:** Change in accounting procedure by a firm often makes ratio analysis misleading.
5. **Window Dressing:** Financial statements can be easily window dressed to present a better picture of its financial and profitability position to outsiders. But it may be very difficult for an outsider to know about the window dressing made by a firm.
6. **Personal Bias:** Ratios have to be interpreted and different people may interpret the same ratio in different ways.
7. **Uncomparable:** Not only industries differ in their nature but also the firms of the similar business widely differ in their size and accounting procedures, etc. It makes comparison of ratios difficult and misleading.
8. **Price Level Changes:** While making ratio analysis, no consideration is made to the changes in price levels and is makes the interpretation of ratios invalid.
9. **Ratios no Substitutes:** Ratios become useless if separated from the statements from which they are computed.

(A) Liquidity or Short-term Solvency Ratios

Liquidity Ratios

Liquidity refers to the ability of a concern to meet its current obligations as and when these become due. The short-term obligations are met by realising amounts from current, floating or circulating assets. If current assets can pay-off current liabilities, then liquidity position will be satisfactory and *vice-versa*. To measure the liquidity of a firm, the following ratios can be calculated.

(i) **Current Ratio:** Current ratio may be defined as, the relationship between current assets and current liabilities. This ratio, also known as working capital ratio.

$$\text{Current ratio} = \frac{\text{Current assets}}{\text{Current liabilities}}$$

Components of Current Ratio

Current assets	Current liabilities
Cash in hand	Sundry creditors
Cash at bank	Bills payable
Sundry debtors	Outstanding expenses
Short-term marketable securities	Provision for taxation
Prepaid expenses	Bank overdraft
Closing stock	Dividends payable
Outstanding income	Income received in advance
Bills receivable	

Interpretation of Current Ratio: A relatively high current ratio is an indication that the firm is liquid and has the ability to pay its current obligations in time as and when they become due. On the other hand, relatively low current ratio represents that the liquidity position of the firm is not good and the firm shall not be able to pay its current liabilities in time without facing difficulties. Standard current ratio is 2:1.

(ii) Quick or Acid Test or Liquid Ratio: The term liquidity refers to the ability of a firm to pay its short-term obligations as and when they become due. Quick ratio is a more rigorous test of liquidity than the current ratio. Quick assets can be converted into cash within a short period without loss of value.

$$\text{Quick/liquid/acid test ratio} = \frac{\text{Quick/liquid assets}}{\text{Quick/liquid liabilities}}$$

Quick assets = Current assets – (Stock and prepaid expenses)

Quick liabilities = Current liability – Bank overdraft

Components:

Quick/liquid assets	Quick liabilities
Cash in hand	Sundry creditors
Cash at bank	Bills payable
Sundry debtors	Outstanding expenses
Short-term marketable securities	Provision for taxation
Outstanding income	Dividends payable
Bills receivable	Income received in advance

Interpretation of Quick Ratio: A high acid test ratio is an indication that the firm is liquid and has the ability to meet its liquid liabilities in time and on the other hand a low quick ratio represents that the firm's liquidity position is not good. A standard ratio is 1:1.

(iii) Absolute Liquid Ratio: Absolute liquid assets include cash, bank and marketable securities or temporary investments. Standard absolute liquid ratio is 0.5:1 or 1:2

Absolute Liquid Ratio

$$= \frac{\text{Cash + Bank + marketable securities}}{\text{Current liabilities}}$$

***Illustration 4*:**

Cash	18,000	Debtors	1,42,000
Closing stock	1,80,000	Bills payable	27,000
Creditors	50,000	Outstanding expenses	15,000
Tax payable	75,000		

From the above information calculate :

(a) Current Ratio (b) Liquid Ratio (c) Absolute Liquid Ratio

Solution:

(a) Current Ratio:

$$= \frac{\text{Current assets}}{\text{Current liabilities}}$$

$$= \frac{18{,}000 + 1{,}42{,}000 + 1{,}80{,}000}{27{,}000 + 50{,}000 + 75{,}000 + 15{,}000}$$

$$= \frac{3{,}40{,}000}{1{,}67{,}000} = 2.04:1$$

(b) Liquid Ratio:

$$= \frac{\text{Liquid assets}}{\text{Liquid liabilities}}$$

$$= \frac{18{,}000 + 1{,}42{,}000}{1{,}67{,}000}$$

$$= \frac{1{,}60{,}000}{1{,}67{,}000} = 0.96:1$$

(c) Absolute Liquid Ratio:

$$= \frac{\text{Absolute liquid assets}}{\text{Current liabilities}}$$

Absolute liquid assets = cash and bank and marketable securities

$$= \frac{18{,}000}{1{,}67{,}000} = 0.11:1$$

(B) Long-term Solvency or Leverage Ratios

(i) Debt Equity Ratio: This ratio indicates the relationship between the external equities or the outsiders funds and the internal equities or the shareholders funds.

$$\text{Debt Equity Ratio} = \frac{\text{External Equities}}{\text{Internal Equities}}$$

External Equities = Current liabilities + Long-term liabilities

Internal Equities = Proprietors fund

Interpretation of Debt Equity Ratio

The debt equity ratio is calculated to measure the extent to which debt financing has been used in a business. The ratio indicates the proportionate claims of owners and the outsiders against the firm's assets. A ratio of 1:1 may be usually considered to be a satisfactory ratio although there cannot be any 'rule of thumb' or standard norm for all types of businesses.

(ii) Proprietary Ratio or Equity Ratio: Proprietary ratio relates to the proprietors' fund to total assets. It reveals the owners' contribution to the total value of assets. This ratio shows the longer-term solvency of the firm. It is calculated by dividing proprietors' funds by the total tangible assets.

$$\text{Proprietary Ratio or Equity Ratio} = \frac{\text{Proprietors' Funds}}{\text{Total Tangible Assets}}$$

Proprietors' Funds = Equity Share Capital + Preference Share Capital + Reserve and Surplus

Interpretation of Proprietary Ratio

As equity ratio represents the relationship of owners fund to total assets, higher the ratio, better is the long-term solvency position of the company.

***Illustration 5*:**

From the following, calculate the proprietary ratio:

Liabilities	*Rs.*	*Assets*	*Rs.*
Preference share capital	1,00,000	Fixed assets	2,00,000
Equity share capital	2,00,000	Current assets	1,00,000
Reserves and surplus	50,000	Good-will	50,000
Debentures	1,00,000	Investments	1,50,000
Creditors	50,000		
	5,00,000		**5,00,000**

Solution:

$$\text{Proprietary Ratio} = \frac{\text{Proprietors' Fund}}{\text{Total Tangible Assets}}$$

$$= \frac{1,00,000 + 2,00,000 + 50,000}{2,00,000 + 1,00,000 + 1,50,000}$$

$$= \frac{3,50,000}{4,50,000} = 0.78 : 1$$

(iii) Fixed Assets to Net Worth Ratio or Fixed Assets to Proprietors' Funds: The ratio establishes the relationship between fixed assets and shareholders' funds. The ratio can be calculated as follows:

$$\text{Fixed Assets to Net Worth Ratio} = \frac{\text{Fixed Assets (After depreciation)}}{\text{Proprietors' Funds}}$$

Desirable Ratio is 1:1

Interest Coverage Ratio

The ratio is used to test the debt-servicing capacity of a firm. It is also known as Debt Service Ratio or Fixed charges cover or Times Interest Earned.

$$\text{Debt Service or Interest Coverage Ratio} = \frac{\text{Net Profit (Before interest and taxes)}}{\text{Fixed Interest Charges}}$$

***Illustration 6*:**

The net profit (after taxes) of a firm is Rs.1,00,000 and its fixed interest charges on long-term borrowings are Rs. 20,000. the rate of income tax is 50%.Calculate interest coverage ratio.

Solution:

$$\text{Interest Coverage Ratio} = \frac{\text{Net Profit (Before interest and taxes)}}{\text{Fixed Interest Charges}}$$

$$= \frac{1,00,000 + 1,00,000 + 20,000}{20,000} = 11 \text{ times.}$$

(iv) Capital Gearing Ratio: The term capital gearing is used to describe the relationship between equity share capital including Reserves and Surplus to Preference share capital and other fixed interest bearing loans. If the Preference share capital and fixed interest bearing securities exceeded the equity shareholders' funds, the company is said to be highly geared and *vice-versa.*

$$\text{Capital Gearing Ratio} = \frac{\text{Preference Capital + Long - term Debt Bearing Fixed Interest}}{\text{Equity Share Capital + Reserve and Surplus}}$$

***Illustration 7*:**

Particulars	*Rs.*
Equity Share Capital	10,00,000
10% Preference Share Capital	5,00,000
18% Debentures	8,00,000
Current Liabilities	3,00,000
General Reserve	8,00,000

Find out Capital Gearing from the above particulars.

Solution:

$$\text{Capital Gearing Ratio} = \frac{\text{Preference Capital + Long - term Debt Bearing Fixed Interest}}{\text{Equity Share Capital + Reserve and Surplus}}$$

$$= \frac{5,00,000 + 8,00,000}{10,00,000 + 8,00,000} = \frac{13,00,000}{18,00,000} = 0.72:1$$

***Illustration 8*:**

Calculate:

(a) Liquid Ratio (b) Proprietary Ratio, (c) Debt Equity Ratio, and (d) Capital Gearing Ratio.

Liabilities	*Rs.*	*Assets*	*Rs.*
5,000 equity shares of Rs.50 each	2,50,000	Building	3,00,000
1000,8% pref. share of Rs.100 each	1,00,000	Machinery	2,50,000
2,000,9% debentures of Rs.100 each	2,00,000	Stock	1,20,000
Reserves	1,50,000	Debtors	1,00,000
Bank overdraft	25,000	Bank	27,500
Creditors	75,000	Prepaid expenses	2,500
	8,00,000		**8,00,000**

Solution:

(a) Liquid Ratio

$$= \frac{\text{Liquid Assets}}{\text{Liquid Liabilities}}$$

$$= \frac{1,00,000 + 27,500}{75,000} = \frac{1,27,500}{75,000} = 1.71$$

(b) Proprietary Ratio:

$$= \frac{\text{Propretors' Fund}}{\text{Total Tangible Assets}}$$

$$= \frac{2,50,000 + 1,00,000 + 1,50,000}{8,00,000}$$

$$= \frac{5,00,000}{8,00,000} = 0.63:1$$

(c) Debt Equity Ratio

$$= \frac{\text{External Equities}}{\text{Internal Equities}}$$

$$= \frac{2,00,000 + 75,00,000 + 25,000}{2,50,000 + 1,00,000 + 1,50,000}$$

$$= \frac{3,00,000}{5,00,000} = 0.60:1$$

(d) Capital Gearing Ratio

$$= \frac{\text{Preference Share Capital} + \text{Long - term Debt Bearing Fixed Interest}}{\text{Equity Share Capital} + \text{Reserve and Surplus}}$$

$$= \frac{1,00,000 + 2,00,000}{2,50,000 + 1,50,000}$$

$$= \frac{3,00,000}{4,00,000} = 0.75 : 1$$

(C) Turnover/Activity Ratios

These ratios are also called turnover ratios because they indicate the speed with which assets are converted or turned over into sales. For example, inventory turnover ratio indicate the rate at which the funds invested in inventories are converted into sale.

(i) **Inventory Turnover or Stock Turnover ratio:** It indicates the number of times the stock has been turned over during the period and evaluates the efficiency with which a firm is able to manage its inventory.

$$\text{Stock turnover ratio} = \frac{\text{Cost of goods sold}}{\text{Average stock}}$$

Cost of goods sold = Sales – Gross profit

Cost of goods sold = Opening stock + Purchases + Direct expenses – Closing stock

$$\text{Average stock} = \frac{\text{Opening stock} + \text{Closing stock}}{2}$$

Interpretation of Stock Turnover Ratio

A high inventory turnover ratio indicates brisk sales. A low inventory turnover implies over-investment in inventory.

Illustration 9:

Calculate Stock turnover ratio from the followings:

Opening stock Rs. 40,000; Closing stock Rs. 44,000

Sales Rs. 4,15,000; Gross profit ratio 20%

Solution:

$$\text{Stock turnover ratio} = \frac{\text{Cost of goods sold}}{\text{Average stock}}$$

Cost of goods sold = Sales – Gross profit

= 4,15,000 – 83,000

= 3,32,000.

$$\text{Average stock} = \frac{40{,}000 + 44{,}000}{2} = \frac{84{,}000}{2} = \text{Rs. } 42{,}000$$

$$\text{Stock turnover ratio} = \frac{3{,}32{,}000}{42{,}000} = 7.9 \text{ times}$$

(ii) **Debtors or Receivables Turnover Ratio or Debtor's Velocity:** Two kinds of ratios can be computed to evaluate the quality of debtors.

(a) **Debtors/Receivables Turnover or Debtor's Velocity:** Debtors turnover ratio indicate the velocity of debt collection of firm. In simple words, it indicates the number of times average debtors (receivables) are turned over during a year.

$$\text{Debtors turnover/ velocity} = \frac{\text{Net credit annual sales}}{\text{Average trade debtors}}$$

$$\text{Average trade debtors} = \frac{\text{Opening trade debtors} + \text{closing trade debtors}}{2}$$

Interpretation of Debtors Turnover/Velocity

The higher the value of debtors turnover the more efficient is the management of debtors/ sales or more liquid are the debtors. Similarly, low debtors turnover implies inefficient management of debtors/ sales and less liquid debtors.

(b) **Average Collection Period:** The average collection period represents the average number of days for which a firm has to wait before its receivables are converted into cash. The ratio can be calculated as follows :

$$\text{Average collection period} = \frac{\text{Debtors} + \text{Bills receivables}}{\text{Net credit sales}} \times \text{No. of working days in a year}$$

Interpretation of Average Collection Period Ratio

The shorter the average collection period the better is the quality of debtors as a short collection period implies quick payment by debtors. Similarly, a higher collection period implies as inefficient collection performance which in turn adversely affects the liquidity or short-term paying capacity of a firm out of its current liabilities.

***Illustration 10*:**

Calculate debtors turnover ratio and average debt collection period from the followings:

Total sales for the year 2007 Rs.1,00,000; Debtors as on 1.1. 2007 Rs.10,000

Cash sales for the year 2007 Rs.20,000; Debtors as on 31.12. 2007 Rs.15,000

B/R as on 1.1. 2007 Rs.7,500; B/R as on 31.12. 2007 Rs.12,500

Solution:

$$\text{Debtor's turnover ratio } = \frac{\text{Net credit sales}}{\text{Average accounts receivable}}$$

Credit sales = Total sales – Cash sales

1,00,000 – 20,000 = 80,000

$$\text{Average accounts receivable} = \frac{17{,}500 + 27{,}500}{2}$$

$$= \frac{45{,}000}{2} = \text{Rs. } 22{,}500$$

$$\text{Debtor's turnover ratio } = \frac{80{,}000}{22{,}500} = 3.56 \text{ times}$$

$$\text{Average debt collection period} = \frac{\text{Debtor's} + \text{B/R}}{\text{Net credit sales}} \times 365$$

$$= \frac{22{,}500}{80{,}000} \times 365 = 103 \text{ days}$$

(iii) Creditors/Payable Turnover Ratio or Creditors Velocity

(a) Creditors/ Payable Turnover Ratio: It indicates the number of times on the average that the creditors turnover each year. It signifies the credit period enjoy by the firm in paying its creditors.

$$\text{Creditors / payable turnover ratio} = \frac{\text{Net credit purchases}}{\text{Average trade creditors}}$$

Interpretation of Creditors Turnover/Velocity

Higher the creditors velocity better it is or otherwise lower the creditors' velocity, less favourable are the results.

(a) Average payment period:

$$\text{Average payment period} = \frac{\text{Creditors} + \text{Bills payable}}{\text{Net credit purchases}} \times \text{No. of days in a year}$$

Interpretation of Average Payment Period Ratio

The average payment period ratio represents the average number of days taken by the firm to pay its creditors. Generally, lower the ratio, the better is the liquidity position of the firm and higher the ratio, less liquid is the position of the firm.

***Illustration 11*:**

Calculate creditors turnover ratio and average debt payment period from the followings:

Credit purchase during 2007 Rs. 2,00,000; Purchase returns Rs. 2,000

Creditors as on 1.1.07 Rs. 30,000; Creditors on 31.12.07 Rs. 22,000

B/P as on 1.1.07 Rs. 6,000; B/P as on 31.12.07 Rs. 10,000

Solution:

$$\text{(a) Creditors turnover ratio} = \frac{\text{Net Credit purchase}}{\text{Average accounts payable}}$$

Net credit purchase = Credit purchase – Purchase returns

= 2,00,000 – 2,000 = Rs.1,98,000

$$\text{Average accounts payable} = \frac{36{,}000 + 32{,}000}{2} = \text{Rs. } 34{,}000$$

$$\text{Creditors turnover ratio} = \frac{1{,}98{,}000}{34{,}000} = 5.82 \text{ times}$$

$$\text{(b) Average debt payment period} = \frac{\text{Creditors} + \text{B/P}}{\text{Net credit purchase}} \times 365$$

$$= \frac{34{,}000}{1{,}98{,}000} \times 365 = 63 \text{ days.}$$

(or)

$$= \frac{\text{No. of days in a year}}{\text{Creditors turnover ratio}} = \frac{365}{5.82} = 63 \text{ days.}$$

(iv) **Working Capital Turnover Ratio:** Working capital turnover ratio indicates the velocity of the utilisation of net working capital. This ratio indicates the number of times the working capital is turned over in the course of a year. This ratio measures the efficiency with which the working capital is being used by a firm. A higher ratio indicates efficient utilisation of working capital and a low ratio indicates otherwise.

Working Capital = Current Assets – Current Liabilities

$$\text{Working capital turnover ratio} = \frac{\text{Cost of sales (or sales)}}{\text{Net working capital}}$$

***Illustration 12*:**

Calculate Working capital turnover ratio:

	Rs.		*Rs.*
Bank	20,000	Stock	25,000
Bills receivable	10,000	Sundry creditors	40,000
Sundry debtors	40,000	Cost of sales	1,75,000

Solution:

$$\text{Working capital turnover ratio} = \frac{\text{Cost of sales}}{\text{Net working capital}}$$

Net working capital = Current assets – Current liabilities

Current assets = 20,000 + 10,000 + 40,000 + 25,000

= Rs.95,000

Current liabilities = 40,000

Net working capital = 95,000 – 40,000 = Rs.55,000

$$\text{Working capital turnover ratio} = \frac{1,75,000}{55,000} = 3.18 \text{ times}$$

(v) **Fixed Assets Turnover Ratio:** It indicates the extent to which the investments in fixed assets contribute towards sales.

$$\text{Fixed assets turnover ratio} = \frac{\text{Cost of goods sold or sales}}{\text{Fixed assets}}$$

***Illustration 13*:**

Sales Rs.10,00,000; Gross profit ratio 25%;

Fixed assets turnover ratio (on cost of sales) 5 times.

Find out value of Fixed assets.

Solution:

$$\text{Fixed assets turnover ratio} = \frac{\text{Cost of sales}}{\text{Fixed assets}}$$

Cost of sales = Sales – Gross profit

= 10,00,000 – 2,50,000 = Rs.7,50,000

Gross profit = 10,00,000 × 25% = 2,50,000

Fixed assets:

$$\text{Fixed assets} = \frac{7,50,000}{5} = \text{Rs.}1,50,000.$$

(vi) Total assets turnover ratio (Turnover to Total assets):

$$\text{Total assets turnover ratio} = \frac{\text{Total assets}}{\text{Net sales}}$$

(vii) Capital turnover ratio: Capital turnover ratio is the relationship between cost of goods sold or sales and the capital employed. This ratio is calculated to measure the efficiency or effectiveness with which a firm utilises its resources or the capital employed. As capital is invested in a business to make sales and earn profits, this ratio is a good indicator of overall profitability of a concern.

$$\text{Capital turnover ratio} = \frac{\text{Cost of goods sold or sales}}{\text{Capital employed}}$$

(D) Profitability Ratios

Analysis of Profitability Ratios

In the words of **Lord Keynes**, "Profit is the engine that drives the business enterprise". A business needs profit not only for its existence but also for expansion and diversification. The investors want an adequate return on their investments, workers want higher wages, creditors want higher security for their interest and loan and so on.

(i) Gross Profit Ratio: Gross profit ratio measures the relationship of gross profit to net sales and is usually represented as a percentage.

$$\text{Gross profit ratio} = \frac{\text{Gross profit}}{\text{Net sales}} \times 100$$

Gross Profit = Sales – Cost of Goods sold

Illustration 14:

Calculate Gross Profit Ratio:

	Rs.		*Rs.*
Sales	3,00,000	Purchases	2,00,000
Sales return	25,000	Purchases return	10,000
Opening stock	20,000	Closing stock	50,000

Solution:

Trading Account

Particulars	*Rs.*	*Particulars*	*Rs.*
To Opening Stock	20,000	By sales 3,00,000	
To Purchases 2,00,000		**Less:** Returns 25,000	2,75,000
Less: Returns 10,000	1,90,000	By Closing Stock	50,000
To Gross Profit	1,15,000		
	3,25,000		**3,25,000**

$$\text{Gross Profit Ratio} = \frac{1,15,000}{2,75,000} \times 100 = 41.82\%$$

(ii) Operating Ratio: Operating ratio established the relationship between cost of goods sold and other operating expenses on the one hand and the sales on the other.

$$\text{Operating ratio} = \frac{\text{Cost of goods sold + Operating expenses}}{\text{Net sales}} \times 100$$

Illustration 15 :

Find out Operating Ratio:

Particulars	*Rs.*
Cost of goods sold	5,00,000
Selling & distribution expenses	50,000
Office & administrative expenses	75,000
Net sales	7,50,000

Solution:

$$\text{Operating ratio} = \frac{\text{Cost of goods sold} + \text{Operating expenses}}{\text{Net sales}} \times 100$$

$$= \frac{5,00,000 + 50,000 + 75,000}{7,50,000} \times 100$$

$$= \frac{6,25,000}{7,50,000} \times 100 = 83.33\%$$

(iii) Operating Profit Ratio: This ratio establishes the relationship between the operating net profit and sales. Operating profit is calculated as :

$$\text{Operating profit ratio} = \frac{\text{Operating Profit}}{\text{Sales}} \times 100$$

(or)

Operating profit ratio = 100 – operating ratio

Operating profit = Net profit + Non-operating expenses – Non-operating income

(or)

= Sales – (Cost of goods sold + administrative expenses +Selling and distribution expenses)

***Illustration 16*:**

From the information given below, Calculate Operating Profit ratio:

Cost of goods sold Rs.5,00,000

Office and administrative expenses Rs. 40,000

Selling and distribution expenses Rs. 50,000

Net sales Rs. 7,00,000

Solution:

$$\text{Operating Profit Ratio} = \frac{\text{Operating Profit}}{\text{Sales}} \times 100$$

Operating Profit = Sales – (Cost of goods sold + administrative expenses + Selling and distribution expenses)

Operating Profit = 7,00,000 – (5,00,000 + 40,000 + 50,000) = 1,10,000

$$\text{Operating Profit Ratio} = \frac{1,10,000}{7,00,000} \times 100 = 15.71\%$$

(iv) Expenses Ratios: Expenses ratios indicate the relationship of various expenses to net sales. The lower the ratio, the greater is the profitability and higher the ratio, lower is the profitability. Individual or specific expenses ratio may be calculated as:

$$\text{(a) Cost of goods sold ratio} = \frac{\text{Cost of goods sold}}{\text{Sales}} \times 100$$

$$\text{(b) Office and Administrative expenses ratio} = \frac{\text{Office and Administrative Expenses}}{\text{Sales}} \times 100$$

$$\text{(c) Selling and Distribution expenses ratio} = \frac{\text{Selling and Distribution Expenses}}{\text{Sales}} \times 100$$

(v) Net Profit Ratio: Net profit ratio establishes a relationship between net profit (after taxes) and sales. This ratio is the overall measure of firm's profitability and is calculated as:

$$\text{Net Profit Ratio} = \frac{\text{Net Profit after tax}}{\text{Net sales}} \times 100$$

(E) Overall Profitability Ratios

Profits are the measure of overall efficiency of a business. The higher the profits, the more efficient is the business considered. Overall profitability or efficiency of a business can be measured in terms of profits related to investments made in the business.

(i) Return on Shareholder Investment or Net Worth: Return on shareholder investment, popularly known as RoI is the relationship between net profits (after interest and tax) and the proprietors funds.

$$\text{Return on shareholders investment} = \frac{\text{Net profit (after interest and tax)}}{\text{Proprietors funds}} \times 100$$

Proprietors' Funds = Equity Share Capital + Preference Share Capital + Reserve and Surplus – (accumulated losses, if any)

***Illustration 17*:**

5,000 equity shares of Rs. 100 each		5,00,000
3,000 10% pref. shares of Rs.100 each		3,00,000
		8,00,000
Reserves and Surplus:		
Revenue Reserve	1,75,000	
Capital Reserve	1,00,000	
Reserves for contingencies	25,000	3,00,000

Net profit before interest and tax			3,00,000
Interest charges			50,000
Tax rate 50%			

Calculate return on shareholders' investment.

Solution:

$$\text{Return on shareholders' investment} = \frac{\text{Net profit (after interest \& tax)}}{\text{Proprietors funds}} \times 100$$

Proprietors' Funds = Equity Share Capital + Preference Share Capital + Reserve and Surplus

Proprietors' Funds = 5,00,000 + 3,00,000 + 3,00,000 = Rs. 11,00,000

Net profit before interest and tax	3,00,000
Less: Interest	50,000
	2,50,000
Less: Income tax at 50%	1,25,000
Net profit after interest and tax	**1,25,000**

$$\text{Operating ratio} = \frac{\text{Cost of goods sold + Operating expenses}}{\text{Net sales}} \times 100$$

Interpretation and Significance of RoI

This ratio is one of the most important ratios used for measuring the overall efficiency of a firm. This ratio is of great importance to the present and prospective shareholders as well as the management of the company. As this ratio reveals how well the resources of a firm are being used, higher the ratio, better are the results.

(ii) Return on Equity Capital: Ordinary shareholders are more interested in the profitability of a company and the performance of a company should be judged on the basis of return on equity capital of the company, return on equity capital, which is the relationship between profits of a company and its equity capital.

$$\text{Return on equity capital} = \frac{\text{Net profit (after tax and preference dividend)}}{\text{Equity share capital (paid - up)}} \times 100$$

Illustration 18:

Following information is given for a company whose accounting year ends on 31st March, 2009.

20,000 equity shares of Rs. 10 each Rs. 8 paid	–	Rs. 1,60,000
10% 5,000 preference shares of Rs. 20 each	–	Rs. 1,00,000
Profit before tax	–	Rs. 1,40,000
Rate of tax	–	50%

Calculate : Return on equity capital

Solution:

$$\text{Return on equity capital} = \frac{\text{Net profit (after tax and preference dividend)}}{\text{Equity share capital (paid - up)}} \times 100$$

Profits available for equity shareholders:

Particulars	*Rs.*
Profits	1,40,000
Less: Tax @ 50%	70,000
Profits after tax	70,000
Less: Preference dividend	10,000
	60,000

Returns on equity capital $= \frac{60,000}{1,60,000} \times 100 = 37.5\%$

MISCELLANEOUS ILLUSTRATIONS

***Illustration 19*:**

Calculate liquidity ratios from the following information and comment on them:

Balance Sheet of Rani Ltd., as on 31.3.2009

Liabilities	*Rs.*	*Assets*	*Rs.*
Equity share capital	6,00,000	Goodwill	1,00,000
7% debentures	3,50,000	Land and building	2,30,000
Long-term debts	2,00,000	Plant and machinery	3,00,000
Bank O/D	75,000	Trade investments	3,00,000
Sundry creditors	60,000	Sundry debtors	1,50,000
Bills payable	30,000	Bills receivable	40,000
Liability for tax	20,000	Cash in hand	50,000

		Cash at bank	60,000
		Stock	1,00,000
		Prepaid rent	5,000
	13,35,000		**13,35,000**

Solution:

(i) Current Ratio:

$$= \frac{\text{Current assets}}{\text{Current liabilities}}$$

$$= \frac{1,50,000 + 40,000 + 50,000 + 60,000 + 1,00,000 + 5,000}{75,000 + 60,000 + 30,000 + 20,000}$$

$$= \frac{4,05,000}{1,85,000} = 2.19:1$$

(ii) Liquid Ratio:

$$= \frac{\text{Liquid assets}}{\text{Liquid liabilities}}$$

$$= \frac{1,50,000 + 40,000 + 50,000 + 60,000}{60,000 + 30,000 + 20,000}$$

$$= \frac{3,00,000}{1,10,000} = 2.73:1$$

(iii) Absolute Liquid Ratio:

$$= \frac{\text{Absolute liquid assets}}{\text{Current liabilities}} = \frac{50,000 + 60,000}{75,000 + 60,000 + 30,000 + 20,000}$$

$$= \frac{1,10,000}{1,85,000} = 0.60:1$$

Comments: Over all short-term financial position is good.

***Illustration 20*:**

Balance Sheet of Sujith Ltd., as on 31.12.2009

Liabilities	*Rs.*	*Assets*	*Rs.*
Share capital	2,00,000	Fixed assets	1,60,000
Reserve and Surplus	30,000	Stock	50,000
Creditors	20,000	Debtors	20,000
B/P	22,000	B/R	15,000
Outstanding expenses	8,000	Prepaid expenses	5,000
Provision for tax	20,000	Bank	30,000
		Cash	20,000
	3,00,000		**3,00,000**

Find out:

(i) Current Ratio, and (ii) Liquid Ratio

Also comment on the liquidity of the firm.

Solution:

(i) Current Ratio:

$$= \frac{\text{Current assets}}{\text{Current liabilities}}$$

$$= \frac{50{,}000 + 20{,}000 + 15{,}000 + 5{,}000 + 30{,}000 + 20{,}000}{20{,}000 + 22{,}000 + 8{,}000 + 20{,}000}$$

$$= \frac{1{,}40{,}000}{70{,}000} = 2:1$$

(ii) Liquid Ratio:

$$= \frac{\text{Liquid assets}}{\text{Liquid liabilities}}$$

$$= \frac{20{,}000 + 15{,}000 + 30{,}000 + 20{,}000}{20{,}000 + 22{,}000 + 8{,}000 + 20{,}000}$$

$$= \frac{85{,}000}{70{,}000} = 1.21:1$$

Comment:

(i) Current ratio is 2:1, which is equal to ideal ratio of 2:1. Hence, the liquidity position is very good.

(ii) Quick ratio of the company is 1.21: 1, while the ideal ratio is 1:1. As the ratio is higher, the company's liquidity position is better.

***Illustration 21*:**

Calculate: (a) Current Ratio, and (b) Liquid Ratio (c) Proprietary Ratio from the following.

Liabilities	*Rs.*	*Assets*	*Rs.*
Eq. share capital	10,00,000	Goodwill	5,00,000
6% Pref. share capital	5,00,000	Plant	6,00,000
General reserve	1,00,000	Land and buildings	7,00,000
Profit and loss A/c	4,00,000	Furniture	1,00,000
Tax provision	1,76,000	Stock	6,00,000
B/P	1,24,000	B/R	30,000
Bank overdraft	20,000	Bank	2,00,000
Creditors	80,000	Debtors	1,50,000
12% debentures	5,00,000	Marketable securities	20,000
	29,00,000		**29,00,000**

Solution:

(a) Current Ratio:

$$= \frac{\text{Current assets}}{\text{Current liabilities}}$$

$$= \frac{6{,}00{,}000 + 30{,}000 + 2{,}00{,}000 + 1{,}50{,}000 + 20{,}000}{1{,}76{,}000 + 1{,}24{,}000 + 20{,}000 + 80{,}000}$$

$$= \frac{10{,}00{,}000}{4{,}00{,}000} = 2.5 : 1$$

(b) Liquid Ratio:

$$= \frac{\text{Liquid assets}}{\text{Liquid liabilities}}$$

$$= \frac{30{,}000 + 2{,}00{,}000 + 1{,}50{,}000 + 20{,}000}{1{,}76{,}000 + 1{,}24{,}000 + 80{,}000}$$

$$= \frac{4,00,000}{3,80,000} = 1.05:1$$

(c) Proprietary Ratio:

$$= \frac{\text{Proprietors' Fund}}{\text{Total tangible assets}}$$

$$= \frac{10,00,000 + 5,00,000 + 1,00,000 + 4,00,000}{24,00,000}$$

$$= \frac{20,00,000}{24,00,000} = 0.83:1$$

Illustration 22:

Balance Sheet of Eswari Ltd., as on 31.12.2009

Liabilities	*Rs.*	*Assets*	*Rs.*
Share capital	2,00,000	Fixed assets	3,60,000
9% Pref. share capital	1,00,000	Stock	50,000
8 % Debentures	1,00,000	Debtors	1,10,000
Profit and loss A/c	40,000	B/R	6,000
Creditors	90,000	Bank	4,000
	5,30,000		**5,30,000**

Find out:

(i) Debt Equity Ratio (ii) Current Ratio, and (iii) Liquid Ratio

Solution:

(i) Debt Equity Ratio:

$$= \frac{\text{External equities}}{\text{Internal equities}}$$

External equities = Long-term debt+ Current liabilities

Internal equities = Proprietors' funds

$$= \frac{1,00,000 + 90,000}{2,00,000 + 1,00,000 + 40,000} = \frac{1,90,000}{3,40,000} = 0.56:1$$

(ii) Current Ratio:

$$=\frac{\text{Current assets}}{\text{Current liabilities}}$$

$$=\frac{50{,}000+1{,}10{,}000+6{,}000+4{,}000}{90{,}000}$$

$$=\frac{1{,}70{,}000}{90{,}000}=1.89:1$$

(iii) Liquid Ratio:

$$=\frac{\text{Liquid assets}}{\text{Liquid liabilities}}$$

Liquid assets = Current assets – (Stock + prepaid exp.)

Liquid liabilities = Current liabilities – Bank O/D

$$=\frac{1{,}10{,}000+6{,}000+4{,}000}{90{,}000}$$

$$=\frac{1{,}20{,}000}{90{,}000}=1.33:1$$

Illustration 23:

Following is the Balance Sheet of Y Ltd.

Liabilities	*Rs.*	*Assets*	*Rs.*
Equity share capital	1,00,000	Cash	2,000
6% Pref. share capital	1,00,000	Bank	10,000
7% debentures -10 years	40,000	Bills receivable	30,000
8% public deposits-5 years	20,000	Investments (short-term)	20,000
Bank O/D	40,000	Debtors	70,000
Creditors	60,000	Stock	40,000
Outstanding expenses	7,000	Furniture	30,000
Proposed dividend	10,000	Machinery	1,00,000
Reserves	1,50,000	Land and buildings	2,20,000
Provision for taxation	20,000	Goodwill	35,000
Profit and loss A/c	20,000	Preliminary expenses	10,000
	5,67,000		**5,67,000**

During the year provision for taxation was Rs. 20,000. Dividend proposed was Rs.10,000. Profit carried forward from the last year was Rs.15,000.

Calculate : (a) Short-term solvency ratios, and (b) Long-term solvency ratios.

Solution:

Short-term solvency ratios:

(i) Current Ratio:

$$= \frac{\text{Current assets}}{\text{Current liabilities}}$$

$$= \frac{2{,}000 + 10{,}000 + 30{,}000 + 20{,}000 + 70{,}000 + 40{,}000}{40{,}000 + 60{,}000 + 7{,}000 + 10{,}000 + 20{,}000}$$

$$= \frac{1{,}72{,}000}{1{,}37{,}000} = 1.3:1$$

(ii) Liquid Ratio:

$$= \frac{\text{Liquid assets}}{\text{Liquid liabilities}}$$

$$= \frac{2{,}000 + 10{,}000 + 30{,}000 + 20{,}000 + 70{,}000}{60{,}000 + 7{,}000 + 10{,}000 + 20{,}000}$$

$$= \frac{1{,}32{,}000}{97{,}000} = 1.35:1$$

Long-term solvency ratios:

(iii) Proprietary Ratio:

$$= \frac{\text{Proprietor s' fund}}{\text{Total tangible assets}}$$

$$= \frac{1{,}00{,}000 + 1{,}00{,}000 + 1{,}50{,}000 + 20{,}000}{5{,}67{,}000 - 35{,}000 - 10{,}000}$$

$$= \frac{3{,}70{,}000}{5{,}22{,}000} = 0.71:1$$

(iv) Capital Gearing Ratio:

$$= \frac{\text{Pre. share capital + Long-term debt bearing fixed interest}}{\text{Equity share capital + Reserve and surplus}}$$

$$= \frac{1,00,000 + 40,000 + 20,000 + 1,60,000}{1,00,000 + 1,50,000 + 20,000 + 2,70,000} = 0.59:1$$

(v) Debt Equity Ratio:

$$= \frac{\text{External equities}}{\text{Internal equities}}$$

$$= \frac{1,97,000}{3,70,000} = 0.53:1$$

Illustration 24:

A Company sells goods on cash as well as on credit basis. The following particulars are extracted from their books of accounts:

Particulars	*Rs.*	*Particulars*	*Rs.*
Total sales	4,00,000	Sales return	28,000
Cash sales	80,000	Debtors at the end	36,000
B/R at the end	8,000	Creditors at the end	25,000
Provision for doubtful debts	3,000		

Cal ulate average collection period.

Solution:

Average Collection Period

$$= \frac{\text{Debtors} + \text{B/R}}{\text{Net credit sales}} \times \text{No. of working days in a year}$$

Net credit sales = Total sales – Cash sales – Sales returns

= 4,00,000 – 80,000 – 28,000

= Rs. 2,92,000

$$= \frac{36,000 + 8,000}{2,92,000} \times 365$$

= 55 days.

Illustration 25:

From the following information calculate average payment period:

Particulars	*Rs.*	*Particulars*	*Rs.*
Total purchases	4,00,000	Creditors at the end	60,000
Cash purchases (included above)	50,000	Reserve for discount on creditors	5,000
Purchases returns	20,000	Bills payable at the end	20,000

Solution:

Average Payment period

$$= \frac{\text{Creditors} + \text{B/P}}{\text{Net credit purchases}} \times \text{No. of days in a year}$$

Net credit purchases = Total purchases – Cash purchases – purchases returns
= 4,00,000 – 50,000 – 20,000
= Rs. 3,30,000

$$= \frac{60{,}000 + 20{,}000}{3{,}30{,}000} \times 365 = 88 \text{ days.}$$

Illustration 26:

JJ Company supplies you the following information for the year ending 31st December, 2009:

Cash sales	Rs. 80,000;	Credit sales	Rs. 2,00,000
Returns inwards	Rs. 10,000;	Opening stock	Rs. 25,000
Closing stock	Rs. 30,000;	Gross profit ratio	25%

Find out inventory turnover.

Solution:

$$\text{Stock turnover ratio} = \frac{\text{Cost of goods sold}}{\text{Average stock}}$$

Cost of goods sold = Cash sales + Credit sales-Returns inwards – Gross Profit
= 80,000 + 2,00,000 – 10,000 – 67,500
= Rs. 2,02,500

$$\text{Average stock} = \frac{\text{Opening stock} + \text{Closing stock}}{2}$$

$$= \frac{25{,}000 + 30{,}000}{2} = 27{,}500$$

$$\text{Stock turnover ratio} = \frac{2{,}02{,}500}{27{,}500} = 7.36 \text{ times}$$

Illustration 27:

Find out the value of creditors from the following:

Sales	Rs. 50,000	Opening stock	Rs. 5,000
G.P. on sales	10%	Closing stock	Rs. 10,000
Creditors velocity	73 days	Bills payable	Rs. 3,000

Solution:

Creditors:

$$\text{Creditors velocity} = \frac{\text{Creditors + B/P}}{\text{Credit purchase}} \times \text{No. of working days in a year}$$

Calculation of Purchase:

Cost of goods sold = Sales – Gross Profit

= Rs. 50,000 – Rs. 5,000 = Rs. 45,000

Purchase = Cost of goods sold + Closing Stock – Opening stock

Purchase = 45,000 +10,000 – 5,000 = Rs. 50,000

$$\frac{\text{Creditors + B/P}}{50{,}000} \times 365 = 73$$

$$\text{Creditors + Bills Payable} = \frac{73 \times 50{,}000}{365} = \text{Rs. } 10{,}000$$

Less: Bills Payable = Rs. 3,000

Creditors = Rs. 7,000

Illustration 28:

Calculate debtors turnover ratio and average debt collection period.

Particulars	***Rs.***
Credit sales	4,00,000
Debtors	20,000
B/R	5,000

Solution:

$$\text{Debtor sturn over ratio} = \frac{\text{Net credit sales}}{\text{Average accounts receivable}}$$

$$= \frac{4,00,000}{25,000} = 16 \text{ times.}$$

$$\text{Average debt collection period} = \frac{\text{Accounts receivable}}{\text{Credit sales}} \times 365$$

$$= \frac{20,000 + 5,000}{4,00,000} \times 365 = 23 \text{ days.}$$

Illustration 29:

From the following calculate:

(a) Debtors turnover ratio (b) Average age of debtors

	2009 (Rs.)	*2008 (Rs.)*
Net sales	18,00,000	15,00,000
Debtors – (Opening)	1,72,000	1,60,000
Debtors – (Closing)	2,34,000	1,72,000

Solution:

$$\text{(a) Debtors turnover ratio} = \frac{\text{Net sales}}{\text{Average debtors}}$$

$$\text{Average debtors} = \frac{\text{Debtors at the beginning} + \text{Debtors at the end}}{2}$$

For 2008:

$$\text{Average debtors} = \frac{1,60,000 + 1,72,000}{2} = 1,66,000$$

$$\text{Debtors turnover ratio} = \frac{15,00,000}{1,66,000} = 9.04 \text{ times}$$

For 2009:

$$\text{Average debtors} = \frac{1,72,000 + 2,34,000}{2} = 2,03,000$$

$$\text{Debtors turnover ratio} = \frac{18,00,000}{2,03,000} = 8.87 \text{ times}$$

(b) Average age of debtors:

$$= \frac{\text{Number of working days in a year}}{\text{Debtors turnover ratio}}$$

For 2008:

$$\text{Average age of debtors} = \frac{366}{9.04} = 40 \text{ days}$$

For 2009:

$$\text{Average age of debtors} = \frac{365}{8.87} = 41 \text{ days}$$

Illustration 30: Find out working capital turnover ratio:

Particulars	*Rs.*	*Particulars*	*Rs.*
Cash	20,000	Bills Receivables	10,000
Sundry debtors	40,000	Stock	25,000
Sundry creditors	40,000	Cost of sales	1,75,000

Solution:

$$\text{Working capital turnover ratio} = \frac{\text{Cost of sales}}{\text{Net working capital}}$$

Net working capital = Current Assets – Current Liabilities

Current assets = 20,000 + 10,000 + 40,000 + 25,000 = 95,000

Current liabilities = 40,000

Net working capital = Rs. 95,000 – 40,000 = 55,000

$$\text{Working capital turnover ratio} = \frac{1,75,000}{55,000} = 3.18 \text{ times}$$

***Illustration 31*:** From the Trading Account of JC Ltd., Calculate Stock turnover ratio:

Particulars	*Rs.*	*Particulars*	*Rs.*
To opening stock	70,000	By sales	4,00,000
To purchases	2,20,000	By closing stock	50,000
To wages	10,000		
To carriage	15,000		

To gross profit	1,35,000		
	4,50,000		**4,50,000**

Solution:

$$\text{Stock turnover ratio} = \frac{\text{Cost of goods sold}}{\text{Average stock}}$$

$$\begin{aligned}\text{Cost of goods sold} &= \text{Sales} - \text{Gross profit} \\ &= 4{,}00{,}000 - 1{,}35{,}000 \\ &= \text{Rs. } 2{,}65{,}000\end{aligned}$$

$$\text{Average stock} = \frac{70{,}000 + 50{,}000}{2} = 60{,}000$$

$$\text{Stock turnover ratio} = \frac{2{,}65{,}000}{60{,}000} = 4.42 \text{ times}$$

***Illustration 32*:**

From the following details calculate:

(i) Fixed assets turnover ratio, and (ii) Working capital turnover ratio

Particulars	*Rs.*	*Particulars*	*Rs.*
Sales during the year 2009	7,50,000	Fixed assets during 2009	3,00,000
Current assets 2009	4,00,000	Current liabilities 2009	2,50,000

Solution:

$$\text{(i) Fixed assets turnover ratio} = \frac{\text{Sales}}{\text{Fixed assets}}$$

$$= \frac{7{,}50{,}000}{3{,}00{,}000} = 2.5 \text{ times}$$

$$\text{(ii) Working capital turnover ratio} = \frac{\text{Sales}}{\text{Net working capital}}$$

Net working capital = Current assets – Current liabilities

= 4,00,000 - 2,50,000 = 1,50,000

$$\text{Working capital turnover ratio} = \frac{7,50,000}{1,50,000} = 5 \text{ times}$$

***Illustration 33*:**

From the following information, calculate average collection period:

Particulars	*Rs.*	*Particulars*	*Rs.*
Total sales	3,00,000	Cash sales	60,000
Debtors	33,000	B/R	12,000
Reserve for bad debts	2,000	Creditor	15,000
Sales return	21,000		

Solution:

$$\text{Average collection period} = \frac{\text{Debtors + B/R}}{\text{Net credit sales}} \times 365$$

Net credit sales = 3,00,000 – 60,000 – 21,000

= Rs. 2,19,000

$$\text{Average collection period} = \frac{33,000 + 12,000}{2,19,000} \times 365 = 75 \text{ days}$$

***Illustration 34*:**

Calculate stock turnover ratio and gross profit ratio.

Trading Account

Particulars	*Rs.*	*Particulars*	*Rs.*
To Opening stock	15,920	By Sales	78,000
To Purchases	39,000	By Closing Stock	14,400
To Carriage	1,000		
To Gross Profit	36,480		
	92,400		**92,400**

Solution:

$$\text{(a) Stock turnover ratio} = \frac{\text{Cost of goods sold}}{\text{Average stock}}$$

Cost of goods sold = Sales – Gross profit

$$= 78,000 - 36,480 = \text{Rs. } 41,520$$

$$\text{Average stock} = \frac{15,920 + 14,400}{2} = \text{Rs.}15,160$$

$$\text{Stock turnover ratio} = \frac{41,520}{15,160} = 2.7 \text{ times}$$

(b) $$\text{Gross profit ratio} = \frac{\text{Gross profit}}{\text{Sales}} \times 100$$

$$= \frac{36,480}{78,000} \times 100 = 46.77\%$$

***Illustration 35*:**

Find out Operating ratio:

Particulars	*Rs.*	*Particulars*	*Rs.*
Cost of goods sold	5,00,000	Selling and distribution expenses	50,000
Office and administrative expenses	75,000	Net sales	7,50,000

Solution:

$$\text{Operating ratio} = \frac{\text{Cost of goods sold} + \text{Operating expenses}}{\text{Net sales}} \times 100$$

$$= \frac{5,00,000 + 50,000 + 75,000}{7,50,000} \times 100$$

$$= \frac{6,25,000}{7,50,000} \times 100 = 83.33\%$$

***Illustration 36*:**

From the following information, calculate

(i) Gross profit ratio (ii) Operating ratio

(iii) Operating profit ratio (iv) Net profit ratio

Particulars	*Rs.*	*particulars*	*Rs.*
Sales	6,00,000	Cost of goods sold	4,00,000
Operating expenses	1,20,000	Non-operating income	12,000
Non-operating expenses	4,000		

Solution:

(i) Gross profit ratio $= \frac{\text{Gross profit}}{\text{Net sales}} \times 100$

Gross profit = Sales – Cost of goods sold

= 6,00,000 – 4,00,000

= Rs.2,00,000

Gross profit ratio $= \frac{2,00,000}{6,00,000} \times 100 = 33\frac{1}{3}\%$

(ii) Operating ratio $= \frac{\text{Cost of goods sold + Operating expenses}}{\text{Net sales}} \times 100$

$= \frac{4,00,000 + 1,20,000}{6,00,000} \times 100 = 86.67\%$

(iii) Operating profit ratio $= \frac{\text{Operating profit}}{\text{Sales}} \times 100$

Operating profit = Gross profit – Operating expenses

= 2,00,000 – 1,20,000 = Rs. 80,000

Operating profit ratio $= \frac{80,000}{6,00,000} \times 100 = 13.33\%$

(or)

Operating profit ratio = 100% – Operating ratio

13.33% = 100% – 86.67%

(iv) Net profit ratio $= \frac{\text{Net profit}}{\text{Net sales}} \times 100$

Net profit = Operating profit + Non-operating income – Non-operating expenses

= 80,000 + 12,000 – 4,000= Rs. 88,000

Net profit ratio $= \frac{88,000}{6,00,000} \times 100 = 14.67\%$

***Illustration 37*:**

From the following information calculate the cost of goods sold

Current liabilities	Rs.9,00,000	Stock velocity	8
Current ratio	2.5:1	Quick ratio	2.1:1

Solution:

(a) Current Ratio:

$$= \frac{\text{Current assets}}{\text{Current liabilities}} = 2.5:1$$

$$\text{Current assets} = \frac{9,00,000}{1.0} \times 2.5 = \text{Rs. } 22,50,000$$

Liquid liability = Current liability – Bank O/D

Liquid liability = Rs. 9,00,000

$$\text{Liquid assets} = \frac{9,00,000}{1} \times 2.1 = \text{Rs.} 18,90,000$$

Closing stock = Current assets – Liquid assets

= 22,50,000 – 18,90,000 = 3,60,000

$$\text{Stock velocity} = \frac{\text{Cost of goods sold}}{\text{Closing stock}}$$

$$8 = \frac{\text{Cost of goods sold}}{3,60,000} = \text{Rs. } 28,80,000$$

(Note: In the absence of sufficient information, closing stock is taken as average stock.)

***Illustration 38*:**

From the followings calculate:

(a) Current liabilities (b) Inventory

Current ratio 2.5 Liquid ratio 1.7 Current assets Rs. 2,50,000

Solution:

$$\text{Current ratio} = \frac{\text{Current assets}}{\text{Current liabilities}} = 2.5:1$$

$$\text{Current liabilities} = \frac{2,50,000}{2.5} \times 1 = \text{Rs.} 1,00,000$$

Liquid liability = Current liability – Bank O/D

Liquid liability = Rs.1,00,000

$$\text{Liquid assets} = \frac{1,00,000}{1} \times 1.7 = \text{Rs.}1,70,000$$

Stock = Current assets – Liquid assets

Stock = 2,50,000 – 1,70,000 = 80,000

***Illustration 39*:**

From the followings calculate:

(a) Current assets (b) Current liabilities (c) Liquid assets (d) Inventory

Current ratio	3.5
Liquid ratio	2.5
Working capital	Rs. 1,00,000

Solution:

Working capital = Current assets – Current liabilities

1,00,000 = 3.5 – 1

1,00,000 = 2.5

$$\text{Current assets} = \frac{1,00,000}{2.5} \times 3.5 = \text{Rs.}1,40,000$$

$$\text{Current liabilities} = \frac{1,00,000}{2.5} \times 1 = \text{Rs. }40,000$$

Liquid liability = Current liability – Bank O/D

Liquid liability = Rs. 40,000

$$\text{Liquid assets} = \frac{40,000}{1} \times 2.5 = \text{Rs.}1,00,000$$

Stock = Current assets – Liquid assets

Stock = 1,40,000 – 1,00,000 = Rs. 40,000

***Illustration 40*:**

Current ratio 2.5 Liquid ratio 1.75

Stock Rs.1,50,000

Calculate Net working capital.

Solution:

Stock = Current ratio – Liquid ratio

1,50,000 = 2.5 – 1.75

1,50,000 = 0.75

$$\text{Current assets} = \frac{1{,}50{,}000}{0.75} \times 2.5 = \text{Rs.}\,5{,}00{,}000$$

$$\text{Current liabilities} = \frac{1{,}50{,}000}{0.75} \times 1 = \text{Rs.}\,2{,}00{,}000$$

Net working capital = Current assets – Current liabilities

= 5,00,000 – 2,00,000

= Rs. 3,00,000

***Illustration 41*:**

Calculate Current ratio, when inventory is Rs. 80,000. Prepaid expenses are Rs. 20,000; Quick ratio is 2.5 to 1 and Current liabilities are Rs. 50,000

Solution:

$$\text{(i) Current ratio} = \frac{\text{Current assets}}{\text{Current liabilities}}$$

$$\text{Current ratio} = \frac{2{,}25{,}000}{50{,}000} = 4.5:1$$

Workings:

Current assets = Stock + Prepaid expenses + quick assets

= 80,000+20,000+ 1,25,000 = Rs. 2,25,000

Quick Assets:

Quick liabilities = Current liabilities – Bank O/D

= 50,000 – NIL

Quick liability = Rs. 50,000

$$\text{Quick assets} = \frac{50{,}000}{1} \times 2.5 = \text{Rs.}\,1{,}25{,}000$$

***Illustration 42*:**

Following ratios are related to the trading activities of National Traders Ltd.,

Debtors velocity	3 months;	Stock velocity	8 months;
Creditors velocity	2 months;	Gross profit ratio	25 %

Gross profit for the year ended 31st December, 2009 amounts Rs. 4,00,000. Closing stock of the year is Rs. 10,000 above the opening stock. Bills receivable amount to Rs. 25,000 and Bills payable Rs. 10,000

Find out (a) Sales (b) Sundry debtors (c) Closing stock (d) Sundry creditors

Solution:

(a) Sales:

$$\text{Gross profit ratio} = \frac{\text{Gross profit}}{\text{Sales}} \times 100$$

$$25\% = \frac{4{,}00{,}000}{\text{Sales}}$$

$$\text{Sales} = \frac{4{,}00{,}000}{25} \times 100$$

= Rs. 16,00,000

(b) Sundry debtors:

Debtors' velocity

$$= \frac{\text{Debtors} + \text{Bills receivable}}{\text{Sales}} \times 12 = 3 \text{ months}$$

$$3 = \frac{\text{Debtors} + \text{Bills receivable}}{16{,}00{,}000} \times 12$$

$$\text{Debtors} + \text{Bills receivable} = \frac{3 \times 16{,}00{,}000}{12} = \text{Rs. } 4{,}00{,}000$$

Less: Bills receivable	= Rs.25,000
Debtors	= 3,75,000

(c) Closing stock:

Stock velocity is given as 8 months. It may be expressed in terms of times.

$$\text{Stock velocity} = \frac{12}{8} = 1.5 \text{ times}$$

$$\text{Stock velocity} = \frac{\text{Cost of goods sold}}{\text{Average stock}} = 1.5$$

Cost of goods sold = Sales – Gross profit

= 16,00,000 – 4,00,000

= Rs. 12,00,000

$$\frac{12,00,000}{\text{Average stock}} = 1.5$$

1.5 × Average stock = 12,00,000

$$\text{Average stock} = \frac{12,00,000}{1.5} = \text{Rs. } 8,00,000$$

Total stock	Rs.16,00,000 (8,00,000 × 2)
Less: Excess stock	Rs. 10,000
	Rs.15,90,000

$$\text{Opening stock} = \frac{15,90,000}{2} = \text{Rs. } 7,95,000$$

Closing stock = 7,95,000 + 10,000 = Rs. 8,05,000.

(d) Sundry Creditors:

Creditors' velocity

$$\frac{\text{Creditors} + \text{Bills payable}}{\text{Credit purchases}} \times 12 = 2 \text{ months}$$

Purchases = Cost of goods sold + Closing stock – Opening stock

= 12,00,000 + 8,05,000 – 7,95,000

Purchases = 12,10,000

$$= \frac{\text{Creditors} + \text{Bills payable}}{12,10,000} \times 12$$

$$\text{Creditors + Bills payable} = \frac{2 \times 12,10,000}{12} = 2,01,667$$

Less : Bills payable 10,000

Creditors Rs. 1,91,667

***Illustration 43*:**

Debtors' velocity	3 months	Creditors' velocity	2 months
Stock velocity	8 times	Capital turnover ratio	2.5 times
Fixed assets turnover ratio	8 times	Gross profit turnover ratio	25%

Gross profit in a year amounts to Rs. 80,000. There is no long-term loan or over draft. Reserve and surplus amount to Rs. 28,000. Liquid assets are Rs. 97,333. Closing stock of the year is Rs. 2,000 more than the opening stock. Bills receivable amount to Rs. 5,000 and bills payable to Rs. 2,000.

Find out:

(a) Sales (b) Sundry Debtors (c) Closing stock

(d) Sundry creditors (e) Fixed assets (f) Proprietors' fund

Prepare a balance sheet with as many details as possible.

Solution:

Balance sheet

Liabilities	*Rs.*	*Assets*	*Rs.*
Share capital	1,00,000	Fixed assets	40,000
Reserve and surplus	28,000	Stock	31,000
Bills payable	2,000	Debtors	75,000
Sundry creditors	38,333	B/R	5,000
		Cash in hand (Bal. fig.)	17,333
	1,68,333		**1,68,333**

Workings:

(a) Gross profit ratio $= \dfrac{\text{Gross profit}}{\text{Sales}} \times 100$

$$25 = \frac{80,000}{\text{Sales}} \times 100$$

$$\text{Sales} = \frac{80{,}000}{25} \times 100 = \text{Rs. } 3{,}20{,}000$$

(b) Sundry Debtors:

Debtors' velocity

$$\frac{\text{Debtors} + \text{Bills receivable}}{\text{Net credit sales}} \times 12 = 3 \text{ months}$$

$$\frac{\text{Debtors} + \text{Bills receivable}}{3{,}20{,}000} \times 12 = 3$$

$$\text{Debtors} + \text{Bills receivable} = \frac{3 \times 3{,}20{,}000}{12} = \text{Rs. } 80{,}000$$

Less: Bills receivable = Rs. 5,000

Debtors = 75,000

(c) Closing stock:

$$\text{Stock velocity} = \frac{\text{Cost of goods sold}}{\text{Average stock}} = 8$$

Cost of goods sold = Sales – Gross profit

= 3,20,000 – 80,000

= Rs. 2,40,000

$$\frac{2{,}40{,}000}{\text{Average stock}} = 8$$

$$\text{Average stock} = \frac{2{,}40{,}000}{8} = \text{Rs. } 30{,}000$$

Total stock Rs.60,000 (30,000 × 2)

Less: Excess stock Rs. 2,000

Rs. 58,000

$$\text{Opening stock} = \frac{58{,}000}{2} = \text{Rs. } 29{,}000$$

Closing stock = 29,000 + 2,000 = Rs. 31,000

(d) Sundry Creditors:

Creditors' velocity

$$\frac{\text{Creditors} + \text{Bills payable}}{\text{Credit purchases}} \times 12 = 2 \text{ months}$$

Purchases = Cost of goods sold + Closing stock – Opening stock

= 2,40,000 + 31,000 – 29,000

Purchases = 2,42,000

Less : Bills payable 2,000

Creditors Rs. 38,333

(e) Fixed assets:

$$\text{Fixed assets turnover ratio} = \frac{\text{Sales}}{\text{Fixed assets}} = 8$$

$$= \frac{3,20,000}{\text{Fixed assets}} = 8$$

Fixed assets = 3,20,000/8 = Rs. 40,000

(f) Captial turnover ratio $= \dfrac{\text{Sales}}{\text{Proprietors' fund}} = 2.5 \text{ times}$

$$= \frac{3,20,000}{\text{Proprietors' fund}} = 2.5$$

$$\text{Proprietors' fund} = \frac{3,20,000}{2.5} = 1,28,000$$

Less: Reserve and surplus 28,000

Share capital 1,00,000

(g) Calculation of Cash in hand:

Particulars	*Rs.*	*Rs.*
Total liquid assets		97,333
Debtors		
Add: B/R	75,000	
	5,000	80,000
Cash (Bal. fig.)		**Rs. 1,77,333**

***Illustration 44*:**

From the following information, prepare a Balance Sheet.

(i)	Current ratio	2.5
(ii)	Liquid ratio	1.5
(iii)	Fixed assets/proprietary funds	0.75
(iv)	Working capital	Rs. 60,000
(v)	Reserves and surplus	Rs. 40,000
(vi)	Bank O/D	Rs. 10,000
(vii)	There is no long-term loan or fictitious asset	

Solution:

Balance Sheet

Liabilities		*Rs.*	*Assets*		*Rs.*
Share capital		2,00,000	Fixed assets		1,80,000
Reserve and surplus		40,000	**Current assets:**		
Current Liabilities:			Liquid assets	45,000	
Liquid liability	30,000		Stock	55,000	1,00,000
Bank O/D	10,000	40,000			
		2,80,000			**2,80,000**

Workings:

Working capital = Current assets – Current liabilities

60,000 = 2.5 – 1

60,000 = 1.5

(i) Current assets $= \frac{60,000}{1.5} \times 2.5 = \text{Rs.}1,00,000$

(ii) Current liabilities $= \frac{60,000}{1.5} \times 1 = \text{Rs.}40,000$

Liquid liability = Current liability – Bank O/D

Liquid liability = Rs. 40,000 – 10,000 = 30,000

Liquid assets $= \frac{30,000}{1} \times 1.5 = \text{Rs.}45,000$

(iii) Stock = Current assets – Liquid assets

Stock = 1,00,000 – 45,000 = Rs.55,000

(iv) Fixed assets:

Fixed assets/proprietary funds 0.75: 1

Total liabilities = Total assets

Current liability + Prop.funds = Fixed assets + Current assets

Prop.funds – Fixed assets = Current assets – Current liability

1.0 - 0.75 = 1,00,000 – 40,000

0.25 = Rs. 60,000

Fixed assets $= \frac{60,000}{0.25} \times 0.75 = \text{Rs.}1,80,000$

Prop.funds $= \frac{60,000}{0.25} \times 1 = \text{Rs.}2,40,000$

Share capital = Prop. funds – Reserves and surplus

2,40,000 – 40,000

Share capital = Rs. 2,00,000

Illustration 45:

From the following information, prepare statement showing the proprietary fund as on 31.12.2009

(i)	Current ratio	2.5:1
(ii)	Liquid ratio	1.5:1
(iii)	Fixed assets to proprietary funds	0.75:1

(iv) Working capital Rs.90,000

(v) Reserve and surplus Rs.60,000

(vi) Bank O/D Rs. 15,000

Solution:

Statement of proprietary fund:

Particulars	***Rs.***	***Rs.***
Fixed assets		2,70,000
Current assets:		
Stock	82,500	
Liquid assets	67,500	
	1,50,000	
Less: Current liabilities	60,000	90,000
Proprietors' fund		**3,60,000**

Represented by:

Particulars	***Rs.***
Share capital	3,00,000
Reserve and surplus	60,000
	3,60,000

Workings:

Working capital = Current assets − Current liabilities

90,000 = 2.5 − 1

90,000 = 1.5

$$\text{(i) Current assets} = \frac{90{,}000}{1.5} \times 2.5 = \text{Rs.}1{,}50{,}000$$

$$\text{(ii) Current liabilities} = \frac{90{,}000}{1.5} \times 1 = \text{Rs.}\,60{,}000$$

Liquid liability = Current liability − Bank O/D

Liquid liability = Rs. 60,000 − 15,000 = 45,000

$$\text{Liquid assets} = \frac{45{,}000}{1} \times 1.5 = \text{Rs.}\,67{,}500$$

(iii) Stock = Current assets – Liquid assets

Stock = 1,50,000 – 67,500 = Rs. 82,500

(iv) Fixed assets:

Fixed assets to proprietary funds = 0.75:1

Total liabilities = Total assets

Current liability + Prop.funds = Fixed assets + Current assets

Prop.funds – Fixed assets = Working capital

1.0 – 0.75 = Rs. 90,000

0.25 = Rs. 90,000

$$\text{Fixed assets} = \frac{90{,}000}{0.25} \times 0.75 = \text{Rs.}2{,}70{,}000$$

$$\text{Prop. funds} = \frac{90{,}000}{0.25} \times 1 = \text{Rs.}3{,}60{,}000$$

Share capital = Prop.funds – Reserve and surplus

3,60,000 – 60,000

Share capital = Rs. 3,00,000

***Illustration 46*:**

You are given the following information pertaining to financial statements of Ding Dong Ltd., Prepare trading and profit and loss as well as Balance Sheet:

Net current assets	Rs. 1,00,000
Paid-up capital	Rs. 3,00,000
Current ratio	1.8:1
Liquid ratio	1.35:1
Fixed assets to shareholders' equity	80%
Gross profit ratio	25%
Net profit to paid-up capital	20%
Stock turnover ratio	5 times
Average age of outstanding customers 36.5 days	

Solution:

Trading and Profit and Loss Account

Particulars	*Rs.*	*Particulars*	*Rs.*
To Cost of goods sold	2,81,250	By Sales	3,75,000
To Gross profit 3,75,000 × 25 %	93,750		
	3,75,000		3,75,000
To indirect exp.(bal. fig.)	33,750	By Gross profit	93,750
To Net profit	60,000		
	93,750		**93,750**

Balance Sheet

Liabilities	*Rs.*	*Assets*		*Rs.*
Share capital	3,00,000	Fixed assets		4,00,000
Reserve and surplus	2,00,000	**Current assets:**		
Current liabilities	1,25,000	Stock	56,250	
		Debtors	37,500	
		Bank	1,31,250	2,25,000
	6,25,000			**6,25,000**

Workings:

Net current assets refers to working capital

Working capital = Current assets – Current liabilities

1,00,000 = 1.8 – 1

1,00,000 = 0.8

(i) Current assets $= \dfrac{1,00,000}{0.8} \times 1.8 =$ Rs. 2,25,000

(ii) Current liabilities $= \dfrac{1,00,000}{0.8} \times 1 =$ Rs.1,25,000

(iii) Liquid liability = Current liability – Bank O/D

Liquid liability = Rs.1,25,000

(iv) Liquid assets $= \frac{1,25,000}{1} \times 1.35 = \text{Rs.}1,68,750$

(v) Stock = Current assets – Liquid assets

Stock = 2,25,000 – 1,68,750 = Rs. 56,250

(vi) Stock velocity $= \frac{\text{Cost of goods sold}}{\text{Closing stock}} = 5$

$$\frac{\text{Cost of goods sold}}{56,250} = 5$$

Cost of goods sold = 56,250 × 5 = Rs. 2,81,250

(vii) Sales:

Cost of goods sold = Sales – Gross profit

= 100 – 25 = 75

If cost of goods sold is Rs.75, sales is Rs.100;

If cost of goods sold is Rs. 2,81,250,

Sales $= \frac{2,81,250}{75} \times 100 = \text{Rs.}3,75,000$

(viii) Debtors:

Average collection period $= \frac{\text{Debtors}}{\text{Credit sales}} \times 365 = 36.5$

$$= \frac{\text{Debtors}}{3,75,000} \times 365 = 36.5$$

Debtors $= \frac{3,75,000}{365} \times 36.5 = \text{Rs.}37,500$

(ix) Bank:

Quick Assets (Debtors + Bank)	Rs. 1,68,750
Less: Debtors	Rs. 37,500
Bank balance	1,31,250

(x) Net Profit:

Net profit to paid-up capital = 20%

3,00,000 × 20% = Rs. 60,000

(xi) Fixed assets:

Fixed assets to shareholders' equity = 80%

Shareholders' funds + Current liabilities = Fixed assets + Current assets

Shareholders' funds = Fixed assets + Current assets – Current liabilities

= Fixed assets + Net current assets (working capital)

100% = 80% + 20%

If working capital is Rs.20, fixed assets are Rs. 80;

If working capital is Rs.1,00,000,

$$\text{Fixed assets} = \frac{1,00,000}{20} \times 80 = \text{Rs. } 4,00,000$$

$$\text{(xii) Shareholders' equity} = \frac{4,00,000}{80} \times 100 = \text{Rs. } 5,00,000$$

Less: Share capital	Rs.	3,00,000
Reserve and surplus	Rs.	2,00,000

***Illustration 47*:**

From the following information, prepare a Balance Sheet. Show the workings.

(i) Current ratio	1.75
(ii) Liquid ratio	1.15
(iii) Fixed assets/proprietary funds	0.75
(iv) Working capital	Rs. 75,000
(v) Reserve and surplus	Rs. 1,00,000
(vi) Bank O/D	Rs. 60,000

(vii) There is no long-term loan or fictitious asset

Solution:

Balance Sheet as on ....

Liabilities		*Rs.*	*Assets*		*Rs.*
Share capital		2,00,000	Fixed assets		2,25,000
Reserve & surplus		1,00,000	**Current assets:**		
Current liabilities:			Liquid assets	46,000	
Bank O/D	60,000		Stock	1,29,000	
Liquid liability	40,000	1,00,000			1,75,000
		4,00,000			**4,00,000**

Workings:

Working capital = Current assets – Current liabilities

75,000 = 1.75 – 1

75,000 = 0.75

(i) Current assets $= \frac{75{,}000}{0.75} \times 1.75 = \text{Rs.}1{,}75{,}000$

(ii) Current liabilities $= \frac{75{,}000}{0.75} \times 1 = \text{Rs.}1{,}00{,}000$

Liquid liability = Current liability – Bank O/D

Liquid liability = Rs.1,00,000 – 60,000 = 40,000

Liquid assets $= \frac{40{,}000}{1} \times 1.15 = \text{Rs.}\ 46{,}000$

(iii) Stock = Current assets – Liquid assets

Stock = 1,75,000 – 46,000 = Rs. 1,29,000

(iv) Fixed assets:

Fixed assets/proprietary funds 0.75 : 1

Total liabilities = Total assets

Current liability + Prop.funds = Fixed assets + Current assets

Prop.funds – fixed assets = Current assets – Current liability

1.0 - 0.75 = 1,75,000 – 1,00,000

$$0.25 = Rs.75,000$$

$$\text{Fixed assets} = \frac{75,000}{0.25} \times 0.75 = Rs.2,25,000$$

$$\text{Prop.funds} = \frac{75,000}{0.25} \times 1 = Rs.\,3,00,000$$

Share capital = Prop.funds – Reserve and surplus

3,00,000 – 1,00,000

Share capital = Rs. 2,00,000

***Illustration 48*:**

From the following information, prepare a statement of proprietary funds with as many details as possible.

Stock velocity	6
Capital turnover ratio (on cost of sales)	2
Fixed assets turnover ratio (on cost of sales)	4
Gross profit turnover ratio	20%
Debtors' velocity	2 months
Creditors' velocity	73 days

Gross profit in a year amounts to Rs. 60,000. Reserve and surplus amounts to Rs. 20,000. Closing stock of the year is Rs. 5,000 more than the opening stock.

Solution:

Statement of Proprietary funds

	Rs.	*Rs.*
Fixed assets		60,000
Current assets:		
Cash	16,500	
Stock	42,500	
Debtors	50,000	
Less: Current liability:	1,09,000	
creditors	49,000	60,000
		1,20,000

Proprietary funds :

Share capital	1,00,000
Reserve and surplus	20,000
	1,20,000

(a) Gross profit ratio $= \frac{\text{Gross profit}}{\text{Sales}} \times 100$

$$20 = \frac{60{,}000}{\text{Sales}} \times 100$$

$$\text{Sales} = \frac{60{,}000}{20} \times 100 = \text{Rs. } 3{,}00{,}000$$

(b) Sundry debtors:

$$\frac{\text{Debtors} + \text{Bills receivable}}{\text{Net credit sales}} \times \text{No. of working days} = 2 \text{ months}$$

$$\frac{\text{Debtors}}{3{,}00{,}000} \times 12 = 2$$

$$\text{Debtors} = \frac{2 \times 3{,}00{,}000}{12} = \text{Rs. } 50{,}000$$

(c) Stock:

$$\text{Stock velocity} = \frac{\text{Cost of goods sold}}{\text{Average stock}} = 6$$

Cost of goods sold = Sales – Gross profit

= 3,00,000 – 60,000

= Rs. 2,40,000

$$\frac{2{,}40{,}000}{\text{Average stock}} = 6$$

$$\text{Average stock} = \frac{2,40,000}{6} = 40,000$$

Total stock	Rs. 80,000 (40,000×2)
Less: Excess stock	Rs. 5,000
	Rs. 75,000

$$\text{Opening stock} = \frac{75,000}{2} = \text{Rs.}37,500$$

Closing stock = 37,500 + 5,000 = Rs. 42,500

(or)

Opening stock = Average stock – 2,500 = Rs. 37,500

Closing stock = Average stock + 2,500 = Rs. 42,500

(Note: If excess, half of the excess amount should be add with average stock and *vice-versa*)

(d) Sundry Creditors:

$$\frac{\text{Creditors} + \text{Bills payable}}{\text{Credit purchases}} \times \text{No. of working days} = 73 \text{ days}$$

Purchases = Cost of goods sold + Closing stock – Opening stock

= 2,40,000 + 42,500 – 37,500

Purchases = 2,45,000

$$\frac{\text{Creditors}}{2,45,000} \times 365 = 73$$

$$\text{Creditors} = \frac{73 \times 2,45,000}{365} = 49,000$$

(e) Fixed assets:

$$\text{Fixed assets turnover ratio (on cost of sales)} = \frac{\text{Cost of sales}}{\text{Fixed assets}} = 4$$

$$= \frac{2,40,000}{\text{Fixed assets}} = 4$$

Fixed assets = 2,40,000/ 4 = Rs. 60,000

(f) Capital turnover ratio (on cost of sales) $= \frac{\text{Cost of sales}}{\text{Proprietors' fund}} = 2$

$$\frac{2,40,000}{\text{Proprietors' fund}} = 2$$

$$\text{Proprietors' fund} = \frac{2,40,000}{2} = 1,20,000$$

Less: Reserve and surplus 20,000

Share Capital 1,00,000

Calculation of cash in hand:

Balance Sheet as on —

Liabilities	*Rs.*	*Assets*	*Rs.*
Share Capital	1,00,000	Fixed assets	60,000
Reserve and surplus	20,000	Stock	42,500
Creditors	49,000	Debtors	50,000
		Cash in hand (bal.fig)	16,500
	1,69,000		**1,69,000**

***Illustration 49*:**

From the following information, prepare a Balance Sheet of the Company, with as many details as possible.

Current ratio	2.5
Liquid ratio	1.5
Net working capital	Rs. 3,00,000
Gross profit ratio	20%
Stock velocity (cost of sales/closing stock)	6 times
Debt collection period	2 months
Fixed assets turnover ratio (on cost of sales)	2 times
Fixed assets to shareholders' net worth	0.80
Reserve and surplus to capital	0.50

Solution:

Balance Sheet

Liabilities	*Rs.*	*Assets*	*Rs.*
Share capital	5,00,000	Fixed assets	6,00,000
Reserve & surplus	2,50,000	Stock	2,00,000
Long term loan (bal.fig.)	1,50,000	Debtors	2,50,000
Current liabilities	2,00,000	Cash	50,000
	11,00,000		**11,00,000**

Workings:

Working capital = Current assets – Current liabilities

3,00,000 = 2.5 – 1

3,00,000 = 1.5

(i) Current assets $= \frac{3,00,000}{1.5} \times 2.5$ = Rs. 5,00,000

(ii) Current liabilities $= \frac{3,00,000}{1.5} \times 1$ = Rs. 2,00,000

(iii) Liquid liability = Current liability – Bank O/D

Liquid liability = Rs. 2,00,000

(iv) Liquid assets $= \frac{2,00,000}{1} \times 1.5$ = Rs. 3,00,000

(v) Stock = Current assets – Liquid assets

Stock = 5.00,000 – 3,00,000 = Rs. 2,00,000

(vi) Cost of goods sold:

$$\text{Stock velocity} = \frac{\text{Cost of goods sold}}{\text{Closing stock}} = 6$$

$$\frac{\text{Cost of goods sold}}{2,00,000} = 6$$

Cost of goods sold = 2,00,000 × 6 = Rs. 12,00,000

(vii) Sales:

Gross profit ratio 20%

Sales – Gross profit = Cost of goods sold

Rs.100 – Rs.20 = Rs. 80

$$\text{Sales} = \frac{12,00,000}{80} \times 100 = \text{Rs.}15,00,000$$

(viii) Debtors:

$$\text{Debtors' velocity} = \frac{\text{Debtors} + \text{Bills receivable}}{\text{Net credit Sales}} \times 12 = 2$$

$$\frac{\text{Debtors}}{15,00,000} \times 12 = 2$$

$$\text{Debtors} = \frac{2 \times 15,00,000}{12} = \text{Rs. } 2,50,000$$

(ix) Fixed assets:

$$\text{Fixed assets turnover ratio} = \frac{\text{Cost of sales}}{\text{Fixed assets}}$$

$$= \frac{12,00,000}{\text{Fixed assets}} = 2$$

Fixed assets = 12,00,000/2

= Rs. 6,00,000

(x) Shareholders' Net worth:

$$\text{Fixed assets to shareholders' net worth} = \frac{\text{Fixed assets}}{\text{Proprietary fund}} = 0.80$$

$$\frac{6,00,000}{\text{Proprietary fund}} = 0.80$$

$$\text{Proprietary fund} = \frac{6,00,000}{0.80} = \text{Rs.}7,50,000$$

(xi) Reserve and surplus:

Proprietary fund = Share capital + Reserve and surplus

Reserve and surplus to capital = 0.50 :1

Proprietary fund = 1 + 0.50 = 1.50

$$\text{Reserve and surplus} = \frac{7,50,000}{1.5} \times 0.5 = \text{Rs. } 2,50,000$$

(xii) Share capital:

Proprietary fund = Rs. 7,50,000

Less: Reserve & surplus = Rs. 2,50,000

Share capital = Rs. 5,00,000

(xiii) Cash:

Total current assets	5,00,000
Less: Stock 2,00,000	
Debtors 2,50,000	
	4,50,000
Cash	50,000

Illustration 50:

From the following information, prepare Balance Sheet of Rakshaa Ltd.,

(i)	Sales for the year	Rs. 20,00,000
(ii)	Gross profit ratio	25%
(iii)	Current ratio	1.50
(iv)	Quick assets (cash and debtors) ratio	1.25
(v)	Stock turnover ratio	15
(vi)	Debts collection period	1.5 months
(vii)	Turnover to fixed assets	1.5
(viii)	Ratio of reserves to share capital	0.33 (i.e., 1/3)
(ix)	Fixed assets to net worth	0.83 (i.e., 5/6)

The term turnover refers to cost of sales and stock refers to closing stock

Solution:

Balance Sheet of Rakshaa Ltd; as on .....

Liabilities	*Rs.*	*Assets*	*Rs.*
Share capital	9,00,000	Fixed assets	10,00,000
Reserves	3,00,000	Stock	1,00,000
Creditors (Bal.fig.)	4,00,000	Debtors	2,50,000
		Cash	2,50,000
	16,00,000		**16,00,000**

Workings:

(i) Gross profit:

$$=\frac{20,00,000}{100}\times 25 = \text{Rs. }5,00,000$$

(ii) Cost of goods sold = Sales – Gross profit

= 20,00,000 – 5,00,000

= 15,00,000

(iii) Stock:

Stock velocity (based on closing stock)

$$\frac{\text{Cost of goods sold}}{\text{Closing stock}} = 15$$

$$=\frac{15,00,000}{\text{Closing stock}} = 15$$

$$\text{Closing stock} = \frac{15,00,000}{1.5} = \text{Rs.}1,00,000$$

(iv) Current assets:

$$\text{Current ratio} = \frac{\text{Current assets}}{\text{Current liabilities}} = 1.5:1$$

$$\text{Liquid ratio} = \frac{\text{Liquid assets}}{\text{Liquid liabilities}} = 1.25:1$$

Liquid liabilities = Current liabilities – Bank overdraft

As number bank O/D, Liquid liabilities = Current liabilities

Therefore, the difference between ratios represents only stock

Current assets – Liquid assets = Stock

1.5 – 1.25 = 0.25

If stock is 0.25, current assets are 1.5

If stock is Rs.1,00,000

Current assets are –

$$= \frac{1,00,000}{0.25} \times 1.5 = \text{Rs.}6,00,000$$

(v) Current liabilities:

$$\text{Current liabilities} = \frac{6,00,000}{1.5} \times 1 = \text{Rs. } 4,00,000$$

(vi) Sundry debtors:

$$\text{Debtors velocity} = \frac{\text{Debtors + Bills receivable}}{\text{Sales}} \times 12 = 1.5 \text{ months}$$

$$= \frac{\text{Debtors}}{20,00,000} \times 12 = 1.5$$

$$\text{Debtors} = \frac{1.5 \times 20,00,000}{12} = \text{Rs. } 2,50,000$$

(vii) Liquid assets:

If the stock is 0.25, quick assets are 1.25

If the stock is Rs. 1,00,000

Liquid assets are

$$= \frac{1,00,000}{0.25} \times 1.25 = \text{Rs. } 5,00,000$$

(viii) Cash:

Liquid assets (Debtors + Cash)	5,00,000
Less: Debtors	2,50,000
Cash	2,50,000

(ix) Fixed assets:

$$\text{Fixed assets turnover ratio (on cost of sales)} = \frac{\text{Cost of sales}}{\text{Fixed assets}} = 1.5$$

$$= \frac{15,00,000}{\text{Fixed assets}} = 1.5$$

Fixed assets = 15,00,000/1.5 = Rs.10,00,000

(x) Net worth:

$$\text{Fixed assets to net worth} = \frac{\text{Fixed assets}}{\text{Net worth}} = 0.83\,(5/6)$$

If fixed assets is Rs. 5, Net worth is Rs. 6

If fixed assets is Rs.10,00,000,

Net worth is —

$$= \frac{10,00,000}{5} \times 6 = \text{Rs.}12,00,000$$

Net worth = Rs.12,00,000

(xi Share capital:

Net worth = Share capital + Reserves

Ratio of reserves to share capital = 1: 3

Net worth = 1+ 3 = 4

$$\text{Share capital} = \frac{12,00,000}{4} \times 3 = \text{Rs. }9,00,000$$

Reserves =12,00,000 – 9,00,000

Reserves = Rs. 3,00,000.

Illustration 51:

From the following information, prepare Balance Sheet of Chandran Ltd., when sales are Rs. 36,00,000

Sales/Total assets	3
Sales/Fixed assets	5
Sales/Current assets	7.5
Sales/Stock	20
Sales/Debtors	15
Current Ratio	2
Total assets/Net worth	2.5
Long-term debt/Equity	1

Balance sheet

Liabilities	*Rs.*	*Assets*	*Rs.*
Net worth		Fixed assets	
Long-term debt		Stock	
Current liabilities		Debtors	
		Liquid assets	

Solution: **Balance Sheet of Chandran Ltd.,**

Liabilities	*Rs.*	*Assets*		*Rs.*
Net worth	4,80,000	Fixed assets		7,20,000
Long-term debt	4,80,000	**Total current assets:**		
Current liabilities	2,40,000	Stock	1,80,000	
		Debtors	2,40,000	
		Liquid assets	60,000	4,80,000
	12,00,000			**12,00,000**

Workings:

(a) Total assets:

$$= \frac{\text{Sales}}{\text{Total assets}} = 3:1$$

$$= \frac{36,00,000}{3} \times 1 = \text{Rs. } 12,00,000$$

(b) Fixed assets:

$$= \frac{\text{Sales}}{\text{Fixed assets}} = 5:1$$

$$= \frac{36,00,000}{5} \times 1 = \text{Rs. } 7,20,000$$

(c) Current assets:

$$= \frac{\text{Sales}}{\text{Current assets}} = 7.5:1$$

$$= \frac{36,00,000}{7.5} \times 1 = \text{Rs. } 4,80,000$$

(d) Inventories:

$$= \frac{\text{Sales}}{\text{Inventories}} = 20:1$$

$$= \frac{36,00,000}{20} \times 1 = \text{Rs. } 1,80,000$$

(e) Debtors:

$$= \frac{\text{Sales}}{\text{Debtors}} = 15:1$$

$$= \frac{36,00,000}{15} \times 1 = \text{Rs. } 2,40,000$$

(f) Current liabilities:

$$\text{Current liabilities} = \frac{4,80,000}{2} \times 1 = \text{Rs. } 2,40,000$$

(g) Net worth:

$$= \frac{\text{Total assets}}{\text{Net worth}} = 2.5:1$$

$$= \frac{12,00,000}{2.5} \times 1 = \text{Rs. } 4,80,000$$

(h) Long-term debt:

(h) Long-term debt:

$$= \frac{\text{Long - term debt}}{\text{Equity}} = 1:1$$

$$= \frac{4,80,000}{1} \times 1 = \text{Rs.}4,80,000$$

(i) Liquid assets = Current assets – (Stock + Debtors)

= 4,80,000 – (1,80,000 + 2,40,000)

= 4,80,000 – 4,20,000

= Rs. 60,000

***Illustration 52*:**

In projecting the financial plan of JC Trading Company Ltd., the use of the following accounting ratio is made.

Estimated annual sales	Rs. 2,00,000
Sales to net worth	2.5 times
Current debt to net worth	25%
Total debt to net worth	60%
Current ratio	3.6 times
Net sales to inventory	4 times
Average collection period	36 days
(taken as 360 days in a year)	
Fixed assets to net worth	70%

On the basis of the above information, prepare a Balance Sheet of the company.

Solution:

Balance Sheet of JC Trading Co. Ltd.

Liabilities	*Rs.*	*Assets*	*Rs.*
Shareholders' funds (Net worth)	80,000	Fixed assets	56,000
Long-term debt	28,000	**Current assets:**	
Current debt	20,000	Stock	50,000
		Debtors	20,000
		Bank	2,000
	1,28,000		**1,28,000**

Workings:

(i) Net worth:

$$\text{Sales to net worth} = \frac{\text{Sales}}{\text{Net worth}} = 2.5:1$$

$$\frac{2,00,000}{2.5} \times 1 = \text{Rs.}\,80,000$$

(ii) Current debt – 25 % on net worth:

80,000 × 25/100 = Rs. 20,000

(iii) Total debt – 60% on net worth:

80,000 × 60/100 = Rs. 48,000

(iv) Long-term debt:

Long-term debt = Total debt – Current debt

= 48,000 – 20,000 = Rs. 28,000

(v) Current assets:

$$\text{Current ratio} = \frac{\text{Current assets}}{\text{Current liabilities}} = 3.6:1$$

$$= \frac{20,000}{1} \times 3.6$$

= Rs. 72,000

(vi) Inventory:

$$\text{Net sales to inventory} = \frac{\text{Net sales}}{\text{Inventory}} = 4:1$$

$$= \frac{2,00,000}{4} \times 1 = \text{Rs.}\ 50,000$$

(vii) Debtors:

$$\text{Average collection period} = \frac{\text{Debtors}}{\text{Sales}} \times \text{No. of days in a year}$$

$$\text{Debtors} = \frac{2,00,000}{360} \times 36 = \text{ Rs. } 20,000$$

(viii) Cash in hand:

Particulars	Rs.	Rs.
Total current assets		72,000
Less: (–) Stock	50,000	
Debtors	20,000	70,000
Cash in hand		**2,000**

(ix) Fixed assets – 70% on net worth:

80,000 × 70/100 = Rs. 56,000

Illustration 53:

From the following particulars, prepare Trading, Profit and Loss Account and Balance Sheet.

Current ratio – 3; Liquid ratio – 1.8

Bank overdraft – Rs.20,000; Working capital – Rs. 2,40,000

Debtors' velocity – 1 month; Gross profit ratio – 20%

Proprietary ratio (Fixed assets/Shareholders' fund) 0.9

Reserve and surplus – 0.25 of share capital.

Opening stock – Rs.1,20,000; 8% Debentures – Rs. 3,60,000

Long-term investments – Rs. 2,00,000

Stock turnover ratio 10 times; Creditors' velocity — ½ month

Net profit to share capital – 20%.

Solution:

Trading, Profit and Loss Account for the year ending..........

Particulars	Rs.	Particulars	Rs.
To Opening stock	1,20,000	By Sales	18,75,000
To Purchases	15,60,000	By Closing stock	1,80,000
To Gross profit	3,75,000		
	20,55,000		20,55,000
To Debenture interest (8% on 3,60,000)	28,800	By Gross profit b/d	3,75,000
To Indirect expenses (Bal.fig.)	2,18,200		
To Net profit	1,28,000		
	3,75,000		**3,75,000**

Balance Sheet as on ....

Liabilities	*Rs.*	*Rs.*	*Assets*	*Rs.*
Share capital		6,40,000	Fixed assets	7,20,000
Reserve and Surplus:			Investments	2,00,000
Reserve (Bal.fig.)	32,000		**Current assets:**	
Profit and loss a/c	1,28,000	1,60,000	Stock	1,80,000
8% Debentures		3,60,000	Debtors	1,56,250
Current liabilities:			Cash (Bal.fig.)	23,750
Bank overdraft	20,000			
Creditors	65,000			
Other liabilities	35,000	1,20,000		
		12,80,000		**12,80,000**

Workings:

(i) Current assets:

Working capital = Current assets – Current liabilities

2,40,000 = 3 – 1

2,40,000 = 2

$$\text{Current assets} = \frac{2,40,000}{2} \times 3$$

(ii) Current liabilities:

$$\frac{2,40,000}{2} \times 1 = \text{Rs.}1,20,000$$

(iii) Liquid liabilities:

= Current liabilities – Bank overdraft

= 1,20,000 – 20,000

= Rs. 1,00,000

(iv) Liquid Assets:

$$= \frac{1,00,000}{1} \times 1.8 = \text{Rs.}1,80,000$$

(v) Stock:

Stock = Current assets – Liquid assets

= Rs. 3,60,000 – Rs. 1,80,000 = Rs. 1,80,000

(vi) Cost of Sales:

$$\text{Stock turnover ratio} = \frac{\text{Cost of sales}}{\text{Average stock}} = 10$$

$$\text{Average Stock} = \frac{\text{Opening stock + closing stock}}{2}$$

$$= \frac{1,20,000 + 1,80,000}{2} = \text{Rs.}1,50,000$$

$$= \frac{\text{Cost of sales}}{1,50,000} = 10$$

Cost of sales = 1,50,000 × 10 = Rs.15,00,000

(vii) Sales and gross profit:

Gross profit ratio = 20% on sales

Cost of sales = Sales – Gross profit

= 100 – 20 = Rs. 80

If cost of sales is Rs. 80, sales is Rs. 100

If cost of sales is Rs. 15,00,000

$$\text{Sales} = \frac{15,00,000}{80} \times 100 = \text{Rs.}18,75,000$$

$$\text{Gross profit} = \frac{18,75,000}{100} \times 20 = \text{Rs.}3,75,000$$

(viii) Debtors:

$$\text{Debtors' velocity} = \frac{\text{Debtors}}{\text{Credit sales}} \times 12 = 1\,\text{month}$$

$$\frac{\text{Debtors}}{18,75,000} \times 12 = 1\,\text{month}$$

(ix) Creditors:

Creditors' velocity

$$= \frac{\text{Creditors}}{\text{Credit purchases}} \times \text{Number of days in a year} = ½ \text{ month}$$

Credit purchases = Cost of sales + Closing stock – Opening stock

Purchases = 15,00,000 +1,80,000 – 1,20,000 = Rs.15,60,000

$$\text{Creditors} = \frac{15{,}60{,}000}{12} \times 0.5 = \text{Rs. } 65{,}000$$

(ix) Proprietary fund and fixed assets:

$$\text{Proprietary ratio} = \frac{\text{Fixed assets}}{\text{Proprietary' fund}} = 0.9:1$$

Proprietary fund + Long-term liability + Current liabilities

= Fixed assets + Investment + Current assets

i.e., P.F. – F.A= Investment + CA – Debentures – CL

- 0.9 = 2,00,000 + 3,60,000 – 3,60,000 – 1,20,000

0.1 = 80,000

$$\text{Fixed assets} = \frac{80{,}000}{0.1} \times 0.9 = \text{Rs. } 7{,}20{,}000$$

$$\text{Proprietary fund} = \frac{80{,}000}{0.1} \times 1 = \text{Rs. } 8{,}00{,}000$$

(xi) Reserve and Surplus and share capital:

Reserve and surplus	= 25% of share capital
Share capital	= Rs. 100
Reserve and surplus	= Rs. 25
Proprietary fund	Rs. 125

If proprietary fund is 125, reserve and surplus = 25

If proprietary fund is 8,00,000,

$$\text{Reserve and surplus} = 8{,}00{,}000 \times \frac{25}{125} = \text{Rs.}\,1{,}60{,}000$$

Share capital = 8,00,000 – 1,60,000 = Rs. 6,40,000

(xii) Net profit:

Net profit = 20% of share capital

$$= \frac{6{,}40{,}000}{100} \times 20 = \text{Rs.}\,1{,}28{,}000$$

DU PONT CONTROL CHART

A system of management control designed by an American company named Du-Pont company is popularly called Du Pont Control Chart. This system uses the ratio inter–relationship to provide charts for managerial attention. The standard ratio of the company are compared to present ratios and changes in performance are judged.

The chart is based on two elements, i.e., net profit and capital employed. Net profit is related to operating expenses. Capital employed consists of current assets and net fixed assets. The ratio will be –

$$= \frac{\text{Profit margin}}{\text{Capital employed}} \times 100$$

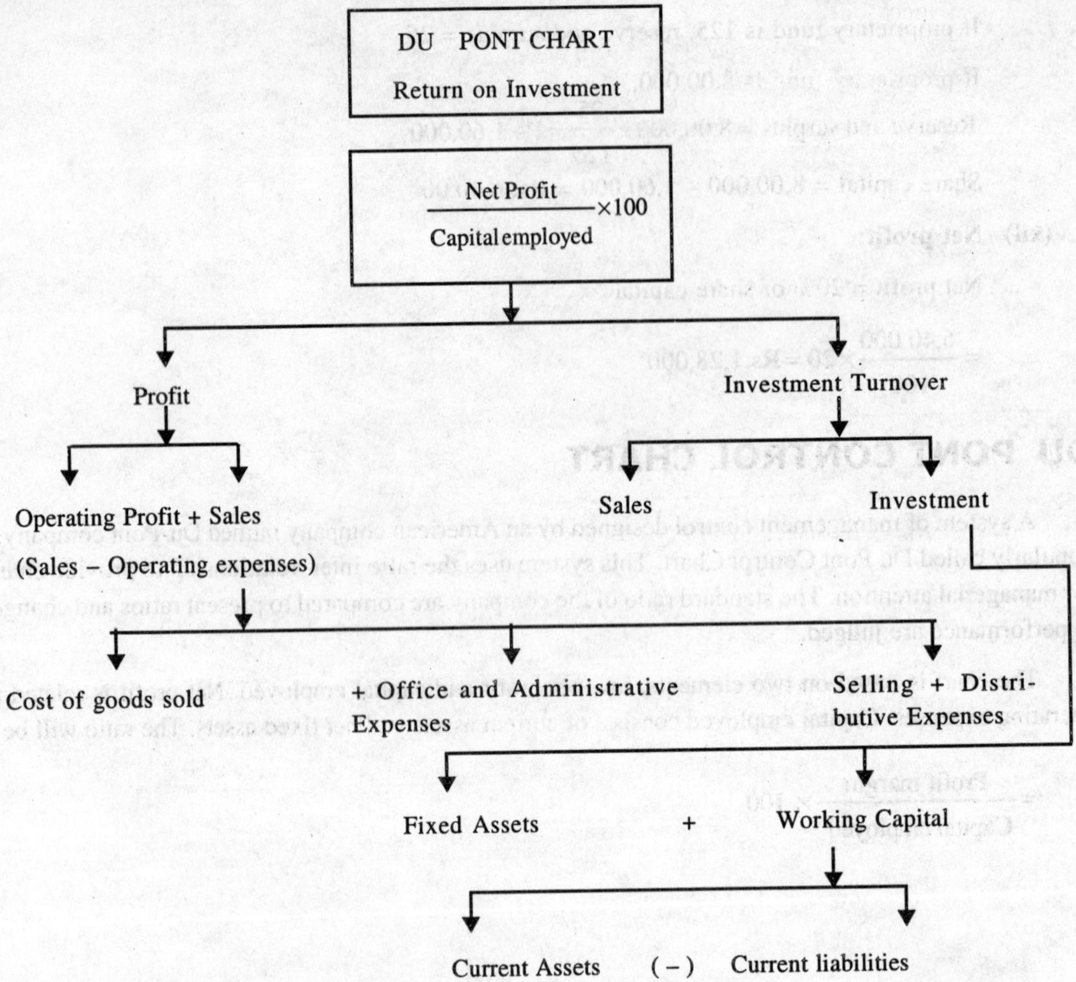

MODEL QUESTIONS

OBJECTIVE TYPE

Choose the best answer from the given alternatives:

1. The standard for absolute liquid ratio is

   (a) 1:2 (b) 1:1

   (c) 1.5:1 (d) 0.75:1

2. The relationship between current assets and current liabilities is

   (a) net profit ratio (b) current ratio

   (c) quick ratio (d) operating profit ratio

3. Solvency ratio is

(a) gross profit ratio (b) capital gearing ratio

(c) current ratio (d) none of the above

4. The term current asset does not include

(a) payments in advance (b) bills receivable

(c) long-term deferred charges (d) stock in trade

5 Long-term solvency ratio is indicated by

(a) current ratio (b) debt/equity ratio

(c) net profit ratio (d) quick ratio

6. Current ratio shows

(a) the change in gross profit (b) the working capital position

(c) the liquidity of assets (d) the change in net profit

7. When the current ratio is 4:1 and the amount of current liabilities is Rs.12,000 what is the amount of working capital

(a) Rs. 48,000 (b) Rs. 36000

(c) Rs. 30,000 (d) Rs. 60,000

8. Capital gearing is one of the

(a) liquidity ratios (b) leverage ratios

(c) activity ratios (d) profitability ratios

9. Return on investment is

(a) a profit and loss account ratio (b) a balance sheet ratio

(c) a combined ratio (d) none of the above

10. The difference between owner's equity at the end and owner's equity at the beginning is the

(a) net assets (b) net profit/loss

(c) net worth (d) equity share capital

11. Who is the user of ratio analysis?

(a) management (b) creditors and financial institutions

(c) investors (d) all of the above

12. Liquid ratio is also known as

(a) net profit ratio (b) current ratio

(c) quick ratio (d) operating profit ratio

Ans: (1) a (2) b (3) c (4) c (5) b (6) b

(7) b (8) b (9) a (10) b (11) d (12) c.

Fill in the blanks:

1. A ratio is an arithmetical relationship of one number to ________
2. Quick ratio is also known as ________
3. Gross capital employed is equal to ________
4. Rule of thumb for a current ratio is ________
5. Two elements of a current ratio are ________ and current liabilities
6. Debt equity ratio is the relationship between outsiders' funds and ________
7. Sales minus cost of goods sold is ________
8. If inventory turnover ratio is 5 times and average stock at cost is Rs.75,000, the cost of goods sold is ________
9. Low turnover of stock ratio indicates ________
10. ________ refers to the ability of a firm to pay its short-term obligations.

Ans:

(1) another number	**(2) liquid or acid test ratio**
(3) assets	**(4) 2:1**
(5) current assets	**(6) shareholders' funds**
(7) gross profit	**(8) Rs. 3,75,000**
(9) over investment in inventory	**(10) liquidity**

State true or false:

1. Liquidity ratio measure the long-term solvency of a concern
2. Inventory is a part of liquid assets
3. Rule of thumb for a quick ratio is 1:1
4. The amount of gross assets is equal to net capital employed
5. Return on investments ratio measures profitability of a business
6. High inventory turnover indicates efficient management of inventory.

Ans:

True: 3, 5, 6 **False: 1, 2, 4.**

Short answer questions

1. What is ratio analysis?
2. What are the significance of ratios?
3. What are liquidity ratios? Discuss their significance
4. What ratios are used to evaluate the long-term solvency of a firm? Explain them.
5. Discuss the significance of turnover ratios.
6. What is meant by shareholders' funds?
7. Discuss the uses of ratio analysis.

Essay type questions

1. What is meant by ratio analysis? Discuss its objectives and limitations.
2. "Ratios are indicators – sometimes pointers but not in themselves powerful tools of management" Explain.
3. Explain the relationship between solvency, liquidity and profitability.
4. What are the important profitability ratios? How are they worked out? Explain and illustrate.
5. Explain the overall profitability ratios of a firm.
6. Discuss the accounting ratios to judge the liquidity position of the business.

EXERCISES

Problem:1

Ram Ltd., has submitted the followingBalance Ssheet as on 30th June, 2009.

Liabilities	*Rs.*	*Assets*	*Rs.*
Equity capital	1,50,000	Fixed assets	1,62,000
Revenue reserves	30,000	**Current assets:**	
6% debentures	20,000	Stock	22,000
Current liabilities:		Debtors	51,000
Sundry creditors	49,000	Bills receivable	2,000
		Bank	12,000
	2,49,000		**2,49,000**

Find out current ratio and liquid ratio

Ans:

Current ratio 1.79:1 **Liquid ratio 1.32:1**

Problem:2

Calculate:

(a) Current Ratio (b) Liquid Ratio (c) Proprietary Ratio (d) Debt Equity Ratio, and (e) Capital Gearing Ratio.

Liabilities	*Rs.*	*Assets*	*Rs.*
5,000 equity shares of Rs.100 each	5,00,000	Building	6,00,000
2,000, 8% Pref. shares of Rs.100 each	2,00,000	Machinery	5,00,000
4,000, 9% debentures of Rs.100 each	4,00,000	Stock	2,40,000
Reserve	3,00,000	Debtors	2,00,000
Bank overdraft	50,000	Bank	55,000
Creditors	1,50,000	Prepaid expenses	5,000
	16,00,000		**16,00,000**

Ans:

(a) **Current ratio 2.5:1** (b) **Liquid ratio 1.7:1**

(c) **Proprietary ratio 0.63:1** (d) **Debt equity ratio 0.6:1**

(e) **Capital gearing ratio 0.75:1**

Problem: 3

The following is the Balance Sheet of Samy Ltd., as on 31st March, 2009.

Liabilities	*Rs.*	*Assets*	*Rs.*
Equity share capital	2,00,000	Land and building	1,50,000
Pref. share capital	2,00,000	Plant and machinery	2,50,000
General reserve	80,000	Furniture	50,000
Profit and loss a/c	40,000	Stock	1,50,000
12% debentures	2,20,000	Debtors	70,000
Creditors	1,00,000	Bills receivable	80,000
Bills payable	50,000	Bank	1,00,000
		Cash	40,000
	8,90,000		**8,90,000**

Calculate:

(i) Current ratio (ii) Liquid ratio

(iii) Debt- equity ratio (iv) Proprietary ratio

(v) Fixed Assets to Net Worth ratio (vi) Capital Gearing ratio

Ans:

(i) 2.93:1 **(ii) 1.93:1** **(iii) 0.71:1**

(iv) 0.58:1 **(v) 0.86:1** **(vi) 1.31:1**

Problem:4

The following information relate to Rani Traders Ltd., for the year ended 31st December, 2009

Trading and Profit and Loss Account

Particulars	*Rs.*	*Particulars*	*Rs.*
To Opening stock	49,750	By Sales	4,25,000
To Purchases	2,72,625	By Closing Stock	74,500
To Incidental expenses	7,125		
To Gross profit	1,70,000		
	4,99,500		4,99,500
To Loss on sale of assets	2,000	By Gross profit	1,70,000
To Adm.expenses	75,000	By Interest	1,500
To Other operating exp.	7,500	By Profit on sale of shares	3,000
To Selling expenses	15,000		
To Net profit	75,000		
	1,74,500		**1,74,500**

Balance Sheet as on 31.12.2009

Liabilities	*Rs.*	*Assets*	*Rs.*
Issued capital: 2,000 shares of Rs.50 each	1,00,000	Land and building Cash	75,000 15,000
Reserves	45,000	Plant and machinery	40,000
Current liabilities	65,000	Debtors	35,500
Profit and loss a/c	30,000	Stock	74,500
	2,40,000		**2,40,000**

Calculate:

(i) Current ratio (ii) Operating ratio (iii) Return on net worth

(iv) Return on total resources (v) Stock turnover ratio (vi) Turnover of fixed assets

(Ans:

(i) 1.92: 1 **(ii) 82.94%** **(iii) 42.85%**

(iv) 31.25% **(v) 4.11 times** **(vi) 3.7:1)**

Problem:5

JC& Company sells goods on cash as well as on credit basis. The following particulars are extracted from their books of accounts:

Particulars	Rs.
Total sales	1,00,000
Cash sales (included in above)	20,000
Sales returns	7,000
Debtors at the end	9,000
B/R at the end	2,000
Provision for doubtful debts	1,000
Total creditors at the end	10,000
Calculate average collection period.	

(Ans: 55 days.)

Problem: 6

From the following information calculate average payment period:

Particulars	*Rs.*	*Particulars*	*Rs.*
Total purchases	5,81,000	Creditors at the end	1,05,000
Cash purchases (included above)	30,000	Bills payable at the end	60,000
Purchases returns	51,000	Reserve for discount on creditors	80,000

(Ans: 120 days)

Problem:7

Calculate stock turnover ratio and stock turnover period from the followings:

Sales Rs. 10,00,000; Gross profit ratio 20%;

Stock at the beginning of the year Rs. 1,75,000;

Stock at the end of the year Rs. 1,45,000.

(Ans: Stock turnover ratio – 5 times; Stock turnover period in months – 2.4 months)

Problem:8

From the following details, calculate stock turnover ratio:

Particulars	*Rs.*
Total Sales	4,40,000
Sales returns	40,000
Gross profit	1,00,000
Closing stock	1,20,000
Excess of closing stock over Opening stock	40,000

(Ans : 3 times)

Problem:9

From the following data, calculate current ratio :

Particulars	*Rs.*
Liquid asset	1,00,000
Stock	90,000
Prepaid expenses	60,000
Working capital	1,50,000

(Ans : Current ratio = 2.5 :1)

Problem:10

Calculate:

(i) Creditors turnover ratio, and (ii) Average payment period

Particulars	*2008 (Rs.)*	*2009 (Rs.)*
Annual credit purchases	6,80,000	7,50,000
Creditors on January 1	80,000	60,000
Creditors on December 31	60,000	90,000
Take 360 days in a year		

(Ans:

2008 (i) 9.71 times: (ii) 37 days

2009 (i) 10 times (ii) 36 days)

Problem:11

Calculate gross profit ratio:

	Rs.		*Rs.*
Sales	2,20,000	Purchases	1,75,000
Sales return	20,000	Purchases return	15,000
Opening stock	30,000	Closing stock	40,000

(Ans: Gross profit ratio = 25%)

Problem:12

Calculate gross profit ratio in the following cases:

Particulars	*Rs.*
(i) Gross profit	75,000
Net sales	3,00,000
(ii) Gross profit	40,000
Sales	3,60,000
Sales return	40,000
(iii) Sales	5,00,000
Cost of goods sold	3,00,000
(iv) Sales	5,00,000
Gross Profit is 25% on cost.	

(Ans :

(i) 25% (ii) 12.5% (iii) 40% (iv) 20%)

Problem:13

Calculate net profit ratio:

Sales : Rs. 3,50,000; Cost of goods sold Rs. 1,50,000;

Administration expenses : Rs. 50,000; Selling expenses Rs. 10,000;

(Ans: Net profit ratio 40%)

Problem:14

Calculate:

(i) Gross profit ratio (ii) Operating ratio

(iii) Operating profit ratio (iv) Net profit ratio

Particulars	*Rs.*	*Particulars*	*Rs.*
Sales	21,000	Income from investments	200
Sales returns	1,000	Depreciation	200
Cost of sales	16,400	Selling expenses	700
Interest expenses (non-operating)	100	Administration expenses	1,300

(Ans:

(i) 18% (ii) 93% (iii) 7% (iv) 7.5%)

Problem:15

Following is the Balance Sheet of Star Ltd., as on 31st December, 2008

Liabilities	*Rs.*	*Assets*	*Rs.*
Equity share capital	50,000	Cash	5,000
7% Pref. share capital	10,000	Debtors	20,000
6% mortgage debentures	70,000	Stock	30,000
Reserves	40,000	Investment (Govt. securities at 10%)	15,000
Creditors	6,000	Fixed assets 1,80,000	
Outstanding expenses	1,000	(–) depreciation 50,000	1,30,000
Provision for taxation	13,000		
Bills payable	10,000		
	2,00,000		**2,00,000**

Additional information:

(i) Net sales Rs. 3,00,000 (ii) Cost of goods sold Rs.2,58,000

(iii) Net income before tax Rs.20,000 (iv) Net income after tax Rs.10,000

Calculate:

(a) Return on capital employed

(b) Capital structure

(c) Gross profit ratio

(Ans:

(a) 15.13% (b) 0.89:1 (c) 14%)

Problem:16

From the following information calculate interest coverage ratio

Net income tax	Rs. 3,12,740	Depreciation	Rs. 40,000
Tax rate	50% of income	Fixed interest charges	Rs. 29,500

(Ans: Interest coverage ratio : 21.2 times)

Problem:17

Current ratio 2.5

Liquid ratio 1.5

Working capital Rs. 90,000

Calculate

(a) Current assets (b) Current liabilities

(c) Liquid assets (d) Stock

(Ans:

(a) Current assets Rs. 1,50,000 (b) Current liabilities Rs. 60,000

(c) Liquid assets Rs. 90,000 (d) Stock Rs. 60,000)

Problem:18

Current ratio 2.6:1

Liquid ratio 1.5:1

Current liabilities Rs. 40,000

Calculate

(a) Current assets (b) Liquid assets (c) Stock

(Ans:

(a) Rs. 1,04,000 (b) Rs. 60,000 (c) Rs. 44,000)

Problem:19

From the followings, calculate the value of debtors

Particulars	***Rs.***
Total sales	6,00,000
Cash sales	2,00,000
Bills receivable	13,333
Debtors' velocity	30 days
No.of working days in a year	**360**

(Ans : Rs. 20,000)

Problem:20

From the following information, prepare Balance Sheet of Rajan Ltd., when sales are Rs. 23,00,000

Sales/Net worth	2.3 times;	Current debt/Net worth	42%
Total debt/Net worth	75%;	Current ratio	2.9 times
Net sales/Inventory	4.6 times;	Average collection period	90 days
Fixed assets/Net worth	53.2%		

Proforma Balance Sheet

Liabilities	*Rs.*	*Assets*	*Rs.*
Net worth		Fixed assets	
Long-term debt		Stock	
Current liabilities		Debtors	
		Cash	

Ans:

Liabilities	*Rs.*	*Assets*	*Rs.*
Net worth	10,00,000	Fixed assets	5,32,000
Long-term debt	3,30,000	Stock	5,00,000
Current liabilities	4,20,000	Debtors	5,75,000
		Cash	1,43,000
	17,50,000		**17,50,000**

Problem:21

Using the following data, complete the Balance Sheet given below:

Particulars	*Rs.*
Gross profit (20% of sales)	60,000
Shareholders' equity	50,000
Credit sales to total sales	80%
Total assets turnover (Sales/Total assets)	3 times
Inventory turnover (to cost of sales)	8 times
Average collection period (360 days a year)	18 days
Current ratio	1.6
Long-term debt to equity	**40%**

Balance Sheet

Particulars	*Rs.*	*Particulars*	*Rs.*
Creditors	....	Cash	....
Long-term debt	....	Debtors	....
Shareholders' equity	....	Inventory	....
		Fixed assets	....
	....		....

(Ans:

Cost of sales Rs. 2,40,000; Creditors Rs. 30,000; Long term debt Rs. 20,000; Shareholders' equity Rs. 50,000; Cash Rs. 6,000; Debtors Rs. 12,000; Inventory Rs. 30,000; Fixed assets Rs. 52,000.)

Problem:22

The following data represents the ratios pertaining to X Co. Ltd., for the year ending 31st March, 2009:

Annual sales	Rs. 40,00,000
Sales to net worth	4 times
Current liabilities to net worth	50%
Total debts to net worth	80%
Current ratio	2.2 times
Sales to inventory	8 times
Average collection period	40 days
Fixed assets to net worth	70%

From the above mentioned particulars, prepare the Balance Sheet of X Company Ltd., as on 31st March, 2009. Assume that all sales are made on credit.

(Ans: Balance Sheet total Rs. 18,00,000)

Problem:23

An engineering company has the following capital structure:

	Rs.
9% preference shares of Rs. 100 each	10,00,000
Equity shares of Rs. 10 each	40,00,000
	50,00,000

The following information's relating to the financial year just ended are –:

Profit after tax Rs. 22,00,000

Equity dividend paid 20%

Market price of equity shares Rs. 20 each

Your are required to state the following :

(i) Dividend yield on equity shares

(ii) Cover for preference and equity dividend

(iii) Earnings yield ratio

(Ans: (i) 10%; (ii) 24.44 times, 2.64 times; (iii) 26.38)

Problem:24

Prepare the Balance Sheet from the following :

Current ratio	2.5
Total assets/Net worth	3.5
Sales/Fixed assets	6
Sales/Current assets	8
Sales/Inventory	15
Sales/Debtors	18
Annual sales	Rs. 25,00,000

(Ans: Rs. 3,95,834.)

☆☆☆

CHAPTER 3

WORKING CAPITAL ANALYSIS, FUND FLOW AND CASH FLOW STATEMENT

- Working Capital
    - Concepts
    - Kinds
    - Importance
- Working Capital Requirements Computation
- Sources of Working Capital
- Fund Flow Analysis
- Cash Flow Analysis

WORKING CAPITAL

MEANING

The fund required for running an organisation is generally called as working capital. The business may need funds for two purposes, i.e., it may be for establishment of the business or for day-to-day operations. The production facilities and profitability can be increased by means of investing more long-term funds in plant and machinery, land and buildings, furniture, etc. On the other hand, funds may also required to meet the day-to-day expenses, e.g., purchase of raw materials, payment of wages, etc., which are all called as short-term funds. These funds are known as working capital. In short, working capital or revolving capital or circulating capital refers to that part of the firm's capital which is required for financing short-term or current assets such as cash, marketable securities, debtors and inventories.

In accounting sense, working capital is the difference between the inflow and outflow of funds. In the other words, it is the net cash inflow.

Definitions

According to Shubin, "Working Capital is the amount of funds necessary to cover the cost of operating the enterprise".

In the works of Genestenberg, "Circulating capital means current assets of a company that are changed in the ordinary course of business from one form to another, for example, from cash to inventories, inventories to receivables, receivables into cash".

CONCEPTS OF WORKING CAPITAL

Gross Working Capital

In a broader sense the term working capital refers to gross working capital. It refers to the firm's investment in total current circulating assets. Under the gross concept, working capital is equal to total current assets. Some of the current assets are:

Ingredients of Current Assets

- Cash in hand
- Cash at bank
- Accounts Receivables
- Sundry debtors
- Short-term loans and advances
- Inventories
- Temporary investment
- Prepaid expenses
- Accrued incomes

Net Working Capital

In a narrow sense, the term working capital refers to the net working capital. The term net working capital can be defined in two different ways:

(i) It is the excess of current assets over current liabilities.

(ii) It is that portion of a firm's current assets which is financed by long-term funds.

Ingredients of Current Liabilities

- Bills Payable
- Sundry Creditors or Accounts Payable
- Accrued or Outstanding Expenses
- Short-term loans, advances and deposits

- Dividends payable
- Bank overdraft
- Provision for taxation.

However, as a general practice, the net working capital is simply referred to as working capital.

OPERATING CYCLE

The operating cycle refers to all stages involved from raw materials to realisation of cash. There is always a time gap in the operating cycle. It is so, because of the time gap between the sales and their actual realisation in cash. The following stages are usually found in the operating cycle of a manufacturing company:-

- Conversion of cash into raw materials
- Conversion of raw material into work-in-progress
- Conversion of work-in-progress into finished goods
- Conversion of finished goods into debtors through sales
- Conversion of debtors into cash
- Direct accumulation of cash through cash sales

The operating cycle of a manufacturing business is represented in the following figure:

OPERATING CYCLE OF A MANUFACTURING BUSINESS

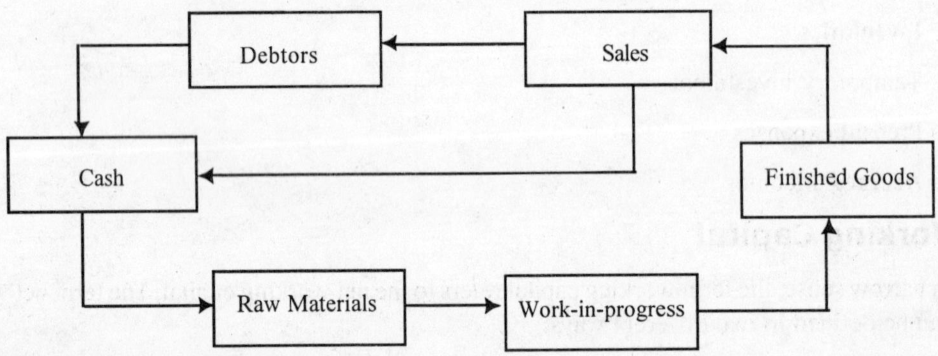

Types of Working Capital

Working capital may be classified into two ways:

(a) On the basis of concept

(b) On the basis of time

On the basis of concept, working capital is again classified into:

(a) Gross working capital, and

(b) Net working capital.

On the basis of time, working capital may be classified as:

(a) Permanent or fixed working capital

(b) Temporary or variable working capital.

The following figure shows the kinds of working capital:

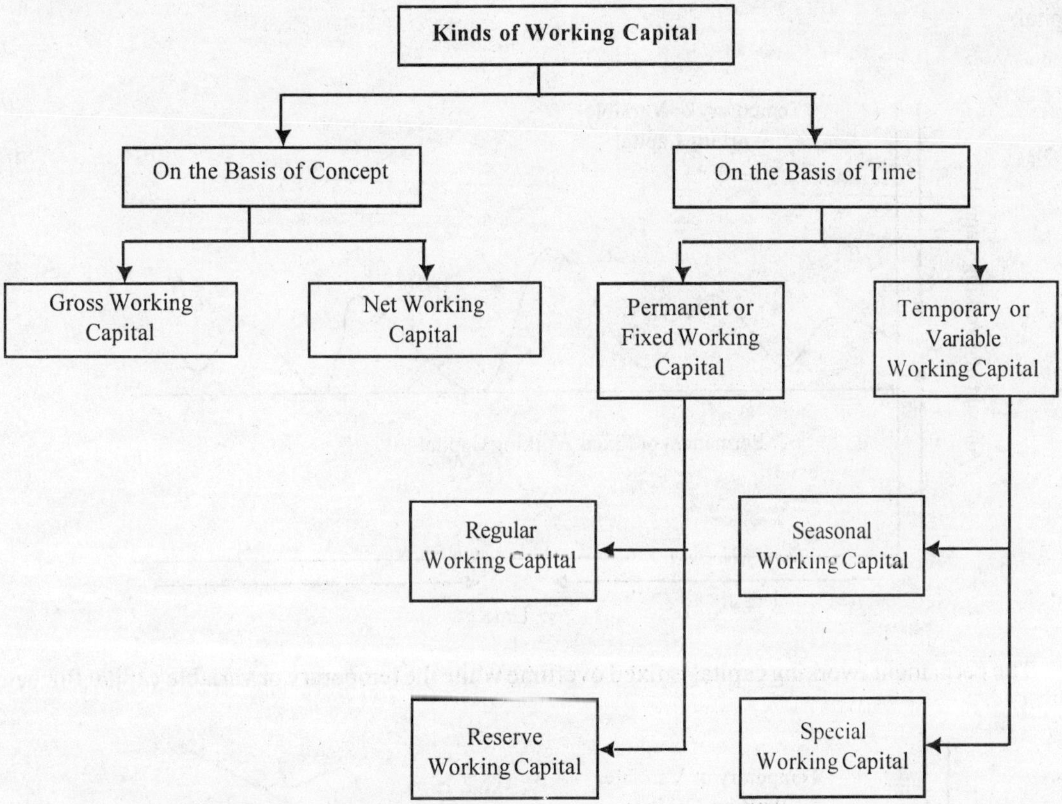

(1) Permanent or Fixed Working Capital:

To carryout the business activities a minimum amount of investment in all current assets is required. In other words, the current assets are required on a continuing basis over the entire year. Such permanent working capital is permanently needed for the business and therefore it should be financed out of long-term funds. The permanent working capital can further be classified as regular working capital and reserve working capital. The regular working capital is required to ensure circulation of operating cycle. Reserve working capital is the excess amount over the requirement for regular working capital which may be provided for contingencies that may arise at unstated periods such as strikes, rise in prices, depression, etc.

(2) Temporary or Variable Working Capital:

Variable working capital is the amount of working capital required for short-term periods. The amount of such working capital keeps on fluctuating from time-to-time on the basis of business activities and economic trend. In such a situation, fixed working capital cannot be employed suitably, hence the requirement of short-term sources are employed to finance variable working capital. Variable working capital can be further classified as seasonal working capital and special working capital. The working capital required to meet the seasonal needs of the business is called seasonal working capital. Special working capital is required to meet special exigencies such as launching of extensive marketing campaigns for conducting research, etc.

The diagrams given below explain the differences between the permanent and variable working capital.

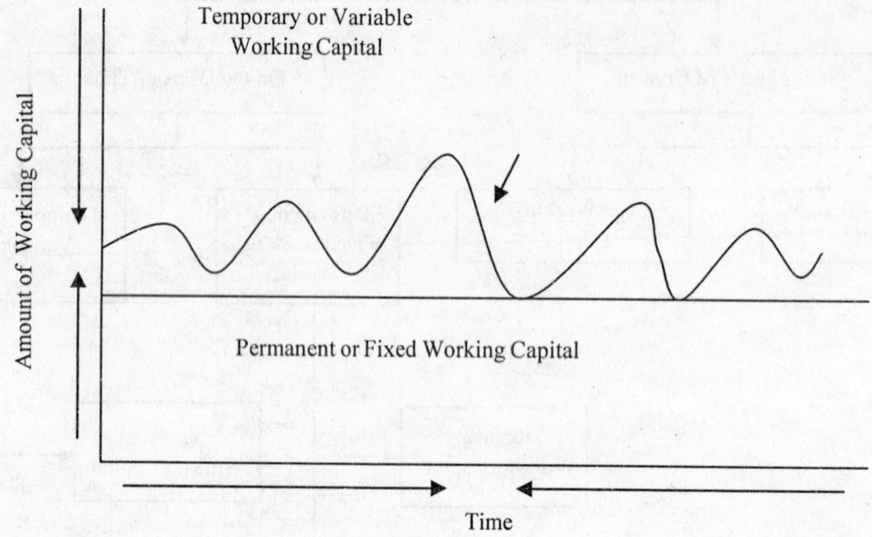

The permanent fworking capital is fixed overtime while the temporary or variable capital flucuates.

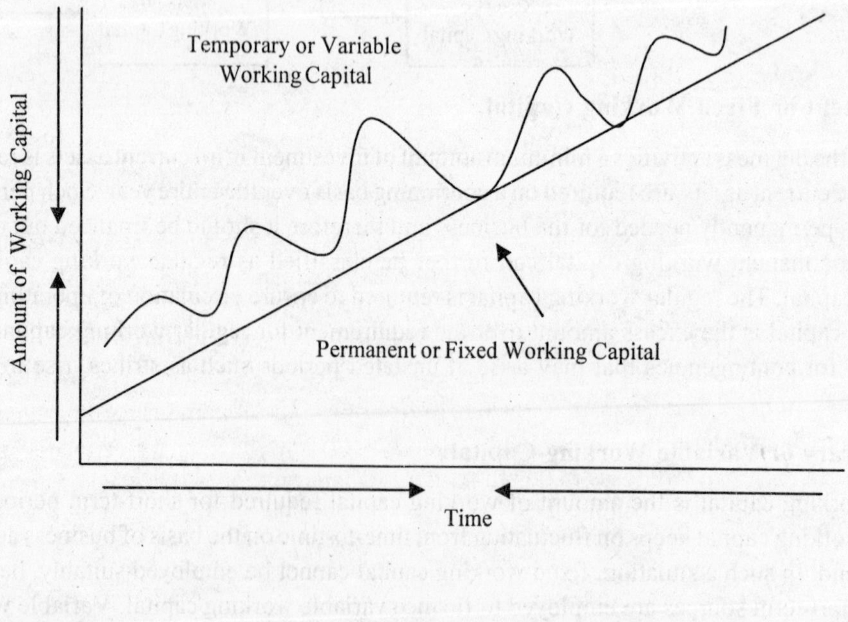

The permanent working capital is also increasing with the passage of time due to the expansion of business. But even then, it does not fluctuate as variable working capital which sometimes increases and sometimes decreases.

Need for Working Capital

The need for working capital arises due to the time gap between production and realisation of cash from sales. There are time gaps in purchase of raw materials and production; production and sales and sales and realisation of cash. Thus, working capital is needed for the following purposes:

- To purchase raw materials, spares and component parts.
- To pay wages and salaries
- To meet day-to-day expenses
- To meet the selling expenses
- To provide credit facilities to the customers.
- To maintain the inventories of raw material, work-in-progress, stores and spares and finished stock.

Advantages of Adequate Working Capital

The advantages of maintaining adequate working capital are as follows:

(1) **Non-stop Production:** Continuous production is inevitable for the success of any organisation. To meet the current demand as well as the expected demand for the product, the company has to produce the goods without any undue stoppage of production because of shortage of raw materials or spares, etc. Hence, maintaining adequate working capital helps to win in the competitive market.

(2) **Solvency of the Business:** Liquidity to meet the day-to-day contingencies and to set right the payment to creditors will create a good morale among the creditors. Maintaining adequate working capital automatically increases the solvency position of the organisation.

(3) **Increased Goodwill:** Sufficient working capital leads a firm to make prompt payments as a result of which a firm can maintain a steady goodwill.

(4) **Possibility of Cash Discounts:** To avail the cash discounts on the purchases, a firm should maintain adequate working capital. Such type of non-operating incomes reduces its costs.

(5) **Regular Supply of Raw Materials:** Adequate working capital ensures regular supply of raw materials and continuous production.

(6) **Regular Payment of Salaries and Wages to Employees:** A company which has adequate working capital can make prompt payment of salaries and wages which raises the morale of its employees, which in turn helps to increase their efficiency, reduces wastage and costs and enhances production and profits.

(7) **Exploitation of Favourable Market Conditions:** Those concerns which have adequate working capital can utilise favourable market conditions. They can buy their requirements of raw material in bulk when the market price is lower. Similarly, they can hold stock of finished goods to realise better prices.

(8) **Ability to Face Crisis:** Adequate working capital facilitates to meet situations of business crisis in emergencies. It enables the business to withstand periods of depression smoothly.

(9) **High Return on Investment:** The continuous production and effective utilisation of fixed assets help to increase the profitability of the organisation.

(10) **High Morale:** Adequacy of working capital creates an environment of security, confidence, high morale creates overall efficiency in a business.

EXCESS OR INADEQUATE WORKING CAPITAL

Working capital is the life blood and nerve centre of a business. In this situation, maintaining adequate working capital is inevitable. It should have neither redundant or excess working capital nor inadequate or shortage of working capital. However, out of the above two, it is the inadequacy of working capital which is more dangerous from the point of view of the firm.

Excessive working capital means idle funds which earn no profits for the business.

Disadvantages of Excessive Working Capital

(1) The business cannot earn adequate return on its investments.

(2) Low rate of return on investments leads to fall in share value.

(3) Excessive working capital may lead to overall inefficiency in the firm.

(4) A firm may be tempted to over trade and lose heavily.

(5) There is no balance between liquidity and profitability because of excessive working capital.

Dangers of Inadequate Working Capital

(1) The inadequate working capital leads to inability to pay the short-term debts in time. This seriously affects the goodwill as well as the reputation of the organisation.

(2) Due to lack of funds, it cannot enjoy the better discount offer, etc.

(3) Favourable market conditions cannot fruitfully be exploited by the organisation.

(4) The rate of return on investments also falls with the shortage of working capital.

(5) Low liquidity position may lead to liquidation of the firm.

(6) Due to inadequate working capital, the fixed assets cannot be effectively utilised.

FACTORS DETERMINING THE WORKING CAPITAL REQUIREMENTS

The following are the important factors generally influencing the working capital requirements.

(1) **Nature or Character of Business:** The working capital requirements of a firm basically depend upon the nature of its business. Public utility undertakings like Electricity, Water Supply and Railways need very limited working capital because they offer cash sales only and supply services, not products, and as such no funds are tied-up in inventories and receivables. On the other hand, trading and financial firms require a very less investment in fixed assets but have to invest large amounts in current assets like inventories, receivables and cash; as such they need large amount of working capital.

(2) **Size of Business/Scale of Operations:** The working capital requirements of a concern are directly influenced by the size of its business which may be measured in terms of scale of operations. Greater the size of business unit, generally, larger will be the requirements of a working capital. However, in some cases, even a smaller concern may need more working capital due to high overhead charges, inefficient use of available resources and other economic disadvantages of small size.

(3) **Production Policy:** In certain industries, the demand is subject to wide fluctuations due to seasonal variations. The requirements of working capital in such cases, depend upon the production policy. The production could be kept either steady by accumulating inventories, during slack periods with a view to meet high demand during the peak seasons or the production could be curtailed during the slack season and increased during the peak season. If the policy is to keep the production steady by accumulating inventories, it will require higher working capital.

(4) **Manufacturing Process/Length of Production Cycle:** In manufacturing business the requirements of working capital increase in direct proportion to the length of manufacturing process. Longer the process period of manufacture, larger is the amount of working capital required. The longer the manufacturing time, the raw materials and other supplies have to be carried for a longer period in the processing with progressive increment of labour and service costs before the finished product is finally obtained.

(5) **Seasonal Variations:** In certain industries, raw materials is not available throughout the year. They have to buy raw materials in bulk during the season to ensure an uninterrupted flow and process them during the entire year. A huge amount is, thus, blocked in the form of material inventories during such season, which give rise to more working capital requirements. Generally during the busy season, a firm requires larger working capital than in the slack season.

(6) **Working Capital Cycle:** In a manufacturing concern, the working capital cycle starts with the purchase of raw material and ends with the realisation of cash from the sale of finished products. This cycle involves purchase of raw materials and stores, its conversion into stocks of finished goods through work-in-progress with progressive increment of labour and service costs, conversion of finished stock into sales, debtors and receivables and ultimately realisation of cash and this cycle continues from again cash to purchase of raw material and so on.

(7) **Credit Policy:** The credit policy of a concern in its dealing with debtors and creditors influences considerably the requirements of working capital. A concern that purchases its requirements on credit and sells its products/services on cash requires lesser amount of working capital. On the other hand, a concern buying its requirements for cash and allowing credit to its customers, shall need larger amount of working capital as very huge amount of funds are bound to be tied-up in debtors or bills receivables.

(8) **Business Cycle:** Business cycle refer to alternate expansion and contraction in general business activity. In a period of boom, i.e. when the business is prosperous, there is a need for larger amount of working capital due to increase in sales, rise in prices, optimistic expansion of business, etc. On the contrary, in the times of depression, i.e., when there is a down swing of the cycle, the business contracts, sales decline, difficulties are faced in collections from debtors and firms may have a large amount of working capital lying idle.

(9) **Rate of Growth of Business:** The working capital requirements of a concern increase with the growth and expansion of its business activities. Although, it is difficult to determine the relationship between the growth in the volume of business and the growth in the working capital of a business, yet it may be concluded that for normal rate of expansion in the volume of business, we may have retained profits to pro[illegible]e for more working capital but fast growing concerns, we shall require larger amount of working capital.

(10) **Earning Capacity and Dividend Policy:** Some firms have more earning capacity that others due to quality of their products, monopoly conditions, etc. Such firms with high earning apacity may generate cash profits from operations and contribute to their working capital.

(11) **Price Level Changes:** Changes in the price level also affect the working capital requirements. Generally, the rising prices will require the firm to maintain larger amount of working capital as more funds will be required to maintain the same current assets. The effect of rising prices may be different for different firms. Some firms may be affected much, while some others may not be affected at all by the rise in prices.

Problem 1 :

You are given the following estimates and are requested to add 10% to your computed figures to allow for contingencies.

	Per annum	*Rs.*
(i)	**Average Amount of Stock:**	
	Finished goods	25,000
	Raw materials	15,000
(ii)	**Average Credit given:**	
	Inland sales 6 weeks	4,16,000
	Export sales 4 weeks	4,68,000
(iii)	**Lag in payment of expenses:**	
	Wages 2 ½ weeks	2,08,000
	Materials and overheads 6 weeks	3,12,000

Prepare a statement of working capital requirement.

Solution:

Statement of Working Capital Requirements

Particulars	*Rs.*	*Rs*
Current Assets:		
Stock of Finished goods		25,000
Stock of raw materials		15,000
Debtors:		
Inlandsales $\frac{4,16,000}{52} \times 6$	48,000	
Exportsales $\frac{4,68,000}{52} \times 4$	36,000	84,000
		1,24,000
Less: Current Liabilities:		
Lag in payment of wages $\frac{2,08,000}{52} \times 2.5$	10,000	
Lag in payment of overheads $\frac{3,12,000}{52} \times 6$	36,000	46,000
		78,000
Add: 10% for contingencies		7,800
Working Capital Requirements		**85,800**

Problem 2 :

From the following information, forecast their working capital requirements.

Projected annual sales	**Rs. 46,80,000**
Percentage of net profit on cost of sales	20%
Average credit period allowed to debtors	10 weeks
Average credit period allowed by creditors	8 weeks
Average stock carrying (in terms of sales requirements)	6 weeks

Add 20% to computed figures to allow for contingencies

Solution:

Particulars	Rs.
Projected annual sales	46,80,000
Less: Profit 1/5th on cost of sales or 1/6th on sales	7,80,000
$46{,}80{,}000 \times 1/6$	
Cost of sales	**39,00,000**

Statement of Working Capital Requirements

Particulars	Rs.
Current Assets:	
Debtors $\frac{39{,}00{,}000}{52} \times 10$	7,50,000
Stock $\frac{39{,}00{,}000}{52} \times 6$	4,50,000
	12,00,000
Less:Current Liability:	
Creditors $\frac{39{,}00{,}000}{52} \times 8$	6,00,000
	6,00,000
Add: 20% for contingencies	1,20,000
Working Capital Requirements	**7,20,000**

Problem 3 :

You are given the following estimates and are instructed to add 15% to your computed figures to allow for contingencies.

Particulars	*Per Annum (Rs.)*
(i) Average amount locked up in stock:	
Stock of finished product	20,000
Stock of stores, material etc.	30,000
(ii) Average credit given:	
Inland sales 8 weeks credit	4,68,000
Export sales 4 weeks credit	1,56,000

(iii) Lag in payment of wages and other outstandings:

Wages 2 ½ weeks	3,12,000
Stores, material, etc., 6 ½ weeks	78,000
Rent, royalties, etc., 4 months	24,000
Clerical staff 1 ½ months	48,000
Manager's salary 2 weeks	10,400
Miscellaneous expenses 2 ½ months	60,000

(iv) Payments in advances:

Insurance (Paid quarterly in advance)	22,000

(v) Undrawn profits on an average throughout the year 25,000

Calculate the average amount of working capital required.

Solution:

Statement of Working Capital Requirements

Particulars	*Rs.*	*Rs.*
Current Assets:		
Stock of finished Goods		20,000
Stock of Stores, Materials, etc.		30,000
Debtors:		
Inland Sales $\frac{4,68,000}{52} \times 8$	72,000	
Export Sales $\frac{1,56,000}{52} \times 4$	12,000	84,000
Advance payment of Insurance $\frac{22,000}{12} \times 3$		5,500
		1,39,500
Less: Current Liabilities:		
Lag in payments:		
Wages $\frac{3,12,000}{52} \times 2.5$	15,000	
Store, material, etc. $\frac{78,000}{52} \times 6.5$		

Rent, royalties etc. $\frac{24,000}{12} \times 4$	8,000	
Clerical staff $\frac{48,000}{12} \times 1.5$	6,000	
Manager salary $\frac{10,400}{52} \times 2$	400	
Miscellaneous salary $\frac{60,000}{12} \times 2.5$	12,500	51,650
		87,850
Add: 15% for contingencies		13,178
Working Capital Requirements		**1,01,028**

Problem 4 :

JC company sells goods in the home market and earns a gross profit of 25% on sales. Its annual figures are as follows:

Particulars	*Rs.*
Sales	5,00,000
Materials used	1,20,000
Wages	1,26,000
Factory expenses	36,000
Administrative expenses	50,000
Depreciation	10,000
Distribution expenses	24,000

Additional Informations:

(a) Credit given by suppliers – 3 ½ months

(b) Credit allowed to customers – 3 months

(c) Lag in payment of wages – 1 month

(d) Lag in payment of factory expenses – 2 months

(e) Distribution expenses are paid quarterly in advance

(f) Raw materials and finished goods are in stock for 1.5 months.

(g) Cash balance estimated to be maintained at Rs. 50,000

You are required to prepare a statement of working capital requirements.

Solution :

Statement of Working Capital Requirements

Particulars	*Rs.*	*Rs.*
Current Assets:		
Cash Balance	50,000	
Debtors $\frac{3,75,000}{12} \times 3$	93,750	
Stock of raw materials $\frac{1,20,000}{12} \times 1.5$	15,000	
Stock of finished goods $\frac{3,75,000}{12} \times 1.5$	46,875	
Distribution expenses paid in advance $\frac{24,000}{12} \times 3$	6,000	
		2,11,625
Less: Current Liabilities:		
Sundry creditors $\frac{1,20,000}{12} \times 3.5$	35,000	
Lag in payment of wages $\frac{1,26,000}{12} \times 1$	10,500	
Lag in payment of factory expenses $\frac{36,000}{12} \times 2$	6,000	51,500
Working Capital Requirements		**1,60,125**

Workings:

(1) Sales 5,00,000

Less : Gross Profit $5,00,000 \times \frac{25}{100}$ 1,25,000

Cost of Sales **3,75,000**

(2) Depreciation is a non-fund item. Hence, it is ignored.

Problem 5 :

From the following details, prepare an estimate of working capital of M/s. Srinivasan Ltd.

	Average period of credit	*Estimated for the year (Rs.)*
Purchase of materials	4 Months	1,80,000
Wages	2 Months	75,000
Overheads:		
Rent, Rates, etc.	4 Months	24,000
Salaries	2 Months	36,000
Other overheads	3 Months	30,000
Cash sales	3,00,000	
Credit sales	4 Months	9,00,000
Average amount of stock		25,000
Average amount of undrawn profits		15,000

Assume that all expenses and income were made at an even rate for the year.

Solution :

Statement of Working Capital Requirements

Particulars	*Rs.*	*Rs.*
Current Assets:		
Stock	25,000	
Debtors $\frac{9,00,000}{12} \times 4$	3,00,000	
		3,25,000
Less: Current Liabilities:		
Creditors $\frac{1,80,000}{12} \times 4$	60,000	
Wages $\frac{75,000}{12} \times 2$	12,500	
Lag in payment of overheads:		
Rent, Rates, etc. $\frac{24,000}{12} \times 4$	8,000	

Salaries $\frac{36,000}{12} \times 2$	6,000	
Other overheads $\frac{30,000}{12} \times 3$	7,500	94,000
Working Capital Required		2,31,000

Problem 6 :

Prepare a statement showing the working capital requirements for level of activity of 36,000 units of output for the year. The cost structure for the company's product for the above mentioned activity level is given below:

Particulars	***Cost per unit (Rs.)***
Raw Materials	30
Direct labour	15
Overheads	10
Total	55
Profit	15
Selling price	70

(a) Raw materials are held in stock, on an average for 3 months.

(b) Work-in-progress (100% complete in regard to materials and 50% for labour and overheads) will be 1.5 months production.

(c) Finished goods are in stock on an average for 2 months.

(d) Credit allowed by suppliers: 3 months

(e) Credit allowed to debtors: 2.5 months

(f) A minimum cash balance of Rs. 20,000 is expected to be maintained.

Prepare a statement of working capital requirements.

Solution:

Output per year = 36,000 units

Output per month $= \frac{36,000}{12} = 3,000$ units

		Rs.
Raw materials	3,000 × 30	90,000
Labour	3,000 × 15	45,000
Overheads	3,000 × 10	30,000
Cost of sales		**1,65,000**

Statement of Working Capital Requirements

Particulars	*Rs.*	*Rs.*
Current Assets:		
Cash		0,000
Stock of raw materials (90,000 × 3)		2,70,000
Work-in-progress:		
Raw materials $\frac{90,000}{1} \times 1.5$	1,35,000	
Labour $\frac{45,000}{1} \times 1.5 \times \frac{1}{2}$	33,750	
Overheads $\frac{30,000}{1} \times 1.5 \times \frac{1}{2}$	22,500	1,91,250
Stock of finished goods (1,65,000 × 2)		3,30,000
Debtors (1,65,000 × 2.5)		4,12,500
		12,23,750
Less: Current Liability:		
Creditors $\frac{90,000}{1} \times 3$		2,70,000
Working Capital Required		**9,53,750**

Problem 7 :

Assuming a year of 50 weeks of 5 days each, calculate the working capital requirements from the following data:

Sales 2,00,000 units sold at Rs. 5 per unit on credit. Customers are allowed 45 days credit.

		Rs.
Production cost:	Raw material	2.00
	Labour	1.50
	Other variable expenses	1.00

The production cycle is 25 days and all materials are issued at the commencement of each cycle.

Credit allowed by suppliers 90 days.

Cash required: to the extent of 10% of the remaining current assets.

Stock levels: Raw materials : 50 days of supply

Finished goods : 25 days of supply

Ignore work-in-progress

Solution:

Production and sales per year = 2,00,000 units

Number of working days in a year = 50 weeks × 5 days = 250 days

Therefore, production per day = $\frac{2,00,000}{250}$ = 800 units.

Cost of production per day

		Rs.
Raw materials	800 units × Rs. 2.00	1,600
Labour	800 units × Rs. 1.50	1,200
Other variable expenses	800 units × Rs. 1.00	800
		3,600

Statement of Working Capital Requirements

Particulars	*Rs.*
Current Assets:	
Stock of raw materials (50 days × Rs. 1,600)	80,000
Stock of finished goods (25 days × Rs. 3,600)	90,000
Debtors (45 days × Rs. 3,600)	1,62,000
	3,32,000
Cash to be maintained (1/10th of Rs. 3,32,000)	33,200

	3,65,200
Less: Current Liability:	
Creditors (90 days x Rs. 1,600)	1,44,000
Working Capital Required	**2,21,200**

Problem 8 :

Mr. Rakesh wishes to commence a new trading business and gives the following informations:

(i) Total estimated sales per annum Rs. 6,00,000

(ii) His fixed expenses are estimated at Rs. 1,000 per month and variable expenses equal to 5% of his turnover.

(iii) He expects to fix a selling price for each product which will be 25% in excess of his cost of purchase.

(iv) He expects to turnover his stock 4 times in a year.

(v) The sales and purchase will be evenly spread throughout the year. All sales will be for cash but he expects one month's credit for purchases.

Calculate: (a) His estimated profit for the year.

(b) His average working capital requirements.

Solution:

(a) Estimated profit of Mr. Rakesh for the year:

		Rs.
Sales		6,00,000
Less: Gross Profit 1/5th on sales		1,20,000
(1/4th on cost or 1/5th on sales)		
Cost of sales/Purchases		4,80,000
Gross Profit		1,20,000
Less: Fixed expenses Rs.1,000 p.m.	12,000	
Variable expenses 5% of turnover	30,000	
6,00,000 @ 5%		42,000
Net Profit		**78,000**

Statement of Working Capital Requirements

Particulars	*Rs.*
Current Assets:	
Average stock	1,20,000
Cash required for fixed expenses per month	1,000
Cash required for variable expenses per month	2,500
Sales per month $= \frac{6,00,000}{12} =$ Rs.50,000	
50,000 @ 5%	
	1,23,500
Less: Current Liability:	
Creditors $\frac{4,80,000}{12} \times 1$	40,000
Working Capital Requirements	**83,500**

Workings:

$$\text{Stock turnover} = \frac{\text{Cost of sales}}{\text{Average stock}} = 4$$

$$= \frac{4,80,000}{\text{Average stock}} = 4$$

$$\text{Therefore, average stock} = \frac{4,80,000}{4} = \text{Rs.}1,20,000$$

Problem 9 :

Jai Ltd., has called for a statement showing the working capital needed to finance a level of activity of 3,60,000 units of output for the year. The cost structure for the company's product, for the above mentioned activity level, is detailed below:

	Cost per units Rs.
Raw materials	40
Direct labour	20
Overheads	25
Total	85
Profit	15
Selling price	100

(a) Raw materials are held in stock, on an average for 3 months.

(b) Work-in-process (100% complete in regard to materials and 50% for labour and overheads) to be one month production.

(c) Finished goods are in stock on an average 2 months

(d) Credit allowed by suppliers 2 months.

(e) One month credit is allowed to debtors, calculation of debtors may be made at selling price.

(f) A minimum cash balance of Rs. 50,000 is expected to be maintained.

(g) The production pattern is assumed to be even during the year.

Prepare the statement of working capital requirements.

Solution:

Estimated production per annum = 3,60,000 units

$$\text{Estimated production per month} = \frac{3,60,000}{12} = 30,000 \text{ units}$$

Cost of sales per month

		Rs.
Raw material	30,000 × 40	12,00,000
Wages	30,000 × 20	6,00,000
Overheads	30,000 × 25	7,50,000
		25,50,000

Statement of Working Capital Requirements

Particulars	*Rs.*	*Rs.*
Current Assets:		
Stock of materials (12,00,000 × 3)		36,00,000
Work-in-process:		
Raw materials (12,00,000 × 1)	12,00,000	
Wages $\left(6,00,000 \times 1 \times \frac{50}{100}\right)$	3,00,000	
Overheads $\left(7,50,000 \times 1 \times \frac{50}{100}\right)$	3,75,000	
		18,75,000
Stock of finished goods (25,50,000 × 2)		51,00,000
Debtors (at selling price as given)		30,00,000
(30,000 × 100 – Rs. 30,00,000)		
Cash Balance		50,000
		1,36,25,000
Less: Current Liability:		
Creditors (12,00,000 × 2)		24,00,000
Working Capital Requirements		**1,12,25,000**

Problem 10 :

Rakshaa Ltd., sells goods in the home market and earns a gross profit of 25% on cost of sales. Its annual figures are as follows:

Particulars	*Rs.*
Sales	4,50,000
Materials used	1,80,000
Wages	1,44,000
Manufacturing expenses	1,50,000
Administrative expenses	48,000
Selling and distribution expenses	24,000
Depreciation	20,000

Additional information is as follows:

(i) Credit given by suppliers of materials is 2.5 months.

(ii) Credit allowed to customers is 2 months

(iii) Wages are paid 1 month in arrear

(iv) Administrative expenses are paid one month in arrear

(v) Selling and distribution expenses are paid quarterly in advance.

(vi) The company wishes to keep 2 months stock of raw materials and also of finished goods.

(vii) The company believes in keeping cash of Rs. 75,000 including the overdraft limit of Rs. 27,000 not yet utilised by the company.

You are required to prepare a statement showing the working capital requirement of the company adding 10% margin for contingencies.

Solution:

Statement showing the Working Capital Requirements

Particulars	*Rs.*	*Rs.*
Current Assets:		
Debtors $= \frac{3,60,000}{12} \times 2$		60,000
Selling and distribution expenses paid in advance $\left(24,000 \times \frac{1}{4}\right)$		6,000
Stock of raw materials $\left(\frac{1,80,000}{12} \times 2\right)$		30,000
Stock of finished goods $\left(\frac{3,60,000}{12} \times 2\right)$		60,000
Cash balance		75,000
		2,31,000
Less: Current Liabilities:		
Creditors $= \frac{1,80,000}{12} \times 2.5$	37,500	

Lag in payment of expenses :		
Wages = $\frac{1,44,000}{12} \times 1$	12,000	
Administrative expenses = $\frac{48,000}{12} \times 1$	4,000	
Bank overdraft (given)	27,000	
		80,500
		1,50,500
Add: 10% for contingencies		15,050
Working Capital Required		**1,65,550**

Workings:

	Rs.
(1) Sales	4,50,000
Less: Gross Profit	90,000
(1/4th on cost of sales or 1/5th on sales)	
Cost of sales	3,60,000

(2) Depreciation is a non-fund item. Hence, it is ignored

Problem 11 :

Vanitha Ltd., gives the following Profit and Loss Account:

Particulars	*Rs.*	*Particulars*	*Rs.*
To Materials	15,00,000	By sales	28,00,000
To Wages	3,00,000		
To Manufacturing expenses	4,00,000		
(Including depreciation Rs. 1,60,000)			
To Administration expenses	2,00,000		
To Selling expenses	2,40,000		
To Net profit	1,60,000		
	28,00,000		**28,00,000**

It is company's policy to maintain the following stocks:

(a) Finished goods 2 months sale.

(b) Materials 2 months consumption

Work-in-process is equal to ½ month production in terms of materials and 1 month wages and manufacturing expenses.

The company extends 2 months credit to its customers and receives 3 months credit from suppliers and pays all expenses and wages ½ month in arrears but selling and distribution expenses are paid 1 month in advance.

The company would like to keep Rs. 75,000 in cash at all times. A safety margin of 5% on total current assets is desirable.

Estimate the working capital requirements for the company.

Solution:

Cost of goods produced/sold:

	Rs.
Materials	15,00,000
Wages	3,00,000
Manufacturing expenses (4,00,000 – 1,60,000)	2,40,000
	20,40,000

Statement of Working Capital

Particulars	*Rs.*	*Rs.*
Current Assets:		
Stock of Finished Goods $\left(20,40,000 \times \frac{2}{12}\right)$		3,40,000
Stock of Materials $\left(15,00,000 \times \frac{2}{12}\right)$		2,50,000
Work-in-Process:		
Materials $\left(15,00,000 \times \frac{0.5}{12}\right)$	62,500	
Wages $\left(3,00,000 \times \frac{1}{12}\right)$	25,000	
Manufacturing Expenses $\left(2,40,000 \times \frac{1}{12}\right)$	20,000	1,07,500
Debtors $\left(20,40,000 \times \frac{2}{12}\right)$		3,40,000

Prepaid selling expenses $\left(2,40,000 \times \frac{1}{12}\right)$		20,000
Cash Balance		75,000
		11,32,500
Add: 5% Safety margin on total current assets		56,625
		11,89,125
Less: Current Liabilities:		
Creditors $\left(15,00,000 \times \frac{3}{12}\right)$	3,75,000	
Lag in payment of expenses:		
Wages $\left(3,00,000 \times \frac{0.5}{12}\right)$	12,500	
Manufacturing expenses $\left(2,40,000 \times \frac{0.5}{12}\right)$	10,000	
(Excluding depreiation)		
Administrative expenses $\left(2,00,000 \times \frac{0.5}{12}\right)$	8,333	4,05,833
Working Capital Requirements		**7,83,292**

FUNDS FLOW STATEMENT

Meaning of Fund

The term fund means change in financial resources arising from changes in working capital items and from financing and investing activities of the enterprises which may involve only non-current items. The fund flow statement analyses only the causes of changes in the firms working capital position. The statement of changes in financial position prepared to determine only the sources and uses of working capital between two dates of Balance Sheets, is known as Fund Flow Statement.

Definition

In the words of Anthony, "The funds flow statement describes the sources from which additional funds were derived and the use to which these sources were put".

Funds Flow Statement

Funds flow statement is a report on the movement of funds or working capital. It explains how working capital is raised and used during an accounting period.

Funds flow statement is a report on financial operational changes, flows or movements during the period. According to Anthony: "The Funds flow statement describes the sources from which additional funds were derived and the use to which these funds were put".

· Various titles are used for the funds flow statement. They are as follows:

- Statement of sources and application of fund
- Statement of sources and uses of fund
- Statement of changes in financial position
- Where got and where gone statement

Sources of Funds

Generally speaking funds are derived from:

(i) Operating of Business

(ii) Income from Investment

(iii) Sale of assets and long-term investment

(iv) Contribution of shareholders.

(v) Gifts, damages awarded in legal actions, etc.

Uses of Funds

(i) Operating losses

(ii) Repayment of long-term loans and debentures

(iii) Redemption of preference share capital

(iv) Payment of cash dividends

(v) Purchase of fixed assets

Objectives or Uses of the Funds Flow Statement

(i) It is a tool of managing working capital

(ii) It shows a picture about a changes in working capital

(iii) It shows the sources of fund like funds from operations, issue of shares, sale of fixed assets or investments, etc.

(iv) It helps to find out how the resources have been obtained and used.

(v) To find out the financial strength and weakness of the business.

Proforma for Schedule of changes in Working Capital

Particulars	*Previous year (Rs.)*	*Current year (Rs.)*	*Increase (Rs.)*	*Decrease (Rs.)*
Current Assets:				
Cash in hand and at bank				
Debtors				
Bills receivable				
Accrued income				
Temporary investment				
Inventories				
Prepaid expenses				
Total Current Assets				
Current Liabilities:				
Sundry creditors				
Outstanding expenses				
Bank overdraft				
Bills payable				
Total Current Liabilities				
Working Capital (CA-CL)				
Decrease(or) Increase in Working Capital				

Problem 1:

From the following informations find out the changes in working capital:

(Rs. in Lakh)

Liabilities	*2008*	*2009*	*Assets*	*2008*	*2009*
Share Capital	545	545	Fixed Assets	3,006	2,343
Reserves	2,459	1,660	Investments	62	62
Long-term Loan	2,796	2,295	Inventories	2,075	1,804
Current Liabilities	1,241	1,533	Debtors	1,157	687
Provisions	434	327	Cash	512	844
			Loans and Advances	663	620
	7,475	**6,360**		**7,475**	**6,360**

Solution:

Schedule of Changes in Working Capital

Particulars	*2008 (Rs.)*	*2009 (Rs.)*	*Increase (Rs.)*	*Decrease (Rs.)*
Current Assets:				
Cash	512	844	332	
Loans and Advances	663	620		43
Inventories	2,075	1,804		271
Debtors	1,157	687		470
Total Current Assets (A)	4,407	3,955		
Current Liabilities:				
Current Liabilities	1,241	1,533		292
Total Current Liabilities (B)	1,241	1,533		
Working Capital (A-B)	3,166	2,422		
Decrease in Working Capital	——	744	744	——
	3,166	**3,166**	**1,076**	**1,076**

Funds From Operations

It can be calculated by adding non-operating expenses and deducting non-operating income from the net profit. If the net amount is positive, it is called funds from operations (Source) and if it is negative, it is called funds lost from operations (application).

Calculation of funds from operations	Rs.	Rs.
Net Profit Shows As P and L Account		
Add:		
1. Depreciation written off		
2. Goodwill written off		
3. Preliminary expenses written off		
4. Provision for taxation		
5. Transfer to reserve		
6. Dividend/Interim/Proposed Dividend paid		
7. Loss on sale of fixed assets		
8. Discount on issue of shares and debentures written off		
9. Patents written off		
Less:		
1. Dividends Received		
2. Profit on sale of fixed assets		
3. Appreciation in the value of fixed Assets		
4. Rent received		
5. Refund of tax		
Funds from operations		

Note:

- If the P&L A/c shows a net loss, the above procedure will be reversed.
- Net profit = Closing balance of P&L A/c — Opening balance of P&L A/c

Sources of Funds	Rs.	Application of Funds	Rs.
1. Funds from operations			
2. Issue of share capital			
3. Issue of debentures			
4. Raising of long-term loan			
5. Sale of fixed assets			
6. Non-trading receipts			
7. Decrease in working capital			

While preparing funds flow statement, the following rules must be remembered:

(i) An increase in a fixed asset indicates an application of funds.

(ii) A decrease in a fixed asset indicates a source of funds.

(iii) An increase in a fixed liability indicates a source of funds.

(iv) An increase in shareholders funds indicates a source of funds.

(v) A decrease in shareholders funds indicates an application of funds.

The following will illustrate these rules:

Source of Funds	*Application of Funds*
– Fixed Assets	+ Fixed Asset
+ Long-term Liabilities	– Long-term Liabilities
+ Shareholders' Funds	– Shareholders' Funds

Hidden Transactions

(i) Fixed Assets: Sometimes, there are certain adjustments of sale and purchases of fixed assets which are given after the two Balance Sheets. Under such circumstances, it is desirable to prepare accounts relating to such fixed assets and provision or reserve for depreciation.

(ii) Proposed Dividend: It can be treated as an item of current liability or non-current liability but preferably it should be treated as non-current liability.

(iii) If dividend paid during the year is not given, then it is assumed that last year balance must have been paid during the year and provision made during the year must be equal to the closing balance.

(iv) Provision for Income Tax: Like proposed dividend it can also be treated as current liability or non-current liability. But preferably it should treated as non-current liability. If income tax paid during the year is not give, then it is assumed that last year balance must have been paid during the year. Provision made during the year must be the closing balance of such account. Income tax payable is a current liability.

(v) Fictitious Assets: If there are certain fictitious assets in the Balance Sheet as discount on issue of shares or debentures, preliminary expenses etc., then the balance to be written off to the Profit and Loss Account can be calculated by preparing the fictitious asset account.

(vi) Net Profit or Drawings: Sometimes, in case of sole trader or partnership concerns, capital of the proprietor or partners is given but figures of drawings or net profit may be missing.

Problem 2 :

Calculate funds from operation from the following P & L Account.

P & L Account

Particulars	*Rs.*	*Particulars*	*Rs.*
To Expenses Paid	3,00,000	By Gross Profit	4,50,000
To Depreciation	70,000	By Gain on Sale of Land	60,000
To Loss on Sale of Machine	4,000		
To Discount	200		
To Goodwill	20,000		
To Net Profit	1,15,800		
	5,10,000		**5,10,000**

Solution:

Calculation of Funds From Operations

Particulars	*Rs.*	*Rs.*
Net Profit		1,15,800
Add: Non-operating Expenses		
Depreciation	70,000	
Loss on Sale of Machine	4,000	
Discount	200	
Goodwill	20,000	94,200
		2,10,000
Less: Non-operating income		
Gain on Sale of Land		60,000
Funds from Operations		**1,50,000**

Problem 3 :

Calculate funds from operation from the following P & L Account.

Particulars	*Rs.*	*Particulars*	*Rs.*
To Expenses Paid and Outstanding	1,50,000	By Gross Profit	2,25,000
To Depreciation	35,000	By Gain on Sale of Land	30,000
To Loss on Sale of Machine	2,000		
To Discount	100		
To Good Will	10,000		
To Net Profit	57,900		
	2,55,000		**2,55,000**

Solution:

Calculation of Funds From Operation

Particulars	*Rs.*	*Rs.*
Net Profit		57,900
Add: Non-operating Expenses:		
Depreciation	35,000	
Loss on Sale of Machine	2,000	
Discount	100	
Goodwill	10,000	47,100
		1,05,000
Less: Non-operating Income:		
Gain on Sale of Land		30,000
Funds from Operation		**75,000**

Problem 4 :

Calculate funds from operations from the following income statement.

Income Statement

Particulars	*Rs.*	*Particulars*	*Rs.*
To Salaries	1,00,000	By Gross profit	5,00,000
To Rent	25,000	By Profit on sale of vehicle	3,000
To Provision for depreciation	50,000	By Refund of tax	2,000
To Commission	5,000	By Dividend received	10,000
To Provision for tax	1,50,000		
To General reserve	3,000		
To Loss on sale of investment	10,000		
To Cost of issue of shares written off	2,000		
To Provision for legal damages	5,000		
To Net Profit	1,65,000		
	5,15,000		**5,15,000**

Solution:

Adj. P& L A/c

Particulars	*Rs.*	*Particulars*	*Rs.*
To Loss on sale of investments	10,000	By Profit on sale of vehicle	3,000
To Provision for tax	1,50,000	By Dividend received	10,000
To Provision for depreciation	50,000	By Refund of tax	2,000
To General reserve	3,000	Fund from operation(b/f)	3,70,000
To Provision for legal damages	5,000		
To Cost of issue of shares written off	2,000		
To Net Profit	1,65,000		
	3,85,000		**3,85,000**

Problem 5 :

From the following, prepare a sources and uses of funds statement for 2009

Particulars	*31.12.2009 (Rs.)*	*31.12.2008 (Rs.)*
Assets:		
Cash	75,000	35,000
Accounts Receivable	90,000	98,000
Stock	1,20,000	87,000
Long-term investment	10,000	15,000
Land	30,000	20,000
	3,25,000	**2,55,000**
Liabilities:		
Creditors	45,000	50,000
Bills Payable	55,000	20,000
Share Capital	1,50,000	1,25,000
Retained Earnings	75,000	60,000
	3,25,000	**2,55,000**

Solution:

Funds Flow Statement for the Year Ended 31.12.2009

Sources	*Rs.*	*Applications*	*Rs.*
Issue of Shares	25,000	Purchase of Land	10,000
Sale of Investment	5,000	Increase in Working Capital	35,000
Funds from Operations	15,000		
	45,000		**45,000**

Workings:

Calculation of funds from operation:

Closing Balance of Profit and Loss A/c.	75,000
Less: Opening Balance of Profit and Loss A/c.	60,000
Funds From Operations	15,000

Problem 6 :

The following is the Comparative Balance Sheet of JC Ltd., Prepare Funds Flow Statement.

Balance Sheet

Particulars	*2008 (Rs.)*	*2009 (Rs.)*	*Particulars*	*2008 (Rs.)*	*2009 (Rs.)*
Share Capital	8,000	8,500	Land	5,000	5,000
P and L a/c	1,450	2,450	Plant	2,400	3,400
Creditors	900	500	Debtors	1,650	1,950
Mortgage Loan	-	500	Stock	900	700
			Cash	400	900
	10,350	**11,950**		**10,350**	**11,950**

Solution:

Schedule of Changes in Working Capital

Particulars	*2008 Rs.*	*2009 Rs.*	*Increase Rs.*	*Decrease Rs.*
Current Assets:				
Debtors	1,650	1,950	300	-
Stock	900	700	-	200
Cash	400	900	500	-
Total Current Assets	2,950	3,550		

Current Liabilities:				
Creditors	900	500	400	-
Total Current Liabilities	900	500		
Working Capital	2,050	3,050		
Increase in Working Capital	1,000	-	-	1,000
	3,050	**3,050**	**1,200**	**1,200**

Funds Flow Statement

Sources	*Rs.*	*Applications*	*Rs.*
Issue of shares	500	Purchase of plant	1,000
Funds from operations	1,000	Increase in working capital	1,000
Mortgage loan	500		
	2,000		**2,000**

Problem 7 :

Calculate funds from operations from the following:

P&L Appropriation A/c

Particulars	*Rs.*	*Particulars*		*Rs.*
To Salary	10,000	By Gross Profit		1,00,000
To Rent	6,000	By Profit on sale of equip.		
To Dep. On Plant	10,000	Book Value	20,000	
To Stationery	6,000	**Less:** Sold for	30,000	10,000
To Preliminary Exp. W/Off	4,000			
To Goodwill Written Off	6,000			
To Provision for Tax	8,000			
To Proposed Dividend	12,000			
To Net Profit	48,000			
	1,10,000			**1,10,000**

Solution:

Calculation of funds from Operation:

	Particulars	*Rs.*	*Rs.*
	Net profit		48,000
Add:	**Non-operating expenses:**		
	Depreciation on plant	10,000	
	Preliminary expenses written off	4,000	
	Goodwill written off	6,000	
	Provision for tax	8,000	
	Proposed dividend	12,000	40,000
			88,000
Less:	**Non-operating income:**		
	Profit on sale of equipment (20,000-30,000)		10,000
	Funds from operations		**78,000**

Problem 8 :

Calculate funds from operations from the following information.

Particulars	*Rs.*	*Particulars*	*Rs.*
Salaries	5,000	Profit on sale of land	5,000
Rent	3,000	Cl. balance of P&L a/c	60,000
Depreciation on plant	5,000	Dis. on issue of debentures	2,000
Provision for tax	4,000	Provision for bad debts	1,000
Loss on sale of plant	2,000	Preliminary exp. written off	3,000
Op. balance of P&L a/c	25,000	Proposed dividend	6,000
Transfer to general reserve	1,000		
Goodwill written off	2,000		

Solution:

Calculation of Funds from Operations

	Paticulars	*Rs.*	*Rs.*
	Closing balance of profit and loss account		60,000
Add:	**Non-fund or non-operating expenses:**		

	Depreciation on plant	5,000	
	Provision for tax	4,000	
	Loss on sale of plant	2,000	
	Transfer to general reserve	1,000	
	Goodwill written off	2,000	
	Discount on issue of debentures	2,000	
	Provision for bad debts	1,000	
	Preliminary expenses written off	3,000	
	Proposed dividend	6,000	26,000
			86,000
Less:	**Non-fund or non-operational Income:**		
	Profit on sale of land	5,000	
	Opening balance of P&L a/c	25,000	30,000
	Funds from operations		**56,000**

Problem 9 :

From the following two Balance Sheets as at 31.12.2008 and 2009. You are required to prepare a statement of sources and uses of funds.

Particulars	***2008 (Rs.)***	***2009 (Rs.)***
Liabilities:		
Share Capital	40,000	45,000
Trade Creditors	10,000	23,000
Profit and Loss a/c	2,30,000	2,50,000
	2,80,000	**3,18,000**
Assets:		
Cash	30,000	47,000
Debtors	1,20,000	1,15,000
Stock	80,000	90,000
Land	50,000	66,000
	2,80,000	**3,18,000**

Solution:

Schedule of Changes in Working Capital

Particulars	*2008 (Rs.)*	*2009 (Rs.)*	*Increase (Rs.)*	*Decrease (Rs.)*
Current Assets:				
Cash	30,000	47,000	17,000	-
Debtors	1,20,000	1,15,000	-	5,000
Stock	80,000	90,000	10,000	
Total Current assets	2,30,000	2,52,000		
Current Liabilities:				
Trade creditors	10,000	23,000	-	13,000
Total Current Liabilities	10,000	23,000		
Working capital	2,20,000	2,29,000		
Increase in working capital	9,000	-	-	9,000
	2,29,000	**2,29,000**	**27,000**	**27,000**

Funds Flow Statement

Sources	*Rs.*	*Applications*	*Rs.*
Issue of shares	5,000	Purchase of land	16,000
Funds from operations	20,000	Increase in working capital	9,000
	25,000		**25,000**

Problem 10 :

From the following two Balance Sheets as at March 31, 2008 and 2009, you are required to prepare a funds flow statement.

Particulars	*31.03.2008 (Rs.)*	*31.03.2009 (Rs.)*	*31.03.2008 (Rs.)*	*31.03.2009 (Rs.)*
Liabilities:				
Share Capital	2,00,000	2,50,000		
Trade Creditors	50,000	45,000		
Profit and Loss a/c	1,00,000	1,25,000		
Assets:				
Cash			50,000	55,000
Debtors			1,00,000	1,20,000
Stock			1,50,000	1,75,000
Land			50,000	70,000
	3,50,000	**4,20,000**	**3,50,000**	**4,20,000**

Solution:

Schedule of Changes in Working Capital

Particulars	*31.03.2008 Rs.*	*31.03.2009 Rs.*	*Increase (Rs.)*	*Decrease (Rs.)*
Current Assets:				
Cash	50,000	55,000	5,000	
Debtors	1,00,000	1,20,000	20,000	
Stock	1,50,000	1,75,000	25,000	
Total Current Assets	3,00,000	3,50,000		
Current Liabilities:				
Trade Creditors	50,000	45,000	5,000	
Total Current Liabilities	50,000	45,000		
Working Capital	2,50,000	3,05,000		
Increase in Working Capital	55,000	—	—	55,000
	3,05,000	**3,05,000**	**55,000**	**55,000**

Funds Flow Statement for the Year Ended 31st March, 2009

Sources	*Rs.*	*Applications*	*Rs.*
Issues of Shares	50,000	Purchase of Land	20,000
Funds from Operations	25,000	Increase in Working Capital	55,000
	75,000		**75,000**

Workings:

Calculation of Funds from Operation

Closing Balance of Profit and Loss a/c.	1,25,000
Less: Opening Balance of Profit and Loss a/c.	1,00,000
Funds from Operations	25,000

Problem 11 :

Followings are summarised Balance Sheet of Rajan Industries Ltd., as on 31st December, 2008 and 2009.

Liabilities	31st December		Assets	31st December	
	2008 (Rs.)	2009(Rs.)		2008 (Rs.)	2009(Rs.)
Capital:			Fixed Assets	41,000	40,000
7% Redeemable Preference Shares	-	10,000	Less: Depreciation	11,000	15,000
Equity Shares	40,000	40,000		30,000	25,000
	40,000	50,000	**Current Assets:**		
General Reserve	2,000	2,000	Debtors	20,000	24,000
Profit and Loss a/c	1,000	1,200	Stock	30,000	35,000
Debentures	6,000	7,000	Prepaid Expenses	300	500
Current Liabilities:			Cash	1,200	3,500
Creditors	12,000	11,000			
Provision for Tax	3,000	4,200			
Proposed Dividend	5,000	5,800			
Bank Overdraft	12,500	6,800			
	81,500	**88,000**		**81,500**	**88,000**

Y ou are require to prepare:

(i) A statement showing changes in the working capital, and

(ii) A statement of sources and application of funds.

Solution :

Schedule of Changes in Working Capital

Particulars	*2008 (Rs.)*	*2009(Rs.)*	*Increase (Rs.)*	*Decrease (Rs.)*
Current Assets:				
Cash	1,200	3,500	2,300	
Debtors	20,000	24,000	4,000	
Stock	30,000	35,000	5,000	
Prepaid Expenses	300	500	200	
Total Current Assets	51,500	63,000		
Current Liabilities:				
Creditors	12,000	11,000	1,000	
Provision for Tax	3,000	4,200		1,200

Proposed Dividend	5,000	5,800		800
Bank Oversdraft	12,500	6,800	5,700	
Total Current Liabilities	32,500	27,800		
Working Capital	19,000	35,200		
Increase in Working Capital	16,200	———	———	16,200
	35,200	**35,200**	**18,200**	**18,200**

Funds Flow Statement for the Year Ended 31.12.2009

Sources	*Rs.*	*Application*	*Rs.*
Issues of 7% Preference Shares	10,000	Increase in Working Capital	16,200
Funds from Operations	4,200		
Issue of Debentures	1,000		
Sale of Fixed Assets	1,000		
	16,200		**16,200**

Adj. P & L A/c

Particulars	*Rs.*	*Particulars*	*Rs.*
To Depreciation on fixed asset	4,000	By balance b/d	1,000
To balance c/d	1,200	By Fund from operation(b/f)	4,200
	5,200		**5,200**

Problem 12 :

Following are the Comparative Balance Sheet of Rajan Company for the years 2008 and 2009.

Liabilities	*2008 (Rs.)*	*2009 (Rs.)*	*Assets*	*2008 (Rs.)*	*2009 (Rs.)*
Share Capital	70,000	74,000	Cash	9,000	7,800
P&L a/c	10,740	11,360	Debtors	14,900	17,700
Creditors	10,360	11,840	Stock	49,200	42,700
Debentures	12,000	6,000	Land	20,000	30,000
			Goodwill	10,000	5,000
	1,03,100	**1,03,200**		**1,03,100**	**1,03,200**

Additional information:

(i) Dividends were paid totalling Rs. 4,000

(ii) Land was purchased for Rs. 15,000

You are required to prepare a Funds Flow Statement

Solution:

Schedule of Changes in Working Capital

Particulars	*2008 (Rs.)*	*2009 (Rs.)*	*Increase (Rs.)*	*Decrease (Rs.)*
Current Assets:				
Cash	9,000	7,800	-	1,200
Debtors	14,900	17,700	2,800	-
Stock	49,200	42,700	-	6,500
Total Current Assets	73,100	68,200		
Current Liabilities:				
Trade creditors	10,360	11,840	-	1,480
Total current liabilities	10,360	11,840		
Working capital	62,740	56,360		
Decrease in working capital		6,380	6,380	
	62,740	**62,740**	**9,180**	**9,180**

Funds Flow Statement

Sources	*Rs.*	*Applications*	*Rs.*
Issue of shares	4,000	Redemption of debentures	6,000
Sale of land	5,000	Purchase of land	15,000
Funds from operations	9,620	Dividend paid	4,000
Decrease in working capital	6,380		
	25,000		**25,000**

Workings:

Land Account

	Rs.		*Rs.*
To Balance b/d	20,000	By Cash a/c (Bal. Fig.)	5,000
To Cash	15,000	By Balance c/d	30,000
	35,000		**35,000**

Adj. P&L A/c

Particulars	*Rs.*	*Particulars*	*Rs.*
To Dividend	4,000	By balance b/d	10,740
To Goodwill written off	5,000		
To balance c/d	11,360	By Fund from operation(b/f)	9,620
	20,360		**20,360**

Problem 13 :

From the following Balance Sheet of RR Ltd., prepare a fund flow statement.

Balance Sheet

Liabilities	*2008 (Rs.)*	*2009 (Rs.)*	*Assets*	*2008 (Rs.)*	*2009 (Rs.)*
Eq. Share Capital	3,00,000	4,00,000	Goodwill	1,15,000	90,000
Pref. Share Capital	1,50,000	1,00,000	Building	2,00,000	1,70,000
General Reserve	40,000	70,000	Plant	80,000	2,00,000
Profit and Loss a/c	30,000	48,000	Debtors	1,60,000	2,00,000
Proposed Dividend	42,000	50,000	Stock	77,000	1,09,000
Creditors	55,000	83,000	Bills Receivable	20,000	30,000
Bills Payable	20,000	16,000	Cash	15,000	10,000
Provision for Taxation	40,000	50,000	Bank	10,000	8,000
	6,77,000	**8,17,000**		**6,77,000**	**8,17,000**

Additional Information :

(i) Depreciation of Rs. 10,000 and Rs. 20,000 has been charged on Plant and Buildings respectively in 2009

(ii) An interim dividend of Rs. 20,000 has been paid in 2009

(iii) Income tax Rs. 35,000 was paid during the year 2009

Solution:

Schedule of Changes in Working Capital

Particulars	*2008 (Rs.)*	*2009 (Rs.)*	*Increase (Rs.)*	*Decrease (Rs.)*
Current Assets:				
Debtors	1,60,000	2,00,000	40,000	
Stock	77,000	1,09,000	32,000	
Bills Receivable	20,000	30,000	10,000	
Cash	15,000	10,000		5,000

Bank	10,000	8,000		2,000
Total Current Assets	2,82,000	3,57,000		
Current Liabilities :				
Sundry Creditors	55,000	83,000		28,000
Bills payable	20,000	16,000	4,000	
Total current liabilities	75,000	99,000		
Working capital	2,07,000	2,58,000		
Increase in working capital	51,000			51,000
	2,58,000	**2,58,000**	**86,000**	**86,000**

Funds Flow Statement

Sources	*Rs.*	*Applications*	*Rs.*
Issue of shares	1,00,000	Redemption of Pref. shares	50,000
Sale of building	10,000	Purchase of plant	1,30,000
Funds from operations	2,18,000	Interim dividend paid	20,000
		Payment of tax	35,000
		Proposed dividend	42,000
		Increase in working capital	51,000
	3,28,000		**3,28,000**

Workings:

Provision for Taxation A/c

Particulars	*Rs.*	*Particulars*	*Rs.*
To bank	35,000	By balance b/d	40,000
To balance c/d	50,000	By profit and loss a/c	45,000
	85,000		**85,000**

Land and Building A/c

Particulars	*Rs.*	*Particulars*	*Rs.*
To balance b/d	2,00,000	By depreciation	20,000
		By bank	10,000
		By balance c/d	1,70,000
	2,00,000		**2,00,000**

Plant A/c

Particulars	Rs.	Particulars	Rs.
To balance b/d	80,000	By profit and loss a/c (dep.)	10,000
To bank	1,30,000	By balance c/d	2,00,000
	2,10,000		**2,10,000**

Adj. P& L A/c

Particulars	Rs.	Particulars	Rs.
To Proposed dividend	50,000	By balance b/d	30,000
To General reserve	30,000		
To Goodwill written off	25,000	By Fund from operation(b/f)	2,18,000
To Depreciation on building	20,000		
To Depreciation on plant	10,000		
To Interim dividend	20,000		
To Provision for taxation	45,000		
To balance c/d	48,000		
	2,48,000		**2,48,000**

Problem 14 :

From the following particulars prepare a statement of sources and application of funds.

(i) Increase in working capital Rs. 4,000

(ii) Net profit Rs.10,750 before writing off goodwill.

(iii) Depreciation provided on fixed asset Rs.1,750.

(iv) Dividend Rs. 3,500.

(v) Goodwill written off out of profit Rs.5,000.

(vi) Rs.5,000 share capital issued for cash.

(vii) Machinery was purchased for Rs.10,000.

Solution:

Funds Flow Statement

Sources	Rs.	Applications	Rs.
Issue of shares	5,000	Purchase of Plant and Machinery	10,000
Funds from operations	12,500	Dividend Paid	3,500
		Increase in Working Capital	4,000
	17,500		**17,500**

Workings:

Calculation of Funds from Operations:

		Rs.
Net profit		5,750
Add: Goodwill written off	5,000	
Depreciation	1,750	
		6,750
Funds from operations		**12,500**

	Rs.
Net profit before writing off goodwill	10,750
(—) Goodwill written off	5,000
Net profit after writing off Goodwill	**5,750**

Problem 15 :

The opening and closing balances of plant and machinery (at cost) amounted to Rs. 2,00,000 and Rs. 3,00,000 respectively. Accumulated depreciation at the beginning and at the end amounted to Rs. 50,000 and Rs. 80,000 respectively. A machine costing Rs. 10,000 (w.d.v. Rs. 6,000) was sold for Rs. 5,000 during the year.

Prepare necessary accounts to show the sources and application of funds during the year relating to plant and machinery.

Solution:

Funds Flow Statement

Sources	*Rs.*	*Applications*	*Rs.*
Sale of Plant and Machinery	5,000	Purchase of Plant and Machinery	1,10,000

Workings

Plant and Machinery A/c.

Particulars	*Rs.*	*Particulars*	*Rs.*
To Balance b/d	2,00,000	By Bank (Sales)	5,000
To Bank (Bal. Fig.)	1,10,000	By Accumulated Dep.	4,000
		By Adj. P and L a/c (Loss)	1,000
		By Balance c/d	3,00,000
	3,10,000		**3,10,000**

Accumulated Depreciation A/c

Particulars	*Rs.*	*Particulars*	*Rs.*
To Plant and Machinery	4,000	By Balance b/d	50,000
To Balance c/d	80,000	By Adj. P&L a/c (b/f)	34,000
	84,000		**84,000**

Problem 16 :

Followings are summarised Balance Sheet of JC Industries Ltd., as on 31st December, 2008 and 2009

Liabilities	*31st December*		*Assets*	*31st December*	
	2008 (Rs.)	*2009 (Rs.)*		*2008 (Rs.)*	*2009 (Rs.)*
11% Cumulative Preference Shares	——	30,000	Land and Building	60,000	50,000
Equity Shares	1,10,000	1,20,000	Plant and Machinery	30,000	50,000
General Reserve	4,000	4,000	Debtors	40,000	48,000
Profit and Loss A/c	2,000	2,400	Stock	60,000	70,000
9% Debentures	12,000	14,000	Bank	2,400	7,000
Provision for Tax	6,000	8,400	Cash	600	1,000
Proposed Dividend	10,000	11,600			
Current Liabilities	49,000	35,600			
	1,93,000	**2,26,000**		**1,93,000**	**2,26,000**

You are required to prepare a Statement of sources and application of funds.

Solution:

Schedule of Changes in Working Capital

Particulars	*2008 (Rs.)*	*2009 (Rs.)*	*Increase (Rs.)*	*Decrease (Rs.)*
Current Assets:				
Debtors	40,000	48,000	8,000	
Stock	60,000	70,000	10,000	
Bank	2,400	7,000	4,600	
Cash	600	1,000	400	
Total Current Assets	1,03,000	1,26,000		
Current Liabilities:				
Current Liabilities	49,000	35,600	13,400	

Total Current Liabilities	49,000	35,600		
Working Capital	54,000	90,400		
Increase in Working Capital	36,400	———	———	36,400
	90,400	**90,400**	**36,400**	**36,400**

Funds Flow Statement for the year ended 31.12.2009

Sources	*Rs.*	*Applications*	*Rs.*
Issues of Preference Shares	30,000	Purchase of Plant and Machinery	20,000
Issues of Equity Shares	10,000	Provision for Tax -2004	6,000
Issue of Debentures	2,000	Proposed Dividend -2004	10,000
Sale of Land and Building	10,000	Increase in Working Capital	36,400
Funds from operations	20,400		
	72,400		**72,400**

Adj. P& L A/c

Particulars	*Rs.*	*Particulars*	*Rs.*
To Proposed dividend	11,600	By Balance b/d	2,000
To Provision for tax	8,400		
To balance c/d	2,400	By Fund from operation(b/f)	20,400
	22,400		**22,400**

Problem 17 :

Balance Sheet of Ramu and Somu as on 2008 and 2009 were as follows:

Liabilities	*2008 (Rs.)*	*2009 (Rs.)*	*Assets*	*2008 (Rs.)*	*2009 (Rs.)*
Capital	1,25,000	1,53,000	Cash	10,000	7,000
Creditors	40,000	44,000	Debtors	30,000	50,000
Mrs. Somu's loan	25,000	———	Stock	35,000	25,000
Loan from bank	40,000	50,000	Machinery	80,000	55,000
			Land	40,000	50,000
			Building	35,000	60,000
	2,30,000	**2,47,000**		**2,30,000**	**2,47,000**

During the year a machine costing Rs.10,000 (accumulated depreciation of Rs. 3,000) was sold for Rs. 5,000. The provision for depreciation for machinery as on 2008 was Rs. 25,000 and on 2009 Rs. 40,000. Net profit for the year 2009 amounted to Rs. 45,000. You are required to prepare funds flow statement.

Solution:

Schedule of Changes in Working Capital

Particulars	*2008 (Rs.)*	*2009 (Rs.)*	*Increase (Rs.)*	*Decrease (Rs.)*
Current Assets:				
Cash	10,000	7,000		3,000
Debtors	30,000	50,000	20,000	
Stock	35,000	25,000		10,000
Total Current Assets	75,000	82,000		
Current Liabilities:				
Creditors	40,000	44,000		4,000
Total Current Liabilities	40,000	44,000		
Working Capital	35,000	38,000		
Increase in Working Capital	3,000			3,000
	38,000	**38,000**	**20,000**	**20,000**

Funds Flow Statement for the year ended 2009

Sources	*Rs.*	*Applications*	*Rs.*
Sale of machinery	5,000	Purchase of land	10,000
Loan from bank	10,000	Purchase of building	25,000
Funds from operations	65,000	Drawings	17,000
		Repayment of Mrs. Somu's loan	25,000
		Increase in Working Capital	3,000
	80,000		**80,000**

Note: To find out the cost of the machinery, the opening value of the provision for depreciation should be add with opening value of the machinery and closing provision with closing value of the machinery.

Workings:

Machinery A/c

	Rs.		Rs.
To balance b/d(80,000+25,000)	1,05,000	By cash (sale)	5,000
		By provision for depreciation	3,000
		By Adj. P&L A/C	2,000
		By balance c/d (55,000+40,000)	95,000
	1,05,000		**1,05,000**

Capital A/c

	Rs.		Rs
To Drawings (bal. fig.)	17,000	By Balance b/d	1,25,000
To Balance c/d	1,53,000	By Net Profit	45,000
	1,70,000		**1,70,000**

Calculation of Funds from Operations:

		Rs.
Net Profit		45,000
Add: Non fund or non-operating esxpenses:		
Depreciation (15,000+3,000)	18,000	
Loss on sale of machinery	2,000	
		20,000
		65,000

Problem 18 :

The following are the summarised Balance Sheets of Good Luck Ltd., as on 31st December, 2008 and 31st December 2009

Liabilities	*2008 (Rs.)*	*2009 (Rs.)*	*Assets*	*2008 (Rs.)*	*2009 (Rs.)*
Equity Share	2,00,000	2,40,000	Land and Building	1,05,000	1,50,000
8% Debentures	50,000	———	Plant and Machinery (at cost)	2,90,000	3,20,000
Share Premium	———	10,000	Furniture (at cost)	9,000	10,000
General Reserve	30,000	50,000	Inventories	1,30,000	1,05,000
P&L A/c	48,000	68,000	S. Debtors	75,000	85,000
S. Creditors	1,30,000	1,50,000	Cash	15,000	26,000
Proposed Dividend	20,000	24,000			

Provision for depreciation on:					
Plant and Machinery	1,40,000	1,50,000			
Furniture	6,000	4,000			
	6,24,000	**6,96,000**		**6,24,000**	**6,96,000**

Additional information is as follows:

(i) Furniture which cost Rs. 5,000, written down value Rs. 1,000 was sold during the year 2009 for Rs. 2,000

(ii) Plant and machinery which cost Rs. 20,000 and in respect of which Rs. 13,000 had been written off as depreciation was sold during the year 2009 for Rs. 3,000

You are required to prepare Funds Flow Statement for the year.

Solution:

Schedule of Changes in Working Capital

Particulars	*31.12.08 (Rs.)*	*31.12.09 (Rs.)*	*Increase (Rs.)*	*Decrease (Rs.)*
Current Assets:				
Cash	15,000	26,000	11,000	
Debtors	75,000	85,000	10,000	
Inventories	1,30,000	1,05,000		25,000
Total Current Assets	2,20,000	2,16,000		
Current Liabilities:				
Creditors	1,30,000	1,50,000		20,000
Total Current Liabilities	1,30,000	1,50,000		
Working Capital	90,000	66,000		
Decrease in Working Capital	———	24,000	24,000	———
	90,000	**90,000**	**45,000**	**45,000**

Funds Flow Statement for the year ended 31.12.2009

Sources	*Rs.*	*Applications*	*Rs.*
Issue of Shares	40,000	Purchase of Plant	50,000
Share Premium	10,000	Purchase of Furniture	6,000
Sale of Furniture	2,000	Purchase of Land	45,000
Sale of Plant	3,000	Dividend Paid	20,000
Decrease in Working Capital	24,000	Redemption of Debentures	50,000
Funds from Operation	92,000		
	1,71,000		**1,71,000**

Workings:

Furniture A/c

Particulars	*Rs.*	*Particulars*	*Rs.*
To Balance b/d	9,000	By Cash	2,000
To Adj P & L a/c (profit)	1,000	By Provision for Depreciation	4,000
To Cash (Bal. Fig.)	6,000	By Balance c/d	10,000
	16,000		**16,000**

Plant & Machinery A/c.

Particulars	*Rs.*	*Particulars*	*Rs.*
To Balance b/d	2,90,000	By Cash	3,000
To Cash (bal. fig.)	50,000	By Depreciation	13,000
		By Adjusted P & L A/c (loss)	4,000
		By Balance c/d	3,20,000
	3,40,000		**3,40,000**

Adj. P& L A/c

To Loss on Sale of Plant	4,000	By Balance b/d.	48,000
To depreciation on Plant (10,000+13,000)	23,000	By Profit on Sale of Furniture	1,000
To dep. on Furniture	2,000	By Funds from Operations	92,000
To General Reserve	20,000		
To Proposed Dividend	24,000		
To Balance c/d	68,000		
	1,41,000		**1,41,000**

Problem 19:

The following are the summarised Balance Sheet of Surya Ltd., As on 31st March, 2008 and 2009..

Liabilities	*2008 Rs.*	*2009 Rs.*	*Assets*	*2008 Rs.*	*2009Rs.*
Equity capital	2,00,000	2,60,000	Goodwill	————	20,000
General reserve	50,000	50,000	Plant and machinery	1,12,950	1,16,200
Profit and loss A/c	39,690	41,220	Land and building	1,48,500	1,44,250
Bills payable	33,780	11,525	Stock	1,11,040	97,370
Sundry Creditors	39,500	41,135	Sundry advances	2,315	735
Bank overdraft	59,510	————	Debtors	85,175	72,625
Provision for taxation	40,000	50,000	Cash	2,500	2,700
	4,62,480	**4,53,880**		**4,62,480**	**4,53,880**

Additional information:

(i) During the year ended 31st March, 2009 an interim dividend of Rs.26,000 was paid.

(ii) The assets of another company was purchased for Rs. 60,000 payable in fully paid shares of the company. These assets consisted of stock Rs. 21,640, machinery Rs.18,360 and goodwill Rs.20,000.

In addition plant were purchased for Rs.5,650.

(iii) Income tax paid during the year Rs.25,000.

(iv) The net profit for the year before tax was Rs. 62,500.

Prepare Funds Flow Statement

Solution :

Schedule of Changes in Working capital

Particulars	*2008 (Rs.)*	*2009 (Rs.)*	*Increase (Rs.)*	*Decrease (Rs.)*
Current assets:				
Cash	2,500	2,700	200	
Debtors	85,175	72,625		12,550
Sundry advances	2,315	735		1,580
Stock	1,11,040	97,370		13,370
Total Current assets	2,01,030	1,73,430		
Current Liabilities:				
Sundry Creditors	39,500	41,135		1,635
Bills payable	33,780	11,525	22,255	

Bank overdraft	59,510	———	59,510	
Total current liabilities	**1,32,790**	**52,660**		
Working capital	68,240	1,20,770		
Increase in working capital	52,530			52,530
	1,20,770	**1,20,770**	**81,965**	**81,965**

Funds Flow Statement

Sources	*Rs.*	*Applications*	*Rs.*
Issue of shares (stock)	21,640	Purchase of machinery	5,650
Funds from operations	87,540	Payment of tax	25,000
		Payment of dividend	26,000
		Increase in working capital	52,530
	1,09,180		**1,09,180**

Workings:

Share Capital Account

Particulars	*Rs.*	*Particulars*	*Rs.*
		By balance b/d	2,00,000
		By stock (source of funds)	21,640
		By machinery	18,360
To balance c/d	2,60,000	By goodwill	20,000
	2,60,000		**2,60,000**

Provision for Taxation A/c

Particulars	*Rs.*	*Particulars*	*Rs.*
To Cash (tax paid)	25,000	By Balance b/d	40,000
To Balance c/d	50,000	By Adjusted profit and loss a/c (bal. fig.)	35,000
	75,000		**75,000**

Land and Building Account

Particulars	*Rs.*	*Particulars*	*Rs.*
To Balance b/d	1,48,500	By Depreciation (bal. fig.)	4,250
		By Balance c/d	1,44,250
	1,48,500		**1,48,500**

Plant and Machinery Account

Particulars	Rs.	Particulars	Rs.
To Balance b/d	1,12,950	By Depreciation (bal. fig.)	20,760
To Share capital	18,360	By Balance c/d	1,16,200
To Cash (purchase)	5,650		
	1,36,960		**1,36,960**

Adj. P & L A/c

Particulars	Rs.	Particulars	Rs.
To Depreciation on land	4,250	By Balance b/d	39,690
To Depreciation on plant	20,760	By Fund from operation (b/f)	87,540
To Provision for tax	35,000		
To Interim dividend	26,000		
To Balance c/d	41,220		
	1,27,230		**1,27,230**

Problem 20 :

Followings are the summarised Balance Sheets of Fire Stone Ltd., as on 31st December, 2008 and 2009:

Liabilities	*2008 (Rs.)*	*2009 (Rs.)*	*Assets*	*2008 (Rs.)*	*2009 (Rs.)*
Share capital	2,00,000	2,50,000	Land & building	2,00,000	1,90,000
General reserve	50,000	60,000	Machinery	1,50,000	1,69,000
Profit & loss a/c	30,500	30,600	Stock	1,00,000	74,000
Bank loan (long-term)	70,000	—	Sundry Debtors	80,000	64,200
Sundry creditors	1,50,000	1,35,200	Cash	500	600
Provision for taxation	30,000	35,000	Bank	—	8,000
			Goodwill	—	5,000
	5,30,500	**5,10,800**		**5,30,500**	**5,10,800**

Additional information during the year ended 31st December, 2009:

(a) Dividend of Rs. 23,000 was paid.

(b) The assets of another company were purchased for a consideration of Rs. 50,000 payable in shares.

The following assets were purchased:

Machinery Rs. 25,000; Stock Rs. 20,000

(c) Machinery was further purchased for Rs. 8,000.

(d) Depreciation written off against machinery Rs. 12,000.

(e) Income tax paid during the year Rs. 33,000.

(f) Loss on sale of machinery Rs. 200 was written off to general reserve.

Prepare funds flow statement.

Solution:

Schedule of changes in working capital

Particulars	*2008 (Rs.)*	*2009 (Rs.)*	*Increase (Rs.)*	*Decrease (Rs.)*
Current assets:				
Stock	1,00,000	74,000	-	26,000
Debtors	80,000	64,200	-	15,800
Cash	500	600	100	-
Bank	-	8,000	8,000	-
Total current assets	1,80,500	1,46,800		
Current liability:				
Sundry creditors	1,50,000	1,35,200	14,800	-
Total current Liabilities	1,50,000	1,35,200		
Working capital	30,500	11,600	22,900	41,800
Decrease in working capital	-	18,900	18,900	-
	30,500	**30,500**	**41,800**	**41,800**

Funds Flow Statement

Sources	*Rs.*	*Applications*	*Rs.*
Sale of machinery	1,800	Repayment of bank loan	70,000
Issue of shares for stock	20,000	Payment of tax	33,000
Funds from operations	93,300	Purchase of machinery	8,000
Decrease in working capital	18,900	Dividend paid	23,000
	1,34,000		**1,34,000**

Workings:

Machinery Account

Particulars	Rs.	Particulars	Rs.
To balance b/d	1,50,000	By Depreciation	12,000
To share capital	25,000	By General reserve	200
To cash	8,000	By cash (bal.fig.)	1,800
		By balance c/d	1,69,000
	1,83,000		**1,83,000**

Share Capital Account

Particulars	Rs.	Particulars	Rs.
		By balance b/d	2,00,000
		By Stock (source of funds)	20,000
		By Machinery	25,000
To balance c/d	2,50,000	By Goodwill (bal.fig.)	5,000
	2,50,000		**2,50,000**

Provision for Taxation Account

Particulars	Rs.	Particulars	Rs.
To cash (tax paid)	33,000	By balance b/d	30,000
To balance c/d	35,000	By adj. P&L A/c (current year's provision) (bal.fig.)	38,000
	68,000		**68,000**

General Reserve Account

Particulars	Rs.	Particulars	Rs.
To machinery (Loss on sale)	200	By Balance b/d	50,000
To balance c/d	60,000	By Adjusted P&L a/c (b/f)	10,200
	60,200		**60,200**

Adj. P& L A/c

Particulars	Rs.	Particulars	Rs.
To Depreciation on land	10,000	By Balance b/d	30,500
To Depreciation on plant	12,000	By Funds from operations (b/f)	93,300
To Provision for tax	38,000		

To Dividend	23,000		
To General reserve	10,200		
To balance c/d	30,600		
	1,23,800		**1,23,800**

Problem 21:

From the following Balance Sheets of Apollo Ltd., Prepare funds Flow Statement

Liabilities	*2008 (Rs.)*	*2009 (Rs.)*	*Assets*	*2008 (Rs.)*	*2009 (Rs.)*
Equity capital	3,00,000	4,00,000	Goodwill	1,00,000	80,000
8% Redeemable preference capital	1,50,000	1,00,000	Land and building	2,00,000	1,70,000
Capital reserve	———	20,000	Plant	80,000	2,00,000
General reserve	40,000	50,000	Investments	20,000	30,000
Profit and loss a/c	30,000	48,000	Sundry debtors	1,40,000	1,70,000
Proposed dividend	42,000	50,000	Stock	77,000	1,09,000
Sundry creditors	25,000	47,000	Bills receivable	20,000	30,000
Bills payable	20,000	16,000	Cash in hand	15,000	10,000
Liability for expenses	30,000	36,000	Cash at bank	10,000	8,000
Provision for taxation	40,000	50,000	Preliminary expenses	15,000	10,000
	6,77,000	**8,17,000**		**6,77,000**	**8,17,000**

(i) A piece land had been sold out in 2009 and the profit on sale has been credited to capital reserve.

(ii) A machine has been sold for Rs. 10,000. The written down value of the machinery was Rs. 12,000. Depreciation of Rs.10,000 is charged to plant in 2009.

(iii) The investments are trade investments. Rs. 3,000 by way of dividend is received including Rs. 1,000 from pre-acquisition profit which has been credited to the investment account.

(iv) An interim dividend of Rs. 20,000 has been paid in 2009.

Solution:

Schedule of Changes in Working Capital

Particulars	*2008 (Rs.)*	*2009 (Rs.)*	*Increase (Rs.)*	*Decrease (Rs.)*
Current Assets:				
Debtors	1,40,000	1,70,000	30,000	
Stock	77,000	1,09,000	32,000	
Bills Receivable	20,000	30,000	10,000	

Cash	15,000	10,000		5,000
Bank	10,000	8,000		2,000
Total current assets	**2,62,000**	**3,27,000**		
Current Liabilities:				
Creditors	25,000	47,000		22,000
Bills payable	20,000	16,000	4,000	
Liabilities for expenses	30,000	36,000		6,000
Provision for taxation	40,000	50,000		10,000
Total current liabilities	**1,15,000**	**1,49,000**		
Working Capital	1,47,000	1,78,000		
Increase in Working Capital	31,000			31,000
	1,78,000	**1,78,000**	**76,000**	**76,000**

Funds Flow Statement

Sources	*Rs.*	*Applications*	*Rs.*
Sale of plant	10,000	Purchase of investments	11,000
Issue of shares	1,00,000	Purchase of plant	1,42,000
Funds from operations	1,33,000	Redemption of preference shares	50,000
Sale of land	50,000	Proposed dividend	42,000
Dividend received	3,000	Interim dividend	20,000
		Increase in Working Capital	31,000
	2,96,000		**2,96,000**

Workings:

Land A/c

	Rs.		*Rs.*
To balance b/d	2,00,000	By cash (bal.fig.)	50,000
To Capital reserve	20,000	By balance c/d	1,70,000
	2,20,000		**2,20,000**

Plant A/c

Paticulars	*Rs.*	*Paticulars*	*Rs.*
To balance b/d	80,000	By Depreciation	10,000
To cash (bal.fig.)	1,42,000	By Cash (sales)	10,000
		By Adj P&L A/c (loss on sale)	2,000
		By Balance c/d	2,00,000
	2,22,000		**2,22,000**

Investment A/c

Paticulars	*Rs.*	*Paticulars*	*Rs.*
To balance b/d	20,000	By Dividend	1,000
To cash (bal.fig)	11,000	By Balance c/d	30,000
	31,000		**31,000**

Entry for dividend received

(i)	Cash A/c Dr.	3,000	–
	To dividend A/c	–	3,000
(ii)	Dividend A/c Dr.	3,000	–
	To Adjusted P&L A/c	–	2,000
	To Investment A/c	–	1,000

Adj. P& L A/c

Particulars	*Rs.*	*Particulars*	*Rs.*
To Goodwill written off	20,000	By Balance b/d	30,000
To Depreciation on plant	10,000	By Dividend received	2,000
To Preliminary expenses written off	5,000	By Funds from operations (b/f)	1,33,000
To Propose Dividend	50,000		
To General reserve	10,000		
To Interim dividend	20,000		
To Loss on sale of plant	2,000		
To Balance c/d	48,000		
	1,65,000		**1,65,000**

Problem 22:

The Balance Sheets of SAMY Machinery Ltd., are given below:

Assets	*2008 (Rs.)*	*2009 (Rs.)*
Cash	90,000	90,000
Debtors	67,000	43,000
Temporary investment	1,10,000	74,000
Prepaid expenses	1,000	2,000
Stock	82,000	1,06,000
Land and Building	1,50,000	1,50,000
Machinery	52,000	70,000
	5,52,000	5,35,000
Liabilities:		
Creditors	1,03,000	96,000
Outstanding expenses	13,000	12,000
8% debentures	90,000	70,000
Depreciation fund	40,000	44,000
Reserve for contingencies	60,000	60,000
Profit and Loss Account	16,000	23,000
Capital	2,30,000	2,30,000
	5,52,000	**5,35,000**

Additional informations:

(i) 10% dividend was paid in cash.

(ii) New machinery for Rs. 30,000 was purchased, but old machinery costing Rs. 12,000 was sold for Rs. 4,000; accumulated depreciation was Rs. 6,000.

(iii) Rs. 20,000 8% Debentures were redeemed by purchase from open market @ 96 for a debenture of Rs. 100.

(iv) Rs. 36,000 investments were sold at book value.

Prepare funds flow statement.

Solution:

Schedule of Changes in Working Capital

Particulars	*2008 (Rs.)*	*2009 (Rs.)*	*Increase (Rs.)*	*Decrease (Rs.)*
Current Assets:				
Cash	90,000	90,000	—	
Debtors	67,000	43,000		24,000
Temporary investment	1,10,000	74,000		36,000
Prepaid expenses	1,000	2,000	1,000	
Stock	82,000	1,06,000	24,000	
Total current assets	3,50,000	3,15,000		
Current Liabilities:				
Creditors	1,03,000	96,000	7,000	
Outstanding expenses	13,000	12,000	1,000	
Total current liabilities	1,16,000	1,08,000		
Working Capital	2,34,000	2,07,000		
Decrease in Working Capital	—	27,000	27,000	—
	2,34,000	**2,34,000**	**60,000**	**60,000**

Funds Flow Statement for the year ended 2009

Sources	*Rs.*	*Applications*	*Rs.*
Sale of machinery	4,000	Purchase of Machinery	30,000
Funds from operations	41,200	Redemption of debentures	19,200
Decrease in Working Capital	27,000	Dividend paid	23,000
	72,200		**72,200**

Machinery A/c

	Rs.		*Rs.*
To Balance b/d	52,000	By Cash (Sales)	4,000
To Cash (Purchases)	30,000	By Depreciation	6,000
		By Adj. P and L (loss)	2,000
		By Balance c/d	70,000
	82,000		**82,000**

Depreciation Fund A/c

	Rs.		Rs.
To Plant and Machinery	6,000	By Balance b/d	40,000
To Balance c/d	44,000	By Adj. P&L (bal. fig.) A/c	10,000
	50,000		**50,000**

Adj. P&L A/c

	Rs		Rs
To Depreciation	10,000	By Balance b/d	16,000
To Loss on sale of Machinery	2,000	By Profit on redemption of debentures (200×4)	800
To Dividend	23,000	By Funds from operations (bal. fig.)	41,200
To Balance c/d	23,000		
	58,000		**58,000**

CASH FLOW STATEMENT

Meaning

A statement prepared from the historical data showing inflows and outflows of cash is called, 'cash flow statement'. A cash flow statement summarises the changes in cash position of the firm. Transactions which increase the cash position are termed as, 'inflows' of cash and those which decrease the cash position are termed as, 'outflows' of cash.

Definition

A cash flow statement can be defined as, 'a statement which summarises the sources of cash inflows and uses of cash outflows of a firm during particular period of time, say a month or a year. Such a statement can be prepared from the data made available from comparative Balance Sheets, Profit and Loss Accounts and additional informations.'

Uses of cash flow statement

The main uses of a cash flow statement are given below:

(i) It helps to evaluate the current cash position of the firm

(ii) It helps in making short-term financial decisions relating to liquidity

(iii) It shows the major sources and uses of cash

(iv) It helps in taking loan from banks and other financial institutions

(v) It helps the management in planning the repayment of loans, replacement of assets, credit arrangements, etc.

(vi) It is also significant for capital budgeting decisions.

(vii) It facilitates to prepare sound financial policies of the firm.

Limitations of cash flow statement

The following are the main limitations:

(i) Cash balance disclosed by the cash flow statement may not depict the true liquid position.

(ii) A cash fund does not mean the net income of the business.

(iii) A funds flow statement presents a more complete picture than cash flow statement.

(iv) It is not suitable for judging the profitability of a firm as non-cash charges are ignored while calculating cash flow from operating activities.

Preparation of cash from operations

It can be calculated by adding non-cash and non-operating expenses and deducting non-cash and non-operating income from the net profit. If the net amount is positive, it is called cash from operations (inflows) and if it is negative, it is called cash lost from operations (outflows).

Calculation of cash from operations

Particulars	*Rs.*	*Rs.*
Net Profit as per P&L Account		
Add: Non-cash and non-operating expenses:		
Depreciation written off		
Goodwill written off		
Preliminary expenses written off		
Provision for taxation		
Transfer to reserve		
Dividend/Interim/Proposed dividend paid		
Loss on sale of any fixed assets		
Discount on issue of shares or debentures written off		
Patents written off		
Less: Non-cash and non-operating income:		
Dividends received		
Profit on sale of fixed assets		
Appreciation in the value of fixed assets		
Rent received		
Refund of tax		
Cash from operations		

Note: If the P&L a/c shows a net loss, the above procedure will be reversed.

- Net profit = Closing Balance of P&L a/c — Opening Balance of P&L a/c.

Procedure for the preparation of cash flow statement

The preparation of cash flow statement involves the following steps:

(i) Opening of accounts for non-current items:

It is prepared to ascertain the inflow or outflow of cash. Additional information is to be considered while preparing accounts for non-current items.

(ii) Preparation of cash from operations:

As stated earlier, it can be calculated by adding non-cash and non-operating expenses and deducting non-cash and non-operating income from the net profit. If the net amount is positive, it is called cash from operations (inflows) and if it is negative, it is called cash lost from operations (outflows).

(iii) Comparison of current items to determine inflow or outflow of cash:

The next step is to compare the individual current assets and current liabilities:

(a) increase in current assets is taken as an outflow of cash and *vice-versa.*

(b) increase in current liabilities is taken as an inflow of cash and *vice-versa.*

(iv) Preparation of cash flow statement:

Finally, the above three steps are incorporated in the preparation of cash flow statement. Opening balance of cash and bank and all other sources are entered on the inflow side. Outflow of cash and closing balance of cash and bank are entered on the outflow side.

Cash Inflows

(i) Cash from operations

(ii) Increase of all current liabilities

(iii) Raising of long-term loan

(iv) Sale of fixed assets and long-term investments

(v) Decrease of all current assets

(vi) Issue of shares and debentures

Cash Outflows

(i) Cash lost in operations ; Repayment of long-term loans

(ii) Payment of cash dividends ; Payment of taxes

(iii) Drawings of a partner ; Increase of all current assets

(iv) Redemption of preference shares and debentures

(v) Purchase of fixed assets and long-term investment

(vi) Decrease of all current liabilities

Account form of Cash Flow Statement

Inflows	*Rs.*	*Outflows*	*Rs.*
Opening balance of Cash/Bank		Purchase of fixed assets or investments	
Add: Inflows		Repayment of loan	
Issue of shares or debentures		Redemption of preference shares or debentures	
Sale of fixed assets or investments		Payment of taxes	
Raising of loans		Payment of dividend	
Dividend received		Drawings	
Cash from operations		Cash lost in operation	
		Closing balance of Cash/Bank	

Differences between Cash Flow and Funds Flow Analysis

The following are the main points of differences between the Cash Flow and Funds Flow Analysis:

Cash Flow Analysis	*Funds Flow Analysis*
(1) It is based on a narrower concept of funds, i.e., cash	It is based on the wider concept of funds, i.e., working capital
(2) It shows the causes of changes in cash position	It indicates the causes for changes in working capital
(3) It is suitable for short range planning	It is suitable for long range planning
(4) The inflow of cash results in inflow of funds and inflow of cash	The inflow of funds may not necessarily result in
(5) The preparation of schedule of changes working capital is not necessary	The schedule of changes in working capital is prepared to find out the increase or decrease of working capital
(6) It is based on cash basis of accounting.	It is based on accrual basis of accounting.

Problem 1:

From the following Profit and Loss Account, you are required to compute cash from operations.

Profit and Loss Account for the year ending 30th June, 2009

Particulars	*Rs.*	*Particulars*	*Rs.*
To Salaries	5,000	By Gross profit	25,000
To Rent	1,000	By Profit on sale of land	5,000
To Depreciation	2,000	By Income tax refund	3,000
To Loss on sale of plant	1,000		
To Goodwill written off	4,000		
To Proposed dividend	5,000		
To Provision for taxation	5,000		
To Net profit	10,000		
	33,000		**33,000**

Solution:

Calculation of Cash From Operations:

Particulars	*Rs.*	*Rs.*
Net profit		10,000
Add: Non-operating expenses:		
Depreciation	2,000	
Loss on sale of plant	1,000	
Goodwill written off	4,000	
Proposed dividend	5,000	
Provision for taxation	5,000	17,000
		27,000
Less: Non-operating Income:		
Profit on sale of land	5,000	
Income tax refund	3,000	8,000
Cash from operations		**19,000**

Problem 2:

Calculate cash from operations from the following:

Particulars	*Rs.*	*Rs.*
	I Year	**II Year**
Profit and loss appropriation a/c	25,000	35,000
Bills receivable	20,000	25,000
Provision for depreciation	45,000	48,000
Outstanding rent	2,500	4,000
Prepaid insurance	3,000	2,500
Goodwill	40,000	25,000
Stock	15,000	5,000

Solution:

Adjusted Profit and Loss Account

Particulars	*Rs.*	*Particulars*	*Rs.*
To Provision for depreciation	3,000	By Balance b/d	25,000
To Goodwill written off	15,000	By Net profit	28,000
To balance c/d.	35,000		
	53,000		**53,000**

Calculation of cash from operations:

Particulars	*Rs.*	*Rs.*
Net profit		28,000
Add: Inflows:		
Increase in outstanding rent	1,500	
Decrease in prepaid insurance	500	
Decrease in stock	10,000	12,000
		40,000
***Less:* Outflows:**		
Increase in Bills receivable		5,000
Cash from operations		**35,000**

Problem 3:

From the following Balance Sheets, prepare a Cash Flow Statement:

Liabilities	*2008 (Rs.)*	*2009 (Rs.)*	*Assets*	*2008 (Rs.)*	*2009 (Rs.)*
Share Capital	2,00,000	2,50,000	Cash	30,000	47,000
Sundry Creditors	70,000	45,000	Debtors	1,20,000	1,15,000
Profit and Loss A/c	10,000	23,000	Stock	80,000	90,000
			Land	50,000	66,000
	2,80,000	**3,18,000**		**2,80,000**	**3,18,000**

Solution:

Cash Flow Statement

Inflows	*Rs.*	*Outflows*	*Rs.*
Opening balance of Cash	30,000	Decrease of sundry creditors	25,000
Add: Inflows:		Increase of stock	10,000
Issue of shares	50,000	Purchase of land	16,000
Decrease of debtors	5,000		
Cash from operations (23,000-10,000)	13,000	Closing balance of cash	47,000
	98,000		**98,000**

Problem 4:

The following are the summarised Balance Sheet of Shankar Ltd., as on 31st March, 2008 and 2009. Prepare a Cash Flow Statement:

Liabilities	*2008 (Rs.)*	*2009 (Rs.)*	*Assets*	*2008 (Rs.)*	*2009 (Rs.)*
Share Capital	8,000	8,500	Land	5,000	5,000
Profit and Loss A/c	1,450	2,450	Plant and Machinery	2,400	3,400
Mortgage Loan	-	500	Stock	900	700
Sundry Creditors	900	500	Debtors	1,650	1,950
			Cash	400	900
	10,350	**11,950**		**10,350**	**11,950**

Solution:

Cash Flow Statement

Inflows	*Rs.*	*Outflows*	*Rs.*
Opening balance of cash	400	Decrease of creditors	400
Add: Inflows:		Purchase of plant	1,000
Issue of shares	500	Increase of debtors	300
Mortgage loan	500		
Decrease of stock	200		
Cash from operations (2450-1450)	1,000	Closing balance of cash	900
	2,600		**2,600**

Problem 5:

Calculate cash from operations from the following Trading and Profit and Loss A/c for the year ending 31.3.09

Particulars	*Rs.*	*Particulars*	*Rs.*
To Purchases	20,000	By sales	30,000
To Wages	5,000		
To Gross profit c/d	5,000		
	30,000		**30,000**
To Salaries	1,000	By Gross profit b/d	5,000
To Rent	1,000	**By profit on sale of building:**	
To Depreciation on plant	1,000	Book value 10,000	
To Loss on sale of furniture	500	Sold for 15,000	5,000
To Goodwill written off	1,000		
To Net Profit	5,500		
	10,000		**10,000**

Solution:

Calculation of cash from operations

Particulars	*Rs.*	*Rs.*
Net Profit		5,500
***Add*: Non-cash and non-operating expenses:**		
Depreciation on plant	1,000	
Loss on sale of furniture	500	
Goodwill written off	1,000	2,500
		8,000
***Less*: Non-cash and non-operating Income:**		
Profit on sale of building		5,000
Cash from operations		3,000

Problem 6:

Calculate cash from operations from the following:

Particulars	*Rs.* *I Year*	*Rs.* *II Year*
Profit and Loss appropriation a/c	25,000	35,000
Bills receivable	20,000	25,000
Provision for depreciation	45,000	48,000
Outstanding rent	2,500	4,000
Prepaid insurance	3,000	2,500
Goodwill	40,000	25,000
Stock	15,000	5,000

Solution:

Adjusted Profit & Loss Account

Particulars	*Rs.*	*Particulars*	*Rs.*
To Provision for depreciation	3,000	By Balance b/d	25,000
To Goodwill written off	15,000	By Net profit	28,000
To Balance c/d.	35,000		
	53,000		**53,000**

Calculation of cash from operations:

Particulars	*Rs.*	*Rs*
Net profit		28,000
Add: Inflows:		
Increase in outstanding rent	1,500	
Decrease in prepaid insurance	500	
Decrease in stock	10,000	12,000
		40,000
Less: Outflows:		
Increase in bills receivable		5,000
Cash from operations		35,000

Problem 7:

Calculate cash from operations from the followings:

(i) Profit made during the year Rs.3,00,000 after considering the following items:

	Particulars	*Rs.*
(a)	Depreciation on fixed assets	20,000
(b)	Transfer to general reserve	10,000
(c)	Amortization of goodwill	10,000
(d)	Profit on sale of land	7,000

(ii) The following is the position of Current Assets and Current Liabilities.

Particulars	*I Year Rs.*	*II Year Rs.*
Debtors	15,000	18,000
Creditors	20,000	10,000
Bills receivable	7,000	5,000
Prepaid expenses	10,000	7,000

Solution:

Adjusted Profit and Loss A/c

Particulars	*Rs.*	*Particulars*	*Rs.*
To Depreciation	20,000	By profit on sale of land	7,000
To General reserve	10,000	By cash trading profit (b/f)	3,33,000
To Goodwill written off	10,000		
To Net profit	3,00,000		
	3,40,000		**3,40,000**

Calculation of cash from operations:

Particulars	*Rs.*	*Rs.*
Cash trading profit		3,33,000
Add: Inflows:		
Decrease in bills receivable	2,000	
Decrease in prepaid expenses	3,000	5,000
		3,38,000

Less: Outflows:		
Increase in debtors	3,000	
Decrease in creditors	10,000	13,000
Cash from operations		**3,25,000**

Problem 8:

From the following balances, compute cash from operations:

Particulars	*December 31 2008 (Rs.)*	*December 31 2009 (Rs.)*
Debtors	50,000	47,000
B/R	10,000	12,500
Creditors	20,000	25,000
Outstanding Expenses	1,000	1,200
B/P	8,000	6,000
Prepaid Expenses	800	700
Accrued Income	600	750
Income Received in advance	300	250
Profit made during the year	---	1,30,000

Solution:

Calculation of cash from operations:

Particulars	Rs.	Rs.
Profit made during the year		1,30,000
Add: **Inflows:**		
Decrease in debtors	3,000	
Increase in creditors	5,000	
Increase in outstanding expenses	200	
Decrease in prepaid expenses	100	8,300
		1,38,300
Less: Outflows:		
Increase in Bills receivable	2,500	
Decrease in Bills payable	2,000	
Increase in accrued income	150	
Decrease in income received in advance	50	4,700
Cash from operations		**1,33,600**

Problem 9:

From the following Balance Sheet, prepare a Cash Flow Statement:

Liabilities	*2008 (Rs.)*	*2009 (Rs.)*	*Assets*	*2008 (Rs.)*	*2009 (Rs.)*
Share capital	2,00,000	2,50,000	Cash	30,000	47,000
Sundry creditors	70,000	45,000	Debtors	1,20,000	1,15,000
P&L A/c	10,000	23,000	Stock	80,000	90,000
			Land	50,000	66,000
	2,80,000	**3,18,000**		**2,80,000**	**3,18,000**

Solution:

Cash Flow Statement

Inflows	*Rs.*	*Outflows*	*Rs.*
Opening balance of cash	30,000	Decrease of Creditors	25,000
Add: Inflows:		Increase of Stock	10,000
Issue of shares	50,000	Purchase of Land	16,000
Decrease of debtors	5,000		
Cash from operations (23,000-10,000)	13,000	Closing Balance of cash	47,000
	98,000		**98,000**

Problem 10:

Prepare a Cash Flow Statement for the year ended 31.12.2009.

Liabilities	*2008 (Rs.)*	*2009 (Rs.)*	*Assets*	*2008 (Rs.)*	*2009 (Rs.)*
Creditors	29,000	25,000	Cash	40,000	30,000
Capital	7,39,000	6,15,000	Debtors	20,000	17,000
			Stock	8,000	13,000
			Building	1,00,000	80,000
			Other Fixed Assets	6,00,000	5,00,000
	7,68,000	**6,40,000**		**7,68,000**	**6,40,000**

Additional Information:

(i) There were no drawings.

(ii) There were no purchase or sale of either building or other fixed assets.

Solution:

Cash Flow Statement

Inflows	*Rs.*	*Outflows*	*Rs.*
Opening Cash Balance	40,000	Decrease in accounts payable	4,000
Add: Inflows:		Increase in stock	5,000
Decrease in debtors	3,000	Cash lost from operation	4,000
		Closing cash balance	30,000
	43,000		**43,000**

Workings:

Capital Account

Particulars	*Rs.*	*Particulars*	*Rs.*
To Net Loss (bal. fig.)	1,24,000	By Balance b/d.	7,39,000
To Balance c/d.	6,15,000		
	7,39,000		**7,39,000**

Calculation of Cash from Operations:

Particulars	*Rs.*	*Rs.*
Net Loss		(-) 1,24,000
Add: Non cash or non-operating expenses:		
Depreciation on Building	20,000	
Depreciation on other fixed assets	1,00,000	1,20,000
Cash lost from operations		(-) 4,000

Problem 11:

The following were the Balance Sheets of the Raman and Kandan as on 1.7.2008 and 30.06.2009

Balance Sheet

Liabilities	*1.7.08 (Rs.)*	*30.6.09 (Rs.)*	*Assets*	*1.7.08 (Rs.)*	*30.6.09 (Rs.)*
Creditors	40,000	44,000	Cash	10,000	7,000
Mrs. Kandan's loan	25,000	-	Debtors	30,000	50,000
SBI Loan	40,000	50,000	Stock	35,000	25,000
Capital	1,25,000	1,53,000	Machinery	80,000	55,000
			Land	40,000	50,000
			Building	35,000	60,000
	2,30,000	**2,47,000**		**2,30,000**	**2,47,000**

Additional Informations

During the year a machine costing Rs. 10,000 (accumulated depreciation Rs. 3,000) was sold for Rs. 5,000. The provision for depreciation against machinery as on 1.7.08 was Rs. 25,000 and on 30.6.09 was Rs. 40,000. Net profit for the year ending 30.06.09 amounted to Rs. 45,000.

Prepare a Cash Flow Statement.

Solution:

Cash Flow Statement

Inflows	*Rs.*	*Outflows*	*Rs.*
Opening balance of cash	10,000	Repayment of Mrs. Kandan's loan	25,000
Increase of creditors	4,000	Increase of debtors	20,000
Loan from SBI	10,000	Purchase of land	10,000
Decrease of stock	10,000	Purchase of building	25,000
Sale of machinery	5,000	Drawings	17,000
Cash from operation	65,000	Closing balance of cash	7,000
	1,04,000		**1,04,000**

Workings

Provision for Depreciation on Machinery A/c

Particulars	*Rs.*	*Particulars*	*Rs.*
To Machinery	3,000	By Balance b/d	25,000
To Balance c/d	40,000	By Adjusted P&L A/c (bal. fig.)	18,000
	43,000		**43,000**

Machinery Account

Particulars		*Rs.*	*Particulars*		*Rs.*
To Balance b/d.	(80,000+25,000)	1,05,000	By cash		5,000
			By provision for dep.		3,000
			By Adj.P&L A/c	(loss)	2,000
			By Balance c/d	(55,000+40,000)	95,000
		1,05,000			**1,05,000**

Capital A/c

Particulars	Rs.	Particulars	Rs.
To Cash a/c (drawings) (b/f)	17,000	By balance b/d	1,25,000
To Balance c/d	1,53,000	By Net profit	45,000
	1,70,000		**1,70,000**

Calculation of Cash From Operations:

Particulars	Rs.	Rs.
Net profit		45,000
Add: Non cash or non-operating expenses:		
Provision for depreciation	18,000	
Loss on sale of machinery	2,000	20,000
Cash from operations		**65,000**

Problem 12:

From the following particulars, prepare a cash flow statement.

Balance Sheet

Liabilities	*2008 (Rs.)*	*2009 (Rs.)*	*Assets*	*2008 (Rs.)*	*2009 (Rs.)*
Share Capital	3,00,000	3,50,000	Fixed Assets	5,10,000	6,20,000
8% Debentures	1,00,000	2,00,000	Dis. on Debentures	10,000	5,000
Reserve and Surplus	80,000	1,00,000	Debtors	40,000	75,000
Creditors	70,000	50,000	Stock	30,000	1,00,000
Bills Payable	50,000	60,000	Bank	10,000	—
Bank Overdraft	—	40,000			
	6,00,000	**8,00,000**		**6,00,000**	**8,00,000**

Additional information

(i) Provision for depreciation as on 31.12.08 Rs. 1,50,000 and on 31.12.09 Rs. 1,90,000.

(ii) A machine costing Rs. 70,000 (depreciation written off Rs. 30,000) was sold for Rs. 25,000.

(iii) Dividend paid was Rs. 30,000.

Solution:

Cash Flow Statement

Inflows	*Rs.*	*Outflows*	*Rs.*
Opening balance of bank	10,000	Decrease of creditors	20,000
Issue of shares	50,000	Increase of stock	70,000
Issue of debentures	1,00,000	Purchase of fixed assets	2,20,000
Increase of bills payable	10,000	Dividend paid	30,000
Increase of bank overdraft	40,000	Increase of debtors	35,000
Sale of fixed assets	25,000		
Cash from operations	1,40,000	Closing balance of bank	Nil
	3,75,000		**3,75,000**

Workings

Calculation of Cash From Operations

Particulars	*Rs.*	*Rs.*
Closing balance of Reserve & Surplus		1,00,000
Add: Non-cash and non-operating expenses		
Discount on debentures written off	5,000	
Depreciation (40,000+30,000)	70,000	
Dividend paid	30,000	
Loss on sale of fixed assets	15,000	1,20,000
Less: Non-cash and non-operating Income		2,20,000
Opening balance of P&L A/c.		80,000
Cash from operations		**1,40,000**

Fixed Assets A/c

Particulars	*Rs.*	*Particulars*	*Rs.*
To Balance b/d. (5,10,000+1,50,000)	6,60,000	By Depreciation	30,000
		By Cash	25,000
To cash a/c. (bal. fig.)	2,20,000	By Adjusted P&L A/c. (loss)	15,000
		By Balance c/d. (6,20,000+1,90,000)	8,10,000
	8,80,000		**8,80,000**

Problem 13:

Malar Ltd., furnish you the following Balance Sheets for the year ending 31st December, 2008 and 2009. You are required to prepare a cash flow statement for the year ended 31.12.2009.

Balance Sheet

Liabilities	*2008 (Rs.)*	*2009 (Rs.)*	*Assets*	*2008 (Rs.)*	*2009 (Rs.)*
Eq.Share Capital	20,000	20,000	Goodwill	2,400	2,400
General Reserves	2,800	3,600	Land	8,000	7,200
P&L a/c.	3,200	2,600	Building	7,400	7,200
Sundry Creditors	1,600	1,080	Investments	2,000	2,200
Outstanding Expenses	240	160	Inventories	6,000	4,680
Prov. for tax	3200	3,600	Accounts Receivable	4,000	4,440
Prov. for bad debts	80	120	Bank	1,320	3,040
	31,120	**31,160**		**31,120**	**31,160**

Following additional information has also been supplied to you:

(a) A piece of land has also been sold for Rs. 800

(b) Depreciation amounting to Rs. 1,400 has been charged on building

(c) Provision for taxation has been made for Rs. 3,800 during the year.

Solution:

Cash Flow Statement

Inflows	*Rs.*	*Outflows*	*Rs.*
Opening balance of bank	1,320	Decrease of creditors	520
Sale of land	800	Decrease of O/S exp.	80
Decrease of Inventories	1,320	Tax paid	3,400
Cash from operations	5,440	Purchase of building	1,200
		Purchase of investments	200
		Increase of Account receivable	440
		Closing balance of bank	3,040
	8,880		**8,880**

Workings

Land A/c

Particulars	Rs.	Particulars	Rs.
To Balance b/d.	8,000	By Cash	800
		By Balance c/d	7,200
	8,000		8,000

Building A/c

Particulars	Rs.	Particulars	Rs.
To Balance b/d.	7,400	By Deprecition	1,400
To Cash A/c. (bal. fig.)	1,200	By balance c/d	7,200
	8,600		**8,600**

Provision for Taxation A/c

Particulars	Rs.	Particulars	Rs.
To Cash A/c (tax paid) (bal. fig.)	3,400	By Balance b/d	3,200
To Balance c/d.	3,600	By Adjusted P&L a/c.	3,800
	7,000		**7,000**

Calculation of cash From operations:

Particulars	Rs.	Rs.
Closing balance of P&L a/c.		2,600
Add: Non-cash and non-operating expenses		
Transfer to general reserve	800	
Depreciation on building	1,400	
Provision for taxation	3,800	
Provision for bad debts	40	6,040
		8,640
Less: Non-cash and non-operating Income		
Opening balance of P&L A/c		3,200
Cash from operations		**5,440**

Problem 14:

The comparative Balance Sheets of a company are given below. Prepare a Cash Flow Statement:

Liabilities	*2008 (Rs.)*	*2008 (Rs.)*	*Assets*	*2008 (Rs.)*	*2009 (Rs.)*
Share Capital	35,000	37,000	Cash	4,500	3,900
Debentures	6,000	3,000	Debtors	7,450	8,850
Creditors	5,180	5,920	Stock	24,600	21,350
Provision for doubtful debts	350	400	Land	10,000	15,000
Profit and loss A/c	5,020	5,280	Goodwill	5,000	2,500
	51,550	**51,600**		**51,550**	**51,600**

Additional Information:

(i) Dividend paid Rs. 1,750.

(ii) Land was purchased for Rs. 5,000

Solution:

Cash Flow Statement

Inflows	*Rs.*	*Outflows*	*Rs.*
Opening balance of cash	4,500	Redemption of debentures	3,000
Issue of shares	2,000	Purchase of land	5,000
Increase of creditors	740	Dividend paid	1,750
Decrease of stock	3,250	Increase of debtors	1,400
Cash from operations	4,560	Closing balance of cash	3,900
	15,050		**15,050**

Workings

Calculation of cash from operations:

Particulars	*Rs.*	*Rs.*
Closing balance of P&L A/c		5,280
Add: Non-cash or Non-operating expenses:		
Provision for doubtful debts	50	
Goodwill written off	2,500	
Dividend paid	1,750	4,300
		9,580
Less: Opening balance of P&L A/c		5,020
Cash from operations		**4,560**

Problem 15:

Following are the comparative Balance Sheet of Indian Paints Ltd., for the year ended 31st December 2008 and 31st December, 2009.

Liabilities	*2008 (Rs.)*	*2009 (Rs.)*	*Assets*	*2008 (Rs.)*	*2009 (Rs.)*
Prov. for doubtful debts	2,000	3,000	Cash	43,000	58,000
Accumulated Depreciation:			Prepaid expenses	2,000	2,000
On machinery	3,000	7,500	Debtors	80,000	90,000
On buildings	12,000	18,000	Stock	32,000	40,000
Creditors	33,000	40,000	Investments (long-term)	50,000	30,000
Outstanding expenses	3,500	4,500	Machinery at cost	25,000	40,000
Debentures	40,000	35,000	Building at cost	75,000	90,000
Equity share capital	2,00,000	2,00,000	Land	10,000	10,000
Profit and loss account	23,500	52,000			
	3,17,000	**3,60,000**		**3,17,000**	**3,60,000**

Additional Information:

(a) Dividend paid during 2009 Rs. 26,500

(b) Investments costing Rs. 20,000 were sold in 2009 for Rs. 25,000.

(c) Machinery costing Rs. 5,000 on which Rs. 1,000 depreciation has been accumulated, was sold for Rs. 6,000 in the year 2009.

(d) The provision for doubtful debts charged to Profit and Loss Account was Rs. 1,500. Prepare a cash flow statement for the year 2009.

Solution:

Cash Flow Statement

Inflows	*Rs.*	*Outflows*	*Rs.*
Opening balance of cash	43,000	Purchase of machinery	20,000
Sale of investments	25,000	Redemption of debentures	5,000
Sale of machinery	6,000	Increase in debtors	10,500
Increase in creditors	7,000	Increase in stock	8,000
Increase in outstanding expenses	1,000	Dividend paid	26,500
		Purchase of building	15,000
Cash from operations	61,000	Closing balance of cash	58,000
	1,43,000		**1,43,000**

Workings:

Investment Account

Particulars	*Rs.*	*Particulars*	*Rs.*
To Balance b/d	50,000	By Cash	25,000
To Adjusted P&L A/c. (profit)	5,000	By Balance c/d	30,000
	55,000		**55,000**

Accumulated Depreciation on Machinery Account

Particulars	*Rs.*	*Particulars*	*Rs.*
To Machinery A/c (depn. on machinery sold)	1,000	By Balance b/d.	3,000
To Balance c/d	7,500	By Adj. P&L A/c (bal.fig.)	5,500
	8,500		**8,500**

Machinery Account

Particulars	*Rs.*	*Particulars*	*Rs.*
To balance b/d.	25,000	By cash	6,000
To Adjusted P&L A/c (profit)	2,000	By Accumulated dep. A/c.	1,000
To cash (bal.fig.)	20,000	By Balance c/d.	40,000
	47,000		**47,000**

Provision for Doubtful Debts A/c

Particulars	*Rs.*	*Particulars*	*Rs.*
To Bad Debts (bal.fig.)	500	By Balance b/d	2,000
To Balance c/d	3,000	By Adjusted P&L A/c	1,500
	3,500		3,500

Calculation of Increase in Debtors:

Particulars	*Rs.*
Debtors on 2009	90,000
Add: Bad debts	500
	90,500
Less: Debtors on 2008	80,000
Increase in debtors	10,500

Adjusted P&L A/c

Particulars	Rs.	Particulars	Rs.
To Depreciation on machinery	5,500	By balance b/d.	23,500
To Depreciation on building	6,000	By Profit on sale of investments	5,000
To Provision for doubtful debts	1,500	By Profit on sale of machinery	2,000
To Dividend	26,500	Cash from operations (b/f)	61,000
To Balance c/d.	52,000		
	91,500		**91,500**

Problem 16:

From the following Balance Sheets of Vasanth Ltd., for 2005 and 2006, draw out a cash flow statement.

Balance Sheets of Cauvery Ltd.

Liabilities	2005 (Rs.)	2006 (Rs.)	Assets	2005 (Rs.)	2006 (Rs.)
Equity share capital	2,00,000	3,00,000	Goodwill	50,000	40,000
8% Redeemable pref. share capital	1,00,000	50,000	Land and Building	1,00,000	75,000
General reserve	20,000	30,000	Plant	90,000	1,91,000
Capital reserve	-	25,000	Trade investments	10,000	35,000
Profit and Loss A/c	18,000	27,000	Sundry debtors	60,000	90,000
Proposed dividend	28,000	39,000	Stock	85,000	78,000
Sundry creditors	25,000	47,000	Bills receivables	15,000	18,000
Bills payable	10,000	6,000	Cash in hand	7,000	6,000
Liabilities for expenses	8,000	6,000	Cash at bank	10,000	22,000
Provision for taxation	28,000	32,000	Preliminary expenses	10,000	7,000
	4,37,000	**5,62,000**		**4,37,000**	**5,62,000**

Additional information

(a) In 2006, Rs. 18,000 depreciation has been written off to plant account and no depreciation has been charged on land and buildings.

(b) A piece of land has been sold out and the balance has been revalued, profit on revaluation and sale being transferred to capital reserve. There is no other entry in capital reserve account.

(c) A plant was sold for Rs. 12,000 (W.D.V. Rs. 15,000).

(d) Rs.2,100 dividend has been received, but it includes Rs.600 pre-acquisition dividend.

(e) An interim dividend of Rs. 10,000 has been paid in 2006.

Solution:

Cash Flow Statement

Inflows	*Rs.*	*Outflows*	*Rs.*
Opening balance of cash and Bank(7,000+10,000)	17,000	Purchase of plant	1,34,000
Add: Inflows:		Redemption of preference shares	50,000
Sale of land and building	50,000	Purchase of investments	25,600
Sale of plant	12,000	Payment of interim dividend	10,000
Issue of shares	1,00,000	Payment of dividend	28,000
Dividend received	2,100	Payment of tax	28,000
Cash from operations	1,32,500	Increase in debtors	30,000
Decrease in stock	7,000	Increase in Bills receivable	3,000
Increase in creditors	22,000	Decrease in Bills payable	4,000
Decrease in liabilities for exp.	2,000		
		Closing balance of cash and Bank(6,000+22,000)	28,000
	3,42,600		**3,42,600**

Land and Building A/c

Particulars	*Rs.*	*Particulars*	*Rs.*
To Balance b/d	1,00,000	By Cash (bal.fig.)	50,000
To Capital reserve(profit on sale)	25,000	By Balance c/d	75,000
	1,25,000		**1,25,000**

Plant A/c

Particular	*Rs.*	*Particular*	*Rs.*
To Balance b/d	90,000	By Adj. P and L A/c (depreciation)	18,000
To Cash(bal.fig.)	1,34,000	By Cash	12,000
		By Adj. P&L A/c (loss on sale)	3,000
		By Balance c/d	1,91,000
	2,24,000		**2,24,000**

Investment A/c

Particulars	*Rs*	*Particulars*	*Rs.*
To Balance b/d	10,000	By Dividend (pre-acquisition)	600
To Cash(bal.fig.)	25,600	By Balance c/d	35,000
	35,600		**35,600**

Journal entries:

		Rs	Rs
(i)	Cash A/c Dr.	2,100	
	To Dividend A/c		2,100
(ii)	Dividend A/c Dr.	2,100	—
	To investments A/c		600
	To Adj. P&L A/c		1,500

Adjusted P&L A/c

Particulars	*Rs.*	*Particulars*	*Rs.*
To Transfer to general reserve	10,000	By Balance b/d	18,000
To Provision for tax (2006)	32,000	Pre-acq. dividend received	1,500
To proposed dividend(2006)	39,000		
To Depreciation on plant	18,000	Cash from operation (b/f)	1,32,500
To Goodwill written off	10,000		
To Preliminary exp. written off	3,000		
To Loss on sale of plant	3,000		
To Interim dividend	10,000		
To Balance b/d	27,000		
	1,52,000		**1,52,000**

Note:

Proposed dividend and provision for taxation are treated as non-current liabilities.

The treatment is as follows:

Last year dividend/tax —— Payment in the current year, i.e., put in the outflow side

Current year dividend/tax —— Add with calculation of cash from operations.

Problem 17:

The following shows the balances in condensed form of Pavitra Ltd., at the beginning as well as at the end of the year 2007.

Balance Sheet

Liabilities	*2006 (Rs.)*	*2007 (Rs.)*	*Assets*	*2006 (Rs.)*	*2007 (Rs.)*
Creditors	52,000	47,500	Cash and bank balance	45,000	45,000
Outstanding expenses	6,000	6,500	Debtors	38,500	26,500
8% Debentures	45,000	35,000	Investments	50,000	32,000
Depreciation fund	20,000	22,000	Prepaid expenses	500	1,000
Res. for contingencies	30,000	30,000	Stock-in-trade	41,000	53,000
P&L A/c.	8,000	11,500	Land and building	77,000	77,000
Share capital	1,15,000	1,15,000	Machinery	24,000	33,000
	2,76,000	**2,67,500**		**2,76,000**	**2,67,500**

The following information is also available:

(a) 10% dividend was paid in cash.

(b) New machinery for Rs. 15,000 was purchased but old machinery costing Rs. 6,000 was sold for Rs. 2,000 on which accumulated depreciation was Rs. 3,000.

(c) Rs. 10,000 8% debentures were redeemed by purchase from open market at Rs. 96 for a debenture of Rs. 100.

(d) Investments were sold at book value.

Prepare a cash flow statement.

Solution:

Cash Flow Statement

Inflows	*Rs.*	*Outflows*	*Rs.*
Opening balance of cash and Bank	45,000	Decrease of creditors	4,500
Add: Inflows		Redemption of debentures	9,600
Increase of O/S exp.	500	Increase of stock	12,000
Decrease of debtors	12,000	Increase of prepaid exp.	500
Sale of investments	18,000	Purchase of machinery	15,000
Sale of machinery	2,000	Dividend paid	11,500
Cash from operations	20,600	Closing balance of cash and Bank	45,000
	98,100		**98,100**

Workings:

Machinery A/c

Particulars	*Rs.*	*Particulars*	*Rs.*
To Balance b/d	24,000	By Cash	2,000
To Cash a/c	15,000	By Depreciation	3,000
		By Adjusted P&L A/c.	1,000
		By balance c/d	33,000
	39,000		**39,000**

Investments A/c.

Particulars	*Rs.*	*Particulars*	*Rs.*
To Balance b/d.	50,000	By Cash A/c. (bal. fig.)	18,000
		By Balance c/d	32,000
	50,000		**50,000**

Depreciation Fund a/c.

Particulars	*Rs.*	*Particulars*	*Rs.*
To Machinery A/c	3,000	By Balance b/d.	20,000
To Balance c/ds	22,000	By Adjusted P&L A/c. (bal.fig.)	5,000
	25,000		**25,000**

Calculation of cash from operations:

Particulars	*Rs.*	*Rs.*
Closing balance of P&L a/c		11,500
Add: Non-operating expense:		
Depreciation	5,000	
Dividend paid	11,500	
Loss on sale of machinery	1,000	17,500
		29,000
Less: Non-cash and non-operating Income		
Profit on redemption of debentures	400	
10,000-9,600(10,000X96/100)		
Opening balance of P&L A/c	8,000	8,400
Cash from operations		**20,600**

Problem 18:

The financial position of M/s. Tall and Short on 1st January, 2009 and December 31, 2009 was as follows:

Liabilities	*1.1.2009 (Rs.)*	*31.12.2009 (Rs.)*	*Assets*	*1.1.2009 (Rs.)*	*31.12.2009 (Rs.)*
Current liabilities	36,000	41,000	Cash	4,000	3,600
Mrs. Tall's loan	---	20,000	Debtors	35,000	38,400
Loan from bank	30,000	25,000	Stock	25,000	22,000
Capital	1,48,000	1,49,000	Land	20,000	30,000
			Building	50,000	55,000
			Machinery	80,000	86,000
	2,14,000	**2,35,000**		**2,14,000**	**2,35,000**

During the year the partners withdrew Rs. 26,000 for domestic expenses. The provision for depreciation against machinery as on 1.1.09 was Rs. 27,000 and 31.12.09 Rs. 36,000

Prepare the cash flow statement for the year ended 31st December, 2009.

Solution:

Cash Flow Statement

Inflows	*Rs.*	*Outflows*	*Rs.*
Opening cash balance	4,000	Purchase of land	10,000
Add: Inflows:		Purchase of building	5,000
Loan from Mrs.Tall	20,000	Purchase of machinery	15,000
Cash from operations	36,000	Drawings	26,000
Decrease in stock	3,000	Repayment of loan	5,000
Increase in current liabilities	5,000	Increase in debtors	3,400
		Closing cash balance	3,600
	68,000		**68,000**

Workings:

Machinery Account

Particulars	*Rs.*	*Particulars*		*Rs.*
To Balance b/d (80,000+27,000)	1,07,000			
To Cash (bal.fig.)	15,000	By Balance c/d	(86,000+36,000)	1,22,000
	1,22,000			**1,22,000**

Capital Account

Particulars	*Rs.*	*Particulars*	*Rs.*
To Cash	26,000	By Balance b/d.	1,48,000
To Balance c/d	1,49,000	By Net profit (bal.fig.)	27,000
	1,75,000		**1,75,000**

Calculation of cash from operations:

Particulars	*Rs.*
Net profit	27,000
Add: **Non cash or non-operating expense:**	
Provision for depreciation on machinery (36,000-27,000)	9,000
Cash from operations	**36,000**

TEST YOUR KNOWLEDGE

WORKING CAPITAL REQUIREMENTS

CHOOSE THE BEST ANSWER:

(1) Hard core working capital is —

(a) Negative working capital (b) That portion of fixed working capital

(c) Excess working capital (d) None of the above

(2) Net working capital is the difference between —

(a) Current assets and fixed assets (b) Current assets and non-current liability

(c) Fixed assets and non-current liability (d) None of the above

(3) Permanent working capital means —

(a) Total current assets (b) Cash in hand and bank

(c) Core current assets (d) Stock in trade

(4) Working capital means —

(a) Current Assets + current liabilities (b) Current assets - current liabilities

(c) Current assets/current liabilities (d) Current assets × current liabilities

(5) Gross working capital represents —

(a) Total current assets (b) Total current liabilities

(c) The excess of current assets over current liabilities (d) None of the above

(Answer:b,d,a,b,d)

STATE TRUE OR FALSE:

(1) The net working capital is that portion of a firm's current assets which is financed by long-term funds.

(2) The terms permanent working capital and core current assets are synonymous.

(3) A large balance of cash in hand should be kept by a firm to meet all contingencies.

(4) The gross working capital refers to the capital invested in the total assets of an enterprise.

(5) Every business concern should have excessive working capital.

(6) Commercial banks provide loans for working capital.

(Ans:True: 2,6 False: 1,3,4,5)

FILL IN THE BLANKS:

(i) The net working capital is the excess ___________ assets over ___________ liabilities.

(ii) Working capital is also known as ___________ or ___________ capital.

(iii) The gross working capital is a ________ concern concept.

(iv) The rate of return on investments _________ with the shortage of working capital.

(Ans : (i) Current Assets and Current Liability (ii) Revolving or Circulating
(iii) Going (iv) Falls)

SHORT ANSWER TYPES:

(1) Define the term working capital.

(2) What is operating cycle of working capital?

(3) What is meant by working capital management?

(4) What are the advantages of adequate working capital?

(5) Name the various kinds of working capital.

(6) What are the dangers of inadequate working capital?

(7) Explain the need for working capital.

(8) What are the sources of short-term working capital?

(9) What is the importance of working capital in a business?

ESSAY TYPES:

(1) Discuss the importance of working capital for a manufacturing concern.

(2) Explain the dangers of: (a) excess working capital, (b) inadequate working capital.

(3) Explain the various factors influencing working capital requirements of an organisation.

(4) Give a lucid account of various sources of working capital available for a firms.

(5) State the signification of permanent working capital.

(6) Define working capital. Distinguish between permanent and temporary working capital.

EXERCISES:

(1) M/s. Sanjiv Bros. who are willing to purchase a business have consulted you and one point, on which you are asked to advice them, is the average amount of working capital which would need to be employed in the first year's trading.

You are given the following estimates and are requested to add 15% to your computed figures to allows for contingencies:

	Per annum Rs.
i. Average amount of stocks: Finished goods	30,000
Raw Materials	60,000
ii. Average credit given:	
Inland sales 4 weeks	2,60,000
Export sales 2 weeks	6,50,000
iii. Lag payment of expenses:	
Wages $1^1/_2$ weeks	2,60,000
Materials and overheads 4 weeks	3,90,000

(Ans : Rs. 1,12,125.)

(2) Calculate working capital from the following particulars :

	Rs.
i. Annual expenses	
Wages	52,000
Stores and material	9,600
Office salaries	12,480
Rent	2,000
Other expenses	9,600
ii. Average amount of stock to be maintained	
Stock of finished goods	1,000
Stock of materials and stores	1,600
Expenses paid in advance :	
Quarterly in advance	1,600 p.a.

iii. Annual sales	
Home market	62,400
Foreign market	15,600
iv. Lag in payment of expenses	
Wages	$1^1/_2$ weeks
Stores	$1^1/_2$ months
Office salaries	½ month
Rent	6 months
Other salaries	$1^1/_2$ months
v. Credit allowed to customers	
Home market	6 weeks
Foreign market	$1^1/_2$ weeks

(Ans : 5,230)

(3) From the following information, prepare a statement showing the working capital requirements:
Budgeted sales (Rs. 10 per unit) Rs. 2,60,000 p.a.

Analysis of one type of sales:

Raw materials	0.30
Direct labour	0.40
Overheads	0.20
Total cost	0.90
Profit	0.10
	Re. 1.00

It is estimated that:

- Raw materials are carried in stock for three weeks and finished goods for two weeks.
- Factory processing will take three weeks.
- Suppliers will given full five weeks credit.
- Customers will require eight weeks' credit.

It may be assumed that production and overheads acquire evenly throughout the year.

(Ans : Rs. 55,000.)

(4) The annual capacity of a manufacturing company is to produce 10,000 units. But owing to scarcity of resources the normal level of activity has been 60%.

From the information given below, calculate the working capital requirements.

			Per unit
i.	Elements of cost		
	Direct material		4
	Direct labour		3
	Overheads 100% of Direct labour		
ii.	Profit per unit : 1/6 of selling price		
iii.	Other particulars :		
	a. Raw materials storage period	-	2 months
	b. Processing time	-	3 months
	c. Finished goods in store	-	1 month
	d. Credit to debtors	-	2 months
	e. Credit form creditors	-	2 months
	f. Lag in wage payment	-	1 month

It may be assured that production and overhead accure evenly throughout the year.

(Ans : Rs. 28,000.)

(5) Sangami Ltd., is engaged in customer retailing. You are requested to forecast their working capital requirements from the following information:

Projected annual sales Rs. 6,50,000.

Percentage of NP to cost of sales 25%

Average credit allowed to debtors 10 weeks

Average credit allowed by creditors 4 weeks

Average stock carrying (in terms of sales requirement) 8 weeks.

Add 20% to allow for contingencies.

(Ans : Rs. 1,68,000.)

(6) X & Co; desirous of purchasing a business and has consulted you and one point on which you are asked to advise them is the average amount of working capital which will be required in the first year's working.

You are given the following estimates and are instructed to add 10% to your computed figure to allow for contingencies.

	Figures for the year Rs.
i. Average amount locked up for stocks:	
Stock of finished goods	5,000
Stock of stores, materials, etc.	8,000
ii. Average credit given:	
Inland sales 6 weeks' credit	3,12,000
Export sales $1^1/_2$ weeks credit	78,000
iii. Lag in payment of wages and other outgoings:	
Wages $1^1/_2$ weeks	2,60,000
Stocks, materials $1^1/_2$ weeks	48,000
Rent, 6 months	10,000
Manager ½ month	4,800
Miscellaneous expenses $1^1/_2$ month	48,000
Clerical staff ½ month	62,400
iv. Payment in advance:	
Sundry expenses (paid quarterly in advance)	8,000
Withdrawn profits on the average throughout the year	11,000

Set up your calculations for the average amount of working capital required.

(Ans : Rs. 28,545.)

(7) Mr. Vass wishes to commence a new trading business and gives the following informations:

i. The total estimated sales in a year will be Rs. 12,00,000.

ii. His expenses are estimated as fixed expenses of Rs. 2,000 per month plus variable expenses equal to 5 per cent of his turnover.

iii. He expects to fix a sales price for each product which will be 25 per cent in excess of his cost of purchase.

iv. He expects the turnover of his stock four times in a year.

v. The sales and purchases will be evenly spread throughout the year. All sales will be for cash but he expects one month's credit for purchases.

Calculate :

a. His estimated profit for the year.

b. His average working capital requirements.

(Ans : (a) Rs. 1,56,000 (b) 1,67,000)

FUND FLOW STATEMENT

MODEL QUESTIONS

OBJECTIVE TYPE:

Choose the best answer from the following alternatives:

(1) Increase in an asset due to purchase, is —

(a) Source of Funds (b) Use of Funds

(c) No Flow of Funds

(2) Current assets include —

(a) Trade Investment (b) Machinery

(c) Sundry Debtors

(3) Net profit earned plus non-working capital expenses is equal to —

(a) Fund Provided by Operation (b) Use of Funds

(c) Sinking Fund

(4) Which of the following is a non-current asset?

(a) Goodwill (b) Cash Balance

(c) Bills Receivable

(5) Tax paid is —

(a) Application of Funds (b) Source of Funds

(c) No Flow of Funds

(6) State which of the following is a non-current liabilities —

(a) Mortgage Loan (b) Bank Balance

(c) Outstanding Salary

(7) Stock at the end results in the —

(a) Application of funds (b) Source of Funds

(c) No Flow of Funds

(8) Depreciation of machinery is —

(a) Source of Funds (b) Application of Funds

(c) No Flow of Funds

(9) Which of the following are non-current item?

(a) Share Premium (b) Bank Balance

(c) Payment of Wages

(10) Stock in the beginning results in —

(a) Application of Funds (b) Source of Funds

(c) No flow of Funds

(11) Which are the following will result into application of fund?

(a) Sale of Plant (b) Issue of Share Capital

(c) Payment of Dividend

(12) An increase in share premium account is —

(a) Application of Funds (b) Source of Funds

(c) No flow of Funds

(13) Sale of investments indicate —

(a) Application of Funds (b) Change in Current Asset

(c) A Source of Funds

(14) Expenditure incurred on fixed asset is allocated over the life of assets as —

(a) Capital Expenditure (b) Depreciation

(c) Revenue Expenditure

(15) Fund flow statement basically likes in analysing the changes between ___ prepared for any two consecutive periods.

(a) Profit and Loss A/c (b) Balance Sheet

(c) Income Expenditure A/c

(Answers

1. b 2. c 3. a 4. a 5. a 6. a 7. b 8. a 9. a 10. a

11. c 12.b 13. c 14. b 15. b.)

Fill in the Blanks:

(1) The word fund means the difference between ______________.

(2) Fund flow refers to changes in __________ Capital.

(3) Purchase of plant will mean ______ in working capital.

(4) Building sold on credit is ________ of funds.

(5) Issue of capital will mean ____ in working capital.

(6) Goods purchased on credit ________ in flow of funds.

(7) Goodwill is a ________ transaction.

(8) Commission outstanding is __________ of funds.

(9) When one account is a current and another a non-current, it results in ____.

(10) Any gain on sale of non-current assets should be ________ from the net profit for determining funds from operation.

(11) Difference between current assets and current liabilities is known as ____.

(12) Depreciation is sometime treated as a ________ of funds.

(13) __________ represents expenditure incurred at the time of forming the company and it is capitalised.

(Answers:

(1)	**Current assets and current liabilities**	**(2)**	**Working.**
(3)	**Decrease**	**(4)**	**A source**
(5)	**Increase**	**(6)**	**Does not result**
(7)	**Non-current**	**(8)**	**An application**
(9)	**Flow of funds**	**(10)**	**Deducted**
(11)	**Working capital**	**(12)**	**A source**
(13)	**Preliminary expenses.)**		

True or False:

(1) Funds is the difference between fixed assets and current assets.

(2) Fund flow statement is a good substitute for income statement.

(3) Purchase of stock-in-trade is an application of funds.

(4) Flow of funds means increase or decrease of working capital.

(5) Any transaction that increase working capital is a source of funds.

(6) Depreciation is a source of fund.

(7) There will be flow of funds when both accounts in a transactions are non-current.

(8) Increase in current-assets means increase in working capital.

(9) Fund flow refers to change in long-term funds.

(10) A decrease in current liability increases working capital.

(11) The fund flow statement shows changes in the individual items comprising working capital.

(12) Fund flow analysis shows the position of business as on the closing date of business period.

(13) Cash or credit sales at a profit, increases the working capital.

(14) Working capital is the difference between fixed and current assets.

(15) Purchase of fixed assets is a use of funds.

(16) Payment of dividend is a use of funds.

(17) Amortisation of preliminary expenses is a use of funds.

(18) For funds flow statement provision for tax will be treated as an item of internal source.

(19) Sale of non-current assets and the cash received is a source.

(20) Increase in current asset results in increases working capital.

Answers:

1. False	**2. False**	**3. False**	**4. True**	**5. True**	**6. True**
7. False	**8. True**	**9. False**	**10. True**	**11. False**	**12. False**
13. False	**14 False.**	**15. True**	**16. True**	**17. False**	**18. True**
19. True	**20. True.**				

Short Answer Type:

(1) What is meant by funds flow statement?

(2) What is funds from operations?

(3) What is the purpose of fund flow analysis? Explain.

(4) Is depreciation a source of funds? Explain.

(5) What is meant by schedule of changes in working capital?

(6) Give a proforma of a funds flow statement.

(7) What do you mean by the term funds?

Essay Type:

(1) Explain the concept of flow of funds.

(2) Discuss the managerial uses of funds flow statement. What are its limitations?

(3) Distinguish between funds flow statement and income statement.

(4) Explain the steps involved in preparation of funds flow statement.

(5) Explain the treatment of provision for taxation and proposed dividend in funds flow statement.

Exercises:

(1) Followings are summarised balance sheet of Ram Industries Ltd. as on 31st December, 2004 and 2005.

Liabilities	*2004 (Rs.)*	*2005 (Rs.)*	*Assets*	*2004 (Rs.)*	*2005 (Rs.)*
Share capital	2,30,000	3,00,000	Land and Building	1,50,000	1,50,000
General reserve	1,00,000	1,20,000	Plant and Machinery	1,00,000	60,000
Profit and Loss A/c	80,000	1,00,000	Furniture	40,000	40,000
Creditors	1,00,000	70,000	Investments	60,000	80,000
Provision for Tax	90,000	30,000	Stock	1,20,000	2,00,000
Loan	—	60,000	Debtors	80,000	60,000
			Cash	50,000	90,000
	6,00,000	**6,80,000**		**6,00,000**	**6,80,000**

Additional information:

(i) Provision for taxation made during the year Rs.15,000

(ii) Investments costing Rs. 15,000 were sold during the year for Rs. 18,000

(iii) During the year plant and machinery costing Rs. 10,000 was sold for Rs. 12,500 the profit was included in the P&L account.

(iv) Dividend paid during the year amounted Rs. 30,000

Prepare funds flow statement.

(Ans: Increase in working capital Rs.1,30,000;funds from operations Rs.1,09,500 Funds flow statement total Rs.2,70,000.)

(2) Calculate funds from operations from the following information.

Particulars	*Rs.*	*Particulars*	*Rs.*
Salaries	40,000	Administrative expenses	25,000
Depreciation	20,000	Goodwill written off	10,000
Interest on investment	10,000	Preliminary exp. written off	5,000
Profit on sale of fixed assets	5,000	Loss on sale of old machinery	5,000
Provision for tax	30,000	Op. balance of P&L A/c	70,000
Interim dividend paid	20,000	Cl. balance of P&L A/c	1,20,000
Proposed dividend	30,000		

(Ans: Funds from operations Rs.1,55,000.)

(3) Calculate funds from operations from the following information.

Particulars	*Rs.*	*Particulars*	*Rs.*
Op. balance of P&L a/c	60,000	Loss on sale of machinery	3,000
Cl. balance of P&L a/c	30,000	General reserve	5,000
Interim dividend paid	20,000	Sinking fund	10,000
Proposed dividend	30,000	Salaries	3,000
Depreciation	50,000	Profit on sale of car	4,000
Preliminary exp. written off	1,000	Tax paid	5,000

(Ans: Funds from operations Rs.90,000.)

(4) From the following particulars prepare a statement of sources and application of funds.

(i) Increase in working capital Rs. 8,000.

(ii) Net profit Rs. 21,000 before writing off goodwill.

(iii) Depreciation provided on fixed asset Rs. 3,500.

(iv) Dividend Rs. 7,000.

(v) Goodwill written off out of profit Rs. 10,000.

(vi) Rs. 10,000 share capital issued for cash.

(vii) Machinery was purchased for Rs. 20,000.

(Ans: Funds from operations Rs. 24,500;

Funds flow statement total Rs. 35,000)

(5) From the followings, calculate funds from operations:

Profit and Loss a/c

Particulars	*Rs.*	*Particulars*	*Rs.*
To Operating expenses	1,00,000	By Gross profit	2,00,000
To Depreciation	40,000	By Gain on sale of plant	20,000
To Loss on sale of building	10,000		
To advertisement suspense a/c	5,000		
To Discount allowed	500		
To Preliminary expenses written off	12,000		
To Net profit	52,500		
	2,20,000		**2,20,000**

(Ans : Funds from operations Rs. 99,500)

(6) The following is the balance sheet of Raj Ltd., as on 2008 and 2009 are as follows:

Liabilities	*2008 (Rs.)*	*2009 (Rs.)*	*Assets*	*2008 (Rs.)*	*2009 (Rs.)*
Capital	36,000	41,000	Cash	4,000	3,600
Loan	30,000	45,000	Debtors	35,000	38,400
Capital	1,48,000	1,49,000	Stock	25,000	22,000
			Machinery	80,000	86,000
			Land	20,000	30,000
			Building	50,000	55,000
	2,14,000	**2,35,000**		**2,14,000**	**2,35,000**

During the year, he withdrew Rs. 26,000 for his personal use. Provision for depreciation on machinery for 2008 amounted Rs. 27,000 and for 2009 Rs. 36,000.

Prepare funds flow statement

(Ans:

Decrease in working capital Rs. 5,000; Funds from operations Rs. 36,000;

Total of funds flow statement Rs. 61,000.)

(7) From the following Balance Sheets, prepare funds flow statement and schedule of changes in working capital:

Liabilities	*2008 (Rs.)*	*2009 (Rs.)*	*Assets*	*2008 (Rs.)*	*2009 (Rs.)*
Share capital	2,40,000	3,60,000	Buildings	1,66,200	3,39,600
Share premium	24,000	36,000	Machinery	1,06,800	1,53,900
Reserve	18,000	27,000	Furniture	7,200	4,500
Profit and Loss A/c	58,500	62,400	Stock	66,300	78,000
8% Debentures	-	78,000	Debtors	1,09,500	1,17,300
Provision for tax	29,400	32,700	Bank	14,400	12,000
Creditors	1,00,500	1,09,200			
	4,70,400	**7,05,300**		**4,70,400**	**7,05,300**

Depreciation written off during the year: On machinery Rs. 38,400:On furniture Rs. 1,200.

(Ans: Net increase in working capital Rs. 5,100; Funds from operations Rs. 52,500;

Total of funds flow statement Rs. 2,64,000.)

(8) From the following Balance Sheets, prepare a statement showing application and sources of fund for the year 2005.

Liabilities	*2004 (Rs.)*	*2005 (Rs.)*	*Assets*	*2004 (Rs.)*	*2005 (Rs.)*
Eq. share capital	5,000	5,300	Cash	2,000	2,500
Debentures	1,400	1,300	Debtors	2,400	2,700
Reserves and Surplus	2,800	3,700	Other Current Assets	800	700
Accumulated depreciation	2,100	2,500	Stock	3,100	3,200
Creditors	2,000	2,100	Fixed Assets	5,000	5,800
	13,300	**14,900**		**13,300**	**14,900**

Additional information:

(i) Fixed assets costing Rs. 1,200 were purchased for cash.

(ii) Fixed assets (original cost Rs. 400 accumulated depreciation Rs. 150) were sold at book value.

(iii) Depreciation for the year 2005 amounted to Rs. 550 and debited to P&L A/c.

(iv) Dividend paid amounted to Rs. 300 in 2005.

(v) Reported income for 2005 was Rs. 1,200.

(Ans: Increase in working capital Rs. 700; Funds from operations Rs. 1,750; Funds flow statement total Rs. 2,300.)

(9) From the following Balance Sheet of XYZ Ltd., prepare a funds flow statement.

Balance Sheet

Liabilities	*2003 (Rs.)*	*2004 (Rs.)*	*Assets*	*2003 (Rs.)*	*2004 (Rs.)*
Eq. share capital	3,00,000	4,00,000	Goodwill	1,15,000	90,000
Pref. share capital	1,50,000	1,00,000	Building	2,00,000	1,70,000
Capital reserve	———	20,000	Plant	80,000	2,00,000
General reserve	40,000	50,000	Investments	20,000	30,000
Profit and Loss A/c	30,000	48,000	Debtors	1,40,000	1,70,000
Proposed dividend	42,000	50,000	Stock	77,000	1,09,000
Creditors	25,000	47,000	Bills receivable	20,000	30,000
Bills payable	20,000	16,000	Cash	15,000	10,000
Liability for expenses	30,000	36,000	Bank	10,000	8,000
Provision for taxation	40,000	50,000	Preliminary expenses	15,000	10,000
	6,77,000	**8,17,000**		**6,77,000**	**8,17,000**

Additional Information:

(a) A piece of land has been sold out in 2003 and the profit on sale has been credited to capital reserve.

(b) A machine has been sold out for Rs. 10,000. The written down value of the machine was Rs. 12,000. Depreciation of Rs.10,000 is charged to plant in 2004.

(c) The investments are trade investments. Rs. 3,000 by way of dividend is received including Rs. 1,000 from preacquisition profit which has been credited to the investment account.

(d) An interim dividend of Rs. 20,000 has been paid in 2004.

(Ans: Increase in working capital Rs. 31,000; Funds from operations Rs. 1,33,000; Funds flow statement total Rs. 2,96,000.)

10. From the following Balance Sheet of Vasanth Ltd., prepare a fund flow statement.

Balance Sheet

Liabilities	*2008 (Rs.)*	*2009 (Rs.)*	*Assets*	*2008 (Rs.)*	*2009 (Rs.)*
Eq. share capital	1,00,000	1,00,000	Goodwill	12,000	12,000
General reserve	14,000	18,000	Building	40,000	36,000
Profit and loss a/c	16,000	13,000	Plant	37,000	36,000
Creditors	8,000	5,400	Investments	10,000	11,000
Bills payable	1,200	800	Debtors	18,000	19,000
Prov. for doubtful debts	400	600	Stock	30,000	23,400
Provision for taxation	16,000	18,000	B/R	2,000	3,200
			Cash	6,600	15,200
	1,55,600	**1,55,800**		**1,55,600**	**1,55,800**

Additional Information:

(a) Depreciation of Rs. 4,000 each has been charged on plant and buildings respectively.

(b) An interim dividend of Rs. 8,000 has been paid in 2009.

(c) Income tax Rs. 17,000 was paid during the year 2009.

(Ans: Increase in working capital Rs. 7,000; Funds from operations Rs. 36,000.)

CASH FLOW STATEMENT

MODEL QUESTIONS

OBJECTIVE TYPE :

Choose the best answer from the given alternatives:

(1) Cash from operatio n is equal to____

(a) net profit plus increase in outstanding expenses

(b) net profit plus increase in debtors

(c) net profit plus increase in stock

(2) Increase in amount of debtors results in____

(a) increase in cash (b) decrease in cash

(c) no change in cash

(3) Cash flow statements are of____

(a) long-term duration (b) short-term duration

(c) medium-term duration

(4) Increase in amount of bills payable results in____

(a) increase in cash (b) decrease in cash

(c) no change in cash

(5) There is no increase or decrease in working capital when cash is paid to____

(a) debtors (b) creditors

(c) shareholders

(6) Which should be taken into account for ascertaining cash from operations apart from adjustment of non-cash charges?

(a) changes in current a/c (b) changes in revenue a/c

(c) changes in capital a/c

(7) An increase in current asset results in____

(a) increase in cash (b) decrease in cash

(c) no change in cash

(Ans: 1.a 2.b 3.b 4.a 5.b 6.a 7.b.)

State TRUE or FALSE :

(1) Cash flow statement is based on accrual basis of accounting.

(2) The basis of concept of cash flow statement is based on a narrow concept of funds.

(3) Cash from operation and funds from operations means the same thing.

(4) Increase in provision for doubtful debts should be added back in order to find out cash from operations.

(5) Funds flow statement and cash flow statement are one and the same.

(6) A cash flow statement can very well be equated with an income statement.

(Ans: True: 2, 4 False: 1, 3, 5, 6.)

Fill in the blanks:

(1) Cash flow statement means the inflows and outflows of ——————

(2) Cash flows are classified into ————, ———— and ——— activities.

(3) Cash payments to suppliers for goods and services are classified as cash flows from ——— activities.

(4) Decrease in creditors is ————of cash.

(5) Income from investments is a cash flow from ———— activities.

(6) ———— reveals the effects of transaction in involved in movement of cash.

(Ans:

(1) cash and cash equivalents **(2) operating, investing, financing**

(3) operating **(4) outflows**

(5) investing **(6) Cash flow statement.)**

Short-answer type questions:

(1) What do you mean by cash flow statement?

(2) What are the limitations of cash flow statement?

(3) What are the sources of cash inflow?

(4) How will you calculate cash from operation?

Essay type questions:

(1) Distinguish between cash flow statement and funds flow statement.

(2) Explain the technique of preparing a cash flow statement with imaginary figures.

(3) Define the term cash flow. Explain the objects of cash flow analysis.

(4) State the uses of cash flow statement.

Exercises:

(1) From the following find out cash from operations.

Profit and Loss A/c

Particulars	*Rs.*	*Particulars*	*Rs.*
To Salaries	2,000	By Gross profit	10,000
To Rent	1,000	By Profit on sale of plant	3,000
To Depreciation	500	By Income tax refund	2,000
To Loss on sale of plant	1,000		
To Goodwill written off	1,000		
To Proposed dividend	3,500		
To Provision for taxation	2,500		
To Net Profit	3,500		
	15,000		**15,000**

(Ans: Cash from operations Rs. 7,000.)

(2) Calculate cash from operations from the following profit and loss A/c.

Particulars	*Rs*	*Particulars*	*Rs*
To Operation	1,00,000	By Gross profit	2,00,000
To Depreciation	40,000	By Gain on sale of plant	20,000
To Loss on sale of building	10,000		
To Advt.suspense a/c	5,000		
To Discount (allowed to customer)	500		
To Discount on issue of shares written off	500		
To Goodwill written off	12,000		
To Net profit	52,000		
	2,20,000		**2,20,000**

(Ans: Cash from operations Rs. 99,500.)

(3) Calculate cash from operations: net profit for 2008 Rs. 25,000: depreciation Rs. 1,000; prepaid expenses 1.1.08 Rs. 2,000; prepaid expenses 31.12.08 Rs. 1,000; outstanding salary 31.12.08 Rs. 500.

(Ans: Cash from operations Rs. 27,500.)

(4) The following are extracted from the B/S of a company.

Liabilities as on	31.12.08 (Rs.)	31.12.09 (Rs.)
P&L A/c	50,000	80,000
Provision for taxation	15,000	

Depreciation on assets during the year 2009 was provided Rs. 10,000. Calculate cash from operation if provision for taxation is treated as a non- current liability.

(Ans: Cash from operations Rs. 50,000.)

(5) The following were the Balance Sheet of Anand and Balu as on 1.1.09 and 31.12.09

Balance Sheet

Liabilities	*1.1.09 (Rs.)*	*31.12.09 (Rs.)*	*Assets*	*1.1.09 (Rs.)*	*31.12.09 (Rs.)*
Creditors	40,000	44,000	Cash	10,000	7,000
Mrs. Anand's loan	20,000	-	Debtors	30,000	50,000
SBI Loan	40,000	50,000	Stock	35,000	30,000
Capital	1,25,000	1,53,000	Machinery	1,00,000	90,000
Provision for depreciation	25,000	40,000	Land	40,000	50,000
			Building	35,000	60,000
	2,50,000	**2,87,000**		**2,50,000**	**2,87,000**

Additional Information:

During the year a machine costing Rs. 10,000,was sold without any loss. Net profit for the year 2009 amounted to Rs. 45,000.

Prepare a cash flow Statement.

(Ans: Cash from operations Rs. 50,000; Cash flow statement Rs. 1,04,000.)

(6) Mala Ltd., furnish you the following Balance Sheet for the year ending 31st December, 2008 and 2009. You are required to prepare a cash flow statement for the year ended 31.12.2009

Balance Sheet

Liabilities	*2008 (Rs.)*	*2009 (Rs.)*	*Assets*	*2008 (Rs.)*	*2009 (Rs.)*
Eq. share capital	10,000	10,000	Goodwill	1,200	1,200
General reserves	1,400	1,800	Land	4,000	3,600
P&L A/c	1,600	1,300	Building	3,700	3,600
Sundry creditors	800	600	Investments	1,000	1,100
Outstanding expenses	120	100	Inventories	3,000	2,400
Prov. for tax	1,600	1,800	Accounts receivable	2,000	2,300
Prov. for bad debts	80	100	Bank	700	1,500
	15,600	**15,700**		**15,600**	**15,700**

Following additional information has also been supplied to you:

- A piece of land has also been sold for Rs. 400.
- Depreciation amounting to Rs. 700 has been charged on building.
- Provision for taxation has been made for Rs. 2,000 during the year.

(Ans: Cash from operations Rs. 2,800; Cash Flow Statement Rs.4,520.)

(7) Malathi Ltd., furnish you the following Balance Sheet for the year ending 31st December, 2008 and 2009. You are required to prepare a cash flow statement for the year ended 31.12.09.

Balance Sheet

Liabilities	*2008 (Rs.)*	*2009 (Rs.)*	*Assets*	*2008 (Rs.)*	*2009 (Rs.)*
Share capital	1,40,000	1,48,000	Goodwill	5,000	3,000
General reserves	2,000	3,000	Land	40,000	60,000
P&L a/c.	18,200	19,600	Investments	15,000	7,000
Sundry creditors	10,000	12,000	Inventories	98,400	85,400
Propsed dividend	14,000	14,800	Accounts	29,800	35,400
Bank loan	22,000	9,000	Receivable Bank	18,000	15,600
	2,06,200	**2,06,400**		**2,06,200**	**2,06,400**

Following additional information has also been supplied to you:

(i) Land costing Rs. 20,000 was sold for Rs. 25,000.

(ii) Investments costing Rs. 10,000 was sold for Rs. 10,500 prepare a cash flow statement.

Ans. : Cash from operations Rs. 13,700; cash flow statement Rs. 90,200.

(8) The comparative Balance Sheet of Sagar Ltd., are given below:

Balance Sheet

Liabilities	*2008 (Rs.)*	*2009 (Rs.)*	*Assets*	*2008 (Rs.)*	*2009 (Rs.)*
Share capital	70,000	74,000	Cash	9,000	7,800
Debentures	12,000	6,000	Stock	49,200	42,700
Creditors	10,360	11,840	Debtors	14,900	17,700
Prov. for bad debts	700	800	Land	20,000	30,000
P&L A/c	10,040	10,560	Goodwill	10,000	5,000
	1,03,100	**1,03,200**		**1,03,100**	**1,03,200**

Additional Information:

(a) Dividend paid amount to Rs. 3,500.

(b) Land was purchased for Rs. 10,000.

(c) Amortisation of goodwill amounted to Rs. 5,000.

(d) Debentures were redeemed to the extent of Rs. 6,000.

You are required to prepare a cash flow statement.

(Ans: Cash from operations Rs. 9,120; cash flow statement Rs. 30,100.)

(9) The summarised Balance Sheet of ABC Ltd., as at 31st Dec., 2008 and 2009 are given below:

Liabilities	*2008 (Rs.)*	*2009 (Rs.)*	*Assets*	*2008 (Rs.)*	*2009 (Rs.)*
Share capital	2,25,000	2,25,000	Fixed assets	2,00,000	1,60,000
General reserves	1,50,000	1,55,000	Investments	25,000	30,000
P&L A/c	28,000	34,000	Stock	1,20,000	1,05,000
Sundry creditors	84,000	67,000	Debtors	1,05,000	2,27,500
Prov.for taxation	37,500	5,000	Bank	74,500	98,500
Mortgage loan	—	1,35,000			
	5,24,500	**6,21,000**		**5,24,500**	**6,21,000**

Additional Information:

(i) Investments costing Rs. 4,000 were sold during the year 2009 for Rs. 4,250.

(ii) Prov.for taxation made during the year Rs. 4,500.

(iii) During the year part of the fixed assets costing Rs. 5,000 were sold for Rs. 6,000.

(iv) Dividend paid during the year Rs. 20,000.

Prepare a cash flow statement.

(Ans. : Cash from operations Rs. 69,250; cash flow statement Rs. 3,04,000.)

(10) The comparative Balance Sheet of SURABI Ltd., for the two years were as follows:

Liabilities	*2008 (Rs.)*	*2009 (Rs.)*	*Assets*	*2008 (Rs.)*	*2009 (Rs.)*
Loan from wife	—	20,000	Cash	11,000	15,000
Bills payable	12,000	8,000	Debtors	40,000	35,000
Creditors	25,000	52,000	Stock	25,000	30,000
Bank o/d	43,000	60,000	Machinery	20,000	14,000
Capital	66,000	34,000	Land and buildings	50,000	80,000
	1,46,000	**1,74,000**		**1,46,000**	**1,74,000**

Additional information:

(i) Net loss for the year 2009 amounted to Rs. 13,000.

(ii) During the year a machine costing Rs. 5,000 (accumulated depreciation Rs. 2,000) was sold for Rs. 2,500. The provision for depreciation against machinery as on 31.12.08 was Rs. 6,000 and on 31.12.09 Rs. 7,000.

Prepare a Cash Flow Statement.

(Ans: Cash lost from operation Rs. 9,500 ; cash flow statement Rs. 82,500.)

(11) The following is the summarised Balance Sheet of VASAN Ltd., as 31st Dec.,2008 and 2009:

Liabilities	*2008 (Rs.)*	*2009 (Rs.)*	*Assets*	*2008 (Rs.)*	*2009 (Rs.)*
Share capital	2,00,000	2,50,000	Land and buildings	2,00,000	1,90,000
General reserve	50,000	60,000	Machinery	1,50,000	1,69,000
Profit and loss a/c	30,500	30,600	Stock	1,00,000	74,000
Bank loan	70,000	——	Debtors	80,000	64,200
Creditors	1,50,000	1,35,200	Cash	500	600
Prov.for tax	30,000	35,000	Bank	——	8,000
			Goodwill	——	5,000
	5,30,500	**5,10,800**		**5,30,500**	**5,10,800**

Additional informations:

(i) Dividend of Rs. 23,000 was paid.

(ii) Assets of another company were purchased for a consideration of Rs. 50,000 payable in shares. The following assets were purchased:

Stock Rs. 20,000, machinery Rs. 25,000.

(iii) Machinery was further purchased for Rs. 8,000.

(iv) Depreciation written off on machinery for Rs. 12,000.

(v) Incometax provided during the year Rs. 33,000.

(vi) Loss on sale reduce of machinery Rs. 200 was written off to general reserve.

Prepare the cash flow statement.

(Ans: Cash from operations Rs. 88,300; cash flow statement Rs. 1,52,400.)

☆☆☆

CHAPTER 4

MARGINAL COSTING

- Marginal Costing
- Concepts of Cost-volume-profit analysis
- Break Even Analysis
- Managerial Applications of Marginal Costing
- Significance and Limitations of Marginal Costing.

INTRODUCTION

Marginal costing is a technique of costing fully oriented towards managerial decision-making and control.These costs tend to vary in direct proportion to the changes in the production level. Hence, the marginal costing can also be called as variable costing or direct costing or incremental costing or differential costing.

Definition of Marginal Cost

According to the Terminology of cost Accountancy of the Institute of Cost and Management Accountants, London, The Marginal Cost represents, "the amount at any given volume of output by which aggregate costs are changed if the volume of output is increased or decreased by one unit". Hence, marginal cost is nothing but the cost of producing an additional unit of output.

Definition of Marginal Costing

According to Dr. Joseph, "Marginal costing is a technique of determining the amount of changes in the aggregate costs due to an increase of one unit over the existing level of production".

Thus, the marginal costing involves the following two aspects:

(i) Ascertainment of marginal cost.

(ii) Deriving of cost-volume-profit relationship by differentiating fixed cost from variable costs.

Characteristics of Marginal Costing

The main characteristics of marginal costing are as follows:

(1) Marginal costing is a technique of control or decision-making.

(2) Only the variable costs (marginal costs) are treated as the cost of the product.

(3) The stock of work-in-progress and finished goods are valued at variable cost. Fixed costs will not be included in the valuation of stocks.

(4) Fixed costs are treated as period costs and are charged to costing profit and loss account.

(5) Prices are based on marginal costs by adding contribution.

(6) The profitability at various levels of activity is ascertained by calculating cost-volume-profit relationship.

Advantages of Marginal Costing

(1) Simple and easy to understand

(2) Inventory Valuation

(3) Removes the problem of under-absorption of Overheads

(4) No-profit, No-loss point

(5) Helpful to Management

(6) Profit Planning

(7) Fixation of selling prices: Marginal costing is immensely helpful in the determination of selling prices under different situations like recession, depression, introduction of new products, etc.

Demerits

However, it also suffers from demerits.

(1) It is difficult to separate fixed and variable costs clearly.

(2) Since variable overheads are apportioned on estimated basis, problem of under or over-recovery cannot be totally eliminated.

(3) Price fixation and comparison between two jobs cannot be done without considering fixed costs.

(4) The stock is valued at marginal cost. Hence, in the case of loss due to fire, full loss cannot be recovered from the insurance company.

(5) Valuation of inventories and profit estimations based on marginal costing are objected by tax authorities.

(6) In controlling costs, marginal costing is not useful in concerns where fixed costs are huge in relation to variable costs.

The systems of budgetary control and standard costing serve the purpose better than marginal costing. Hence, this technique is not required.

Concepts and Terms Used in Cost-Volume-Profit Analysis

1. **Variable Costs:** These costs are varying in proportion to the level of production and sales. Hence, these costs are also called, **'Product Cost' or 'Marginal Cost'.** Examples: direct material, direct wages, direct expenses and variable overheads.
2. **Fixed Cost:** Irrespective of the level of activity, these costs are fixed in nature. Hence, these costs are called **sunk cost or period cost or time costs.** Examples: Office rent, factory rent, manager's salary, etc.
3. **Contribution:** Contribution is the difference between sales and variable cost. Contribution is the amount that is contributed towards fixed expenses and profit. In practice a majority of the managerial decisions are based on the principle of contribution.

   Contribution can be ascertained as given below:

   Contribution = Sales – Variable Cost **(C=S-V)**

   Contribution = Fixed Expenses + Profit **(C=FE+P)**

   Contribution = Fixed Expenses – Loss **(C=FE-L)**
4. **Profit Volume Ratio (P/V Ratio) or Contribution to Sales Ratio (C/S Ratio):** The proportion of contribution to sales is called P/V ratio. This ratio may also be called **contribution ratio or marginal ratio.** The P/V ratio is generally expressed as a percentage. A high P/V ratio indicates high profitability and a low P/V ratio indicates low profitability.
5. **Break Even Analysis:** Break even analysis is a method of studying the relationship between revenue and costs in relation to sales volume of a business enterprise. According to Matx Curry and Frank "break even analysis determines at what level cost and revenue are in equilibrium". This is so because the break even analysis is the most widely known form of cost-volume-profit analysis.

   Assumptions of break even analysis:

   The break even analysis assumes the following:

   (i) All elements of costs are divided into fixed and variable costs.

   (ii) Variable costs vary in relation to the volume of production.

   (iii) Fixed costs remain constant at all volumes of output.

   (iv) The selling price remains constant at all levels of output.

   (v) The volume of production is the only factor that influences cost.

   (vi) There is only one product or in the case of multiple products, sales mix remains stable.

6. **Break even point:** The point which breaks the total cost and the selling price evenly to show the level of output or sales at which there shall be no profit or no loss is called break even point. In other words, that point of sales volume at which total revenue is equal to total cost. The break even point may also be called, 'Critical Point' or 'Equilibrium Point' or 'Balancing Point' or 'No profit, No Loss Point' or 'Zero Profit and Zero Loss Point'.

The following chart clearly illustrates the break even point:

Margin of Safety

The excess of actual or budgeted sales over the break even sales is called the margin of safety. The margin of safety is calculated in rupees, units or even in percentage form. One of the indicators to analyse

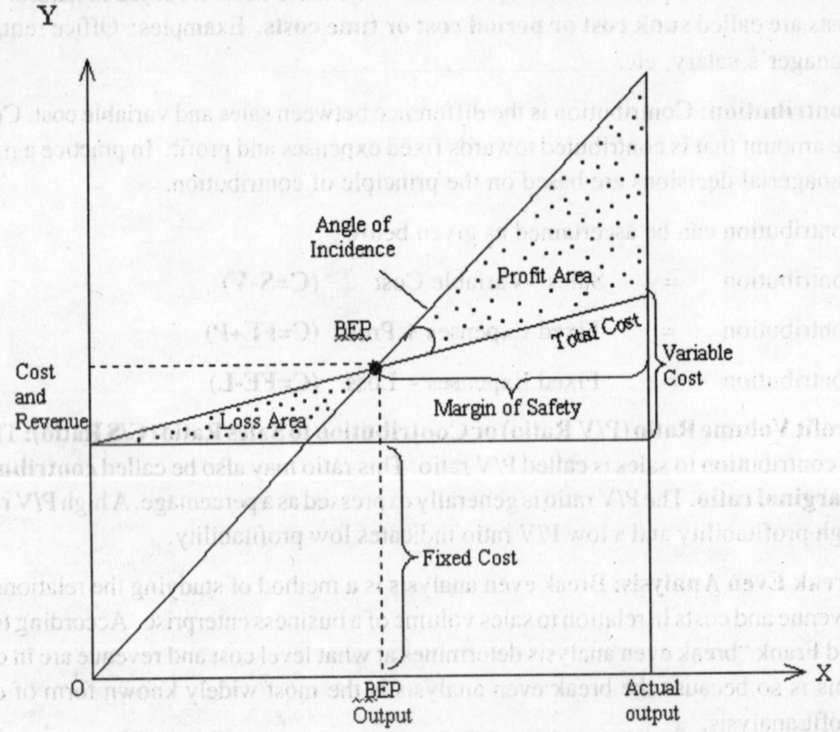

the strength of the business is the size of margin of safety. The large margin of safety shows the soundness of the business and even if there is any fall in the sales volume, then they can be able to earn some profit. This margin of safety can be improved by adopting the following steps:

1. By increasing the volume of production.
2. By increasing the sale price of the product.
3. By reducing the fixed cost through adopting the innovative technologies.
4. By reducing the variable cost by means of cost-reduction and cost-consciousness principles.
5. By eliminating unprofitable products.

6. By adopting the optimal sales mix to increase the viability of the product.

Angle of Incidence

The angle of incidence shows the profit earning capacity of a business. A large angle of incidence indicates a higher rate of profit and *vice-versa*. The intersection of total cost line and sales line is called break even point and the angle lies at this point is called the "Angle of Incidence".

Problem 1:

From the following information prepare a Marginal Cost Statement:

Variable Cost:	***Rs.***
Direct Material	5,000
Direct Wages	3,000
Factory Overheads	1,500
	9,500
Fixed Cost	3,400
Total Cost	**12,900**
Profit	3,100
Sales	**16,000**

Solution:

Marginal Cost Statement

Particulars	***Rs.***	***Rs.***
Sales		16,000
Less: Variable Costs:		
Direct Material	5,000	
Direct Wages	3,000	
Factory Overheads	1,500	9,500
Contribution		6,500
Less: Fixed Cost:		3,400
Profit		**2,100**

Problem 2:

From the following data, find out the amount of fixed expenses:

Particulars	***Rs.***
Sales	3,00,000
Direct Material	99,000
Direct Labour	55,000
Variable Overheads	30,000
Profit	**60,000**

Solution:

Calculation of fixed expenses:

Marginal Cost Statement

Particulars	***Rs.***	***Rs.***
Sales		3,00,000
Less: Variable Costs:		
Direct Material	99,000	
Direct Wages	55,000	
Variable Overheads	30,000	1,84,000
Contribution		1,16,000
Less: Fixed Expenses (bal. fig.)		56,000
Profit		**60,000**

Problem 3:

Calculate break even point in terms of rupees:

Sales	8,00,000
Fixed Expenses	2,00,000
Variable Costs:	
Direct Material	2,00,000
Less: Direct Labour	1,30,000
Other Variable Expenses	**70,000**

Solution:

$$BEP\ (\text{in Rs.}) = \frac{\text{Fixed Expenses}}{\text{Contribution}} \times \text{Sales}$$

$$\text{Contribution} = \text{Sales} - \text{Variable Cost}$$

$$= 8,00,000 - 4,00,000$$

$$= \text{Rs. } 4,00,000$$

$$BES. = \frac{2,00,000}{4,00,000} \times 8,00,000$$

$$= \text{Rs. } 4,00,000.$$

Problem 4:

The following information are given for two companies:

Particulars	***J Ltd.,***	***C Ltd.,***
Units produced and sold	20,000	20,000
	Rs.	**Rs.**
Revenues	2,50,000	2,50,000
Fixed Costs	90,000	40,000
Operating Income	69,000	65,000
Variable Costs	91,000	1,45,000

Find out the break even point of each company both in units as well as volume.

Solution:

Particulars	***J Ltd., Rs.***	***C Ltd., Rs.***
Sales	2,50,000	2,50,000
Less: Variable Cost	91,000	1,45,000
Contribution	1,59,000	1,05,000
Less: Fixed Cost	90,000	40,000
Profit **(Operating Income)**	**69,000**	**65,000**

$$BEP\ (\text{in Rs.}) = \frac{\text{Fixed Cost}}{\text{Contribution}} \times \text{Sales}$$

$$= \frac{90,000}{1,59,000} \times 2,50,000 \quad = \frac{40,000}{1,05,000} \times 2,50,000$$

$$= \text{Rs. } 1{,}41{,}509 \qquad = \text{Rs } 95{,}238$$

$$\text{Selling Price Per Unit} = \frac{2{,}50{,}000}{20{,}000} = \text{Rs. } 12.50$$

$$\text{BEP (in Units)} = \frac{\text{BES}}{\text{Selling Price p.u.}}$$

$$\frac{1{,}41{,}509}{12.50} = 11{,}321 \text{ units} \qquad \frac{95{,}238}{12.50} = 7{,}619 \text{ units}$$

(rounded off) (rounded off)

Problem 5:

Calculate BEP from the following details:

Fixed expenses Rs 1,50,000

Variable cost per unit Rs. 10

Selling price per unit Rs. 15.

Solution:

$$\text{BEP (in Units)} = \frac{\text{Fixed Expenses}}{\text{Contribution per unit}} \times \text{Sales}$$

$$= \text{Rs. } 15 - \text{Rs. } 10 = \text{Rs. } 5$$

$$\text{BEP (in Units)} = \frac{1{,}50{,}000}{5} = 30{,}000 \text{ units.}$$

$$\text{BEP(in Units)} = \frac{\text{Fixed Expenses}}{\text{Contribution per unit}} \times \text{Selling Price Per Unit}$$

$$= \frac{1{,}50{,}000}{5} \times 15 = \text{Rs. } 4{,}50{,}000$$

Problem 6:

From the following particulars find out the BEP What will be selling price per unit if BEP is to be brought down to 10,000 units?

Particulars	**Rs.**
Variable Cost Per Unit	80
Fixed Expenses	2,90,000
Selling Price Per unit	100

Solution:

$$\text{BEP (in Units)} = \frac{\text{Fixed Expenses}}{\text{Contribution per unit}}$$

$$= \frac{2,90,000}{100-80} = \frac{2,90,000}{20} = 14,500 \text{ units}.$$

If break even point is brought down to 10,000 units, fixed expenses are to be recovered from 10,000 units.

$$\text{Fixed Expenses Per Unit} = \frac{\text{Fixed Expenses } 2,90,000}{\text{Number of units}} = \text{Rs. } 29.$$

When BEP is 10,000 units, selling price per unit is calculated as follows:

Selling Price = Fixed Expenses Per Unit + Variable Expenses Per Unit

= Rs. 29 + Rs. 80 = Rs. 109.

Problem 7:

From the following data calculate:

(i) Number of units to be sold to earn a profit of Rs. 2,50,000.

(ii) Sales to earn a profit of Rs. 2,50,000.

Selling price per unit Rs. 50.

Variable selling cost per unit Rs. 3.

Variable manufacturing cost per unit Rs. 22.

Fixed factory overhead Rs. 1,75,000.

Fixed selling cost Rs. 25,000.

Solution:

(i) Number of units to be sold to earn a profit of Rs. 2,50,000

$$= \frac{\text{Fixed Expenses} + \text{Desired Profit}}{\text{Contribution per unit}}$$

$$= \frac{2,00,000 + 2,50,000}{50 - 25} = \frac{4,50,000}{25} \times 50$$

(ii) Sales to earn a profit of Rs. 2,50,000

$$= \frac{\text{Fixed Expenses} + \text{Desired Profit}}{\text{Contribution per unit}} \times \text{Selling Price}$$

$$= \frac{2,00,000+2,50,000}{50-25} = \frac{4,50,000}{25} \times 50$$

$$= \text{Rs.}9,00,000$$

MANAGERIAL APPLICATIONS OF MARIGINAL COSTING

Pricing Decisions

Fixing price of a product is the most important factor, because it is the base to determine the profit of the organisation as well as the marketability of the product. Normally, the price of a product is based on the total cost of sales plus a margin of profit. But under certain circumstances the price of the product can be fixed below the total cost of the product.

For instance, under the following circumstances, the price of a product can be fixed even below the marginal cost of the product.

(i) To launch a new product in the market.

(ii) To Explore the market in the overseas.

(iii) To Avoid the competitor from the existing market.

(iv) To Assist the sale of joint products.

(v) To Avoid the retrenchment of workers.

(vi) To Dispose off the perishable type of products.

(vii) To Make use of optimum capacity.

(viii) To Retain the existing customers to prevent the loss of future orders.

(ix) To Dispose off the surplus stocks.

(x) To Popularize a particular product.

Problem 8:

P.V. Ratio is 50%. Marginal cost is Rs. 60. What is the selling price per unit?

Solution:

P/V Ratio is 50%

Therefore, contribution is Rs. 50 when sales are Rs. 100

Therefore, variable cost = Sales – Contribution

= 100 – 50 = Rs. 50.

If variable cost is Rs. 50, selling price is Rs. 100.

If variable cost is Rs. 60, selling price $= \frac{100}{50} \times 60 =$ Rs. 120.

Therefore, selling price p.u. = Rs. 120.

Problem 9:

A company producing 70,000 units of a product working at 70% capacity receives an order from a foreign dealer for 30,000 units at Rs. 60.00 per unit although the local price is Rs. 110 per unit.

Particulars	*Per Unit Rs.*
Material	25.00
Labour:	
Skilled Labour (fixed)	15.00
Unskilled Labour	15.00
Variable Overheads	10.00
Fixed Overheads	25.00
Total	**90.00**

(i) Advise the management whether to accept the foreign order or not.

(ii) What will be your advice if the order has come from the local merchant?

(iii) If there is temporary fall in demand what will be minimum selling price to be charged?

Solution:

Calculation of Contribution

Particulars		*Per Unit Rs.*	*For 3,000 units Rs.*
Selling Price		60.00	18,00,000
Less : Variable Cost :			
Material	25.00		
Unskilled Labour	15.00		
Variable Overhead	10.00	50.00	15,00,000
Contribution		**10.00**	**3,00,000**

Decision:

(i) **Foreign Order:** Foreign order should be accepted because it gives an additional contribution of Rs. 10 per unit and in total Rs. 3,00,000.

(ii) **Local Order:** Local order should be rejected because existing selling price in the local market is Rs. 110. Foreign order price, (i.e., Rs. 60) will affect the relationship with other customers in the local market.

(iii) **Minimum Selling Price:** If there is a temporary fall in demand, the selling price should not be less than variable cost. Therefore, minimum selling price should be equal to variable cost, i.e. Rs. 50.

Problem 10:

The cost sheet of a product is given below:

Particulars	*Rs.*	*Rs.*
Direct Material		5.50
Direct Wages		3.50
Factory Overheads:		
Fixed	0.75	
Variable	0.50	
		1.25
Administrative Expenses		0.75
Selling and Distributive Overheads:		
Fixed	0.50	
Variable	0.50	1.00
Total		**12.00**

Selling price per unit is Rs. 13.00

The above figures are for an output of 60,000 units. The capacity for the firm is 75,000 units. A foreign customer is desirous of buying 15,000 units at a price of Rs. 11 per unit.

Advice the manufacturer whether the order should be accepted. What will be your advise if the order were from a local merchant?

Solution:

Marginal Cost Statement for additional units of 15,000

Particulars	*Rs.*	*Per units* *Rs.*	*15,000 units* *Rs.*
Selling Price		11.00	1,65,000
Less : Variable Cost :			
Direct Material	5.50		
Direct Wages	3.50		
Factory Overheads	0.50		
Selling and Distribution Overheads	0.50	10.00	1,50,000
Contribution		**1.00**	**15,000**

Decision

(i) **Foreign Order:** The foreign order should be accepted, because additional contribution of Rs.15,000 will increase the profit by this amount as fixed expenses remain constant up to 100% capacity.

(ii) **Local Order:** The order from the local merchant should be rejected. Since, existing selling price in the local market is Rs.13.

Profit Planning and Maintaining a Desired Level of Profit

Profit planning is an important activity of every management. Achieving maximum profit is the preamble of every business activity. The marginal costing technique helps management to fix prices as well as to maintain a desired level of profit.

Problem 11:

A company produces and markets industrial goods. Due to heavy competition the company proposes to reduce the selling price. If the present level of profit is to be maintained indicate the number of units to be sold if the proposed reduction in selling price is (1) 10%; (2) 15%; (3) 20%.

The following additional information is available:

Particulars	*Rs.*
Present Sales (30,000 Units)	6,00,000
Variable Cost (30,000 Units)	3,60,000
Contribution	2,40,000
Less: Fixed Cost	1,40,000
Profit	**1,00,000**

Solution:

Present selling price per unit is Rs. 20 (6,00,000 / 30,000)

If the reduction is 10% = 20 – 10% = Rs. 18.00

If the reduction is 15% = 20 – 15% = Rs. 17.00

If the reduction is 20% = 20 – 20% = Rs. 16.00

Contribution at various proposed selling prices:

Particulars	*10%*	*15%*	*20%*
Selling Price	18	17	16
Less: Variable Cost (3,60,000/30,000)	12	12	12
Contribution per unit	6	5	4

Total contribution required to maintain the present level of profit is as follows:

	Rs.
Present Sales	6,00,000
Less : Variable Cost	3,60,000
Total Contribution	**2,40,000**

Units to be sold to earn the total contribution of Rs. 2,40,000 to maintain the present level of profits.

$$= \frac{\text{Total Contribution}}{\text{Contribution per unit}}$$

(a) If the price is reduced by 10% $= \frac{2,40,000}{6} =$ 40,000 units.

(b) If the price is reduced by 15% $= \frac{2,40,000}{5} =$ 48,000 units.

(c) If the price is reduced by 20% $= \frac{2,40,000}{4} =$ 60,000 units.

Make or Buy Decisions

In "make or buy" decisions, the management compares the quotation fixed by the supplier with the marginal cost of the particular product. If outside supplier's rate is lower than the marginal cost then, the management can decide to produce the product in their firm itself. Otherwise it can be purchased from the outside supplier or from the open market. In this situation, the management takes the decision based on marginal cost only with the assumption that the fixed expenses do not increase and the production facilities can be fruitfully utilised.

Problem 12:

The management of a company finds that while the cost of making a component part is Rs.15, the same is available in the market at Rs.13 with an assurance of continuous supply.

Give a suggestion whether to make or buy this part. Give also your views in case the supplier reduces the price from Rs.13 to Rs.11.

The cost information is as follows:

Particulars	*Rs.*
Material	3.50
Direct Labour	5.50
Other Variable Expenses	3.00
Fixed Expenses	3.00
Total	**15.00**

Solution:

Marginal Cost Statement

Particulars	*Rs.*
Material	3.50
Direct Labour	5.50
Other Variable Expenses	3.00
Total	**12.00**

Decision

The company should produce the part if the part is available in the market at Rs.13, because the production will give to the company a margin of Re.1 per unit (Rs.13 – Rs.12).

The company should buy the part from the market if the part is available in the market at Rs.11. Because additional cost of producing the part is Re.1 more than the price at which it is available in the market (Rs.12 – Rs.11).

Problems of Key or Limiting Factor

Limiting factors always restrict production or sales because of shortage of such factor. For example, the shortage of raw material, labour, capital, plant capacity, etc., may affect the production process. Hence, such limiting factor should be utilised in the best possible manner and to maximise the profits. In this situation, the management decisions should not be based on the highest P/V ratio. Instead of that, it should be on the basis of highest contribution per unit of key factor.

Problem 13:

From the following data, which product would you recommend to be manufactured in a factory, time being the key factor?

Particulars	***Per Unit of Product X*** ***Rs.***	***Per Unit of Product Y*** ***Rs.***
Direct Material	20	12
Direct Wages @ Rs. 2 per hour	4	6
Variable Overhead @ Rs. 3 per hour	6	9
Selling Price	60	81
Standard time to produce	2 hours	3 hours

Solution:

Calculation of contribution per unit:

Particulars		***Product X*** ***Rs.***		***Product Y*** ***Rs.***
Selling Price		60		81
Less : Variable Cost:				
Direct Material	20		12	
Direct Wages	4		6	
Variable Overhead	6	30	9	27
Contribution		30		54
Standard time to produce		2 hours		3 hours
Contribution per hour		$\frac{30}{2}$ = **Rs. 15**		$\frac{54}{3}$ = **Rs. 18**

Contribution per hour of product Y is more than that of product X by Rs. 3. Hence, product Y is recommended to be produced.

Problem 14:

The following particulars are obtained from costing records of a factory:

Particulars	***Product R (Per Unit)*** ***Rs.***	***Product J (Per Unit)*** ***Rs.***
Selling Price	250	600
Direct Material (Rs. 25 per Kg.)	75	200
Direct Labour (Rs. 15 per hour)	60	105
Variable Overheads	25	70
Total fixed overheads Rs. 20,000		

Comment on the Psdrofitablity of each product when:

a. Raw material is in short supply;

b. Production capacity is limited;

c. Sales quantity is limited;

d. Sales value is limited;

e. Only 1,000 kgs., of raw material is available for both type of products in total and maximum sales quantity of each product is 300 units.

Solution:

Calculation of Contribution Per Unit

	Product R		***Product J***	
	Rs.	***Rs.***	***Rs.***	***Rs.***
Selling Price		250		600
Less : Marginal Costs :				
Direct Material	75		200	
Direct Labour	60		105	
Variable Overheads	25	160	70	375
Contribution Per Unit		90		225
(i) $\text{P V Ratio} = \frac{C}{S} \times 100$		$\frac{90}{250} \times 100$ =36%		$\frac{225}{600} \times 100$ =37.5%
(ii) Contribution per kg.		$\frac{90}{3\,\text{kgs}} = \text{Rs.}30$ $\frac{75}{25} = 3\,\text{kgs}$		$\frac{225}{8\,\text{kgs}} = \text{Rs.}28.10$ $\frac{200}{25} = 8\,\text{kgs}$
(iii) Contribution per hour		$\frac{90}{4\,\text{hrs}} = \text{Rs.}22.50$ $\frac{60}{15} = 4\,\text{hrs.}$		$\frac{225}{7\,\text{hrs}} = \text{Rs.}32.14$ $\frac{105}{15} = 7\,\text{hrs.}$
(iv) $\text{BES} = \frac{\text{Fixed Cost}}{\text{P V Ratio}}$		$\frac{20{,}000}{36} \times 100$ **= Rs. 55,556.**		$\frac{20{,}000}{37.5} \times 100$ **Rs. 53,333.**

(a) When raw material is in short supply, contribution per kg. of product 'R' is more and hence product R is more profitable.

(b) When production capacity is limited contribution per hour of product 'J' is higher and hence product 'J' is more profitable.

(c) When sales quantity is limited, contribution per unit of product 'J' is more and hence product 'J' is more profitable.

(d) When sales value is limited, the BES of product 'J' is lower and hence product 'J' is more profitable.

(e) When raw material as well as sales quantity are limited, the raw materials should first be used for maximum number of units of product R, i.e., for 300 units. This will consume 900 kgs. of material and the balance 100 kgs., shall be used for producing 12 units of product 'J'.

The profit in such a case would be as follows:

Particulars	*Rs.*
Contribution from 300 units of product R (300 × 90)	27,000
Contribution from 12 units of product J (12 × 225)	2,700
Total Contribution	29,700
Less : Fixed Overheads	20,000
Profit	**9,700**

Selection of a Suitable Product Mix

On production of more number of products by a concern, a problem repeatedly arises to find out the product mix which will yield the maximum profits. In determining the optimum sales, the products which give the maximum contribution are to be retained and their production should be increased.

Problem 15:

The cost per unit of the three products X, Y and Z of a company are given below:

Particulars	Product		
	X Rs.	Y Rs.	Z Rs.
Direct Materials	22	18	20
Direct Labour	14	16	14
Variable Overheads	7	9	8
Fixed Expenses	7	7	3
Total Cost	50	50	45

Profit	22	15	9
Selling Price	72	65	54
No. of Units Produced	**15,000**	**8,000**	**10,000**

Production arrangements are such that if one product is given up the production of the others can be raised by 50%. The directors propose that Z should be given up because the contribution from that product is the lowest. Do you agree?

(i) Total Fixed Expenses:

	Rs.
A – 15,000 units x Rs. 7 per unit	1,05,000
B – 8,000 units x Rs. 7 per unit	56,000
C – 10,000 units x Rs. 3 per unit	30,000
	1,91,000

(ii) Contribution per unit:

	X *Rs.*	*Y* *Rs.*	*Z* *Rs.*
Selling Price Per Unit	72	65	54
Less : Variable Cost	43	43	42
	29	**22**	**12**

(a) Total Profit if Product X is given up:

Rs.

Y = 8,000 units + 4000 units, i.e., 8000 × 50% = 12000 units × Rs. 22=2,64,000

Z = 10,000 units + 5000 units, i.e., 10000 × 50% = 15000 units × Rs. 12=1,80,000

Total Contribution	4,44,000
Less : Fixed Expenses	1,91,000
Total Profit	**2,53,000**

(b) Total Profit if Product Y is given up:

X = 15,000 units + 7500 units, i.e., 15000 × 50% = 22500 units × Rs.29 = 6,52,500

Z = 10,000 units + 5000 units, i.e., 10000 × 50% = 15000 units × Rs. 12 = 1,80,000

Total Contribution	8,32,500
Less: Fixed Expenses	1,91,000
Total Profit	**6,41,500**

(c) Total Profit if Product Z is given up:

X = 15,000 units + 7500 units, i.e.,	15000 × 50%	= 22500 units × Rs. 29 =	6,52,500
Y = 8,000 units + 4000 units, i.e.,	8000 × 50%	= 12000 units × Rs. 22 =	2,64,000
		Total Contribution	9,16,500
		Less : Fixed Expenses	1,91,000
		Total Profit	**7,25,500**

If product 'Z' is given up the profit is the maximum. So, the proposal to give up 'Z' is advisable.

Alternative Methods of Production

The marginal costing technique is very much helpful to the management to decide about the use of different methods of production possibilities also.

Problem 16:

Product A can be produced either by machine X or Machine Y, Machine X can produce 200 units of A per hour and Machine Y 250 units per hour. Total machine hours available during the year are 3,000. Taking into account the following data determine the profitable method of manufacture :

	Per Unit of A	
Particulars	***Machine X*** ***Rs.***	***Machine Y*** ***Rs.***
Marginal Cost	6	7
Selling Price	15	15
Fixed Cost	3	3

Solution:

Profitability Statement

Particulars	***Machine X*** ***Rs.***	***Machine Y*** ***Rs.***
Selling Price Per Unit	15	15
Less : Marginal Cost	6	7
Contribution Per Unit	9	8
Output per hour	200 units	250 units
Contribution per hour	Rs. 1,800	Rs. 2,000
Machine Hours per year	3,000	3,000
Annual Contribution	**Rs. 54,00,000**	**Rs. 60,00,000**

Hence, production by Machine Y is more profitable.

Selection of suitable Production/Sales Mix

Problem 17:

Following informations has been made available from the cost records of Kamlesh Ltd., manufacturing spare parts.

	Direct Material Per Unit
R	24 hours at 40 paise per hour
J	24 hours at 40 paise per hour
Variable Overheads	100% of Wages
Fixed expenses	Rs. 1000
Selling Price:	
R	Rs. 34
J	Rs. 30

The directors want to be acquainted with the desirability of adopting any one of the following alternative sales mixes in the budget for the next period.

(a) 300 units of R and 300 units of J.

(b) 600 units of J only

(c) 400 units of R and 200 units of J

(d) 250 units of R and 250 units of J

State which of the alternative sales mixes you would recommend to the management?

Solution:

Calculation of Contribution per unit

	Products			
	R	(Rs.)	J	(Rs.)
Selling Price		34		30
Less: Variable Cost:				
Direct Materials	10.80		7.80	
Direct Wages	9.60		9.60	
Variable Overheads	9.60	30	9.60	27
Contribution		4		3

a. 300 units of R and 300 units J:

Contribution:

R : 300 × 4	1,200
J : 300 × 3	900
	2,100
Less : Fixed Expenses	1,000
Profit	**1,100**

b. 600 units of J only:

Contribution:

J : 600 × 3	1,800
Less : Fixed Expenses	1,000
Profit	**800**

c. 400 units of R and 200 units J:

Contribution:

R : 400 × 4	1,600
J : 200 × 3	600
	2,200
Less : Fixed Expenses	1,000
Profit	**1,200**

d. 250 units of R and 350 units J:

Contribution:

R : 250 × 4	1,000
J : 350 × 3	1,050
	2,050
Less : Fixed Expenses	1,000
Profit	**1,050**

The alternative C is most profitable, since it gives the maximum profits of Rs. 1,200.

Determination of Optimum Level of Activity

The technique of marginal costing helps the management in determining the optimum level of activity. To make such a decision, contribution at different levels of activity can be found. The level of activity which gives the highest contribution will be the optimum level.

Problem 18:

A factory engaged in manufacturing school bags is working at 50% capacity and produces 15,000 bags per annum.

The present cost break-up for bag is as under:

Material	Rs. 12
Labour	Rs. 4
Overheads	Rs. 6 (50% fixed)

The selling price is Rs. 25 per bag.

If it is decided to work the factory at 60% capacity, the selling price falls by 5%. At 90% capacity the selling price falls by 10% accompanied by a similar fall in the price of material.

You are required to calculate the profit at 60% and 85% capacities and also calculate the break even point for the same capacity productions.

Solution:

Statement showing profit at 60% and 85% capacity levels

Capacity Levels	***60%***		***85%***	
Production (in units)	***18,000***		***25,500***	
	Per unit	***Total***	***Per unit***	***Total***
	Rs.	***Rs.***	***Rs.***	***Rs.***
Sales	**23.75**	**4,27,500**	**22.505,**	**73,750**
Less: Variable Cost:				
Material	12.00	2,16,000	10.80	2,75,400
Labour	4.00	72,000	4.00	1,02,000
Variable Overheads	3.00	54,000	3.00	76,500
Total Variable Overheads	**19.00**	**3,42,000**	**17.80**	**4,53,900**
Contribution	4.75	85,500	4.70	1,19,850
Less: Fixed Costs (15,000 × 3)	45,000	45,000		
Profit	**40,500**			**74,850**

(i) BEP (in units) $= \dfrac{\text{Fixed Expenses}}{\text{Contribution per unit}}$ $\dfrac{45,000}{4.75} = 9,474$ units $\dfrac{45,000}{4.70} = 9,574$ units

(ii) BES = BEP (in units) × Selling Price P U 9,474 × 23.75 9,574 × 22.50

= Rs. 2,25,008. = Rs. 2,15,415.

Evaluation of Performance

Evaluation of performance efficiency of various departments or product-lines can be made with the help of marginal costing. The management has to think about the discontinuance of the production of non-profitable products or departments so as to maximise the profits. In this regard, the decisions are based on the lowest contribution or P/V ratio of the respective departments or products.

Problem 19:

The management of a company considered that Product JJ, one of its three main lines, is not as profitable as the other two with the result that no particular efforts are being made to push its sales. The selling prices and costs of the three products are:

Product	*Selling Price*	*Direct Material*	*Direct Labour*		
			Dept. X	*Dept. Y*	*Dept.Z*
	Rs.	*Rs.*	*Rs.*	*Rs.*	*Rs.*
R	70	12	8	3	3
N	60	8	3	8	3
V	66	10	3	3	8

Overhead rates for each department per rupee of direct labour are as follows:

	Dept. X	*Dept. Y*	*Dept. Z*
	Rs.	*Rs.*	*Rs.*
Variable Overhead	1.25	0.50	1.00
Fixed Overheads	1.25	2.00	1.50
Total	**2.50**	**2.50**	**2.50**

What advice would you give to the management about the profitability of product N? Give reasons.

Solution:

Statement showing comparative profitability

	R		N		V	
	Rs.	**Rs.**	**Rs.**	**Rs.**	**Rs.**	**Rs.**
Selling Price		70.00		60.00		66.00
Less : Variable Cost :						
Direct Material	12.00		8.00		10.00	
Direct Labour	14.00		14.00		14.00	
Variable Overhead:						

Department X	10.00		3.75		3.75	
Department Y	1.50		4.00		1.50	
Department Z	3.00	40.50	3.00	32.75	8.00	37.25
Contribution		29.50		27.25		28.75
PV Ratio		42.14 %		45.42%		43.56%

Comment: Hence, P.V. ratio of profit 'N' is the highest, it is the most profitable one.

MISCELLANEOUS ILLUSTRATIONS

Problem 20:

Find the profit from the following data:

Sales	Rs. 1,20,000
Marginal Cost	Rs. 90,000
Break even Sales	Rs. 90,000

Solution:

Profit = Contribution – Fixed Expenses

$$\text{P V Ratio} = \frac{\text{Contribution}}{\text{Sales}} \times 100$$

$$= \frac{1{,}20{,}000 \quad 90{,}000}{\text{Sales}} \times 100$$

$$= \frac{30{,}000}{1{,}20{,}000} \times 100 = 25\%$$

Fixed Expenses:

$$\text{BES} = \frac{\text{Fixed Expenses}}{\text{P V Ratio}}$$

$$90{,}000 = \frac{\text{Fixed Expenses}}{25\%}$$

$$\text{Therefore, fixed expenses} = 90{,}000 \times \frac{25}{100} = \text{Rs. } 22{,}500$$

Profit = Contribution – Fixed Expenses

	Rs.
Contribution	30,000
Less: Fixed Expenses	22,500
Profit	**7,500**

Problem 21:

The following information relating to Murali company is given to you:

Particulars	***Rs.***
Sales	4,00,000
Fixed Cost	1,80,000
Variable Cost	2,50,000

Ascertain how much the value of sales must be increased for the company to break even.

Solution:

$$\text{BEP (in Rs.)} = \frac{\text{Fixed Expenses}}{\text{Contribution}} \times \text{Sales}$$

Contribution = Sales – Variable Cost

= 4,00,000 – 2,50,000

= Rs. 1,50,000

$$\text{BEP (in Rs.)} = \frac{1,80,000}{1,50,000} \times 4,00,000 = \text{Rs.}4,80,000$$

BES = Rs. 4,80,000

Present sales = Rs. 4,00,000

Therefore, sales are to be increased by Rs. 80,000 to break even.

Problem 22:

From the following data, calculate break even point expressed in terms of units and also the new BEP if selling price is reduced by 10%.

Fixed Expenses:

Depreciation	Rs. 1,20,000
Salaries	Rs, 1,10,000

Variables Expenses:

Materials	Rs. 4 per unit
Labour	Rs. 3 per unit
Selling Price	Rs.15 per unit

Solution:

(i) BEP (in Units) $= \dfrac{\text{Fixed Expenses}}{\text{Contribution per unit}}$

$$= \frac{2,30,000}{15-7} = \frac{2,30,000}{8} = 28,750 \text{ units}$$

(ii) New BEP (in Units) when selling price is reduced by 10%

Selling Price	Rs. 15.00
Less : 10% Reduction	Rs. 1.50
New Selling Price	Rs. 13.50

$$= \frac{2,30,000}{13.50-7} = \frac{2,30,000}{6.50} = 35,385 \text{ units.}$$

Problem 23:

Given:

Fixed cost	Rs. 12,000
Break even sales (in units)	5,000
Sales	10,000 Units
Selling price per unit	Rs. 10

Calculate:

(a) Variable Cost

(b) Profit when sales are 10,000 units.

Solution:

Break Even Sales = 5,000 units

Selling Price Per Unit = Rs. 10

Break Even Sales (in Rs.) = 5,000 × 10 = Rs. 50,000

(a) Calculation of variable Cost:

At Break Even Sales, Profit is NIL.

	Rs.
Break Even Sales	50,000
Less: Variable Cost (bal.fig.)	38,000
Contribution	12,000
Less: Fixed Cost	12,000
Profit	**0**

Variable cost p.u.=38000/5000 units = Rs. 7.60

b. Profit when sales are 10,000 units:

Sales (10,000 × Rs. 10)	1,00,000
Less: Variable Cost (10,000 × 7.60)	76,000
Contribution	24,000
Less: Fixed Cost	12,000
Profit	**12,000**

Problem 24:

From the following data calculate:

(i) P/V ratio

(ii) Profit when sales are Rs. 25,000

(iii) New break even sales if selling price is reduced by 10%

Fixed expenses	Rs. 6,000
Break even Sales	Rs. 15,000.

Solution:

(i) P V Ratio:

$$\text{BES} = \frac{\text{Fixed Expenses}}{\text{P V Ratio}}$$

$$15{,}000 = \frac{6{,}000}{\text{P V Ratio}}$$

$$\text{P V Ratio} = \frac{6{,}000}{15{,}000} = \frac{6}{15} = 0.4 \times 100 = 40\%$$

(ii) Profit when sales are Rs. 25,000.

Profit = Contribution – Fixed Expenses

Contribution = Sales × P V Ratio

$$= 25000 \times \frac{40}{100} = \text{Rs.}10{,}000$$

Profit = 10,000 – 6,000 = Rs. 4,000.

(iii) New Break Even Sales if Selling Price is Reduced by 10%

Contribution is Rs. 40 when selling price is Rs. 100.

S – V = C

100 – V = 40

V = 60.

	Rs.
Selling Price	100
Less: 10% reduction	10
Revised Selling Price	90
Less: Variable Cost	60
New Contribution	30

$$\text{New P V Ratio} = \frac{30}{90} \times 100 = 33.33\%$$

$$\text{New BES} = \frac{6{,}000}{33.33\%} \text{ (or) } \frac{6{,}000}{1} \times 3 = \text{Rs. } 18{,}000$$

Problem 25:

You are required to calculate the Break Even Sales from the following data :

Profit Rs. 7,500 (25% of Sales)

P V Ratio is 40%

Solution:

Sales:

Profit is Rs. 25 when sales are Rs. 100.

$$\text{If profit is Rs. 7,500, Sales} = \frac{7{,}500}{25} \times 100 = \text{Rs.}30{,}000$$

Sales = Rs. 30,000

Fixed Cost:

Contribution = Sales × P V Ratio

$$= 30{,}000 \times \frac{40}{100} = \text{Rs.}12{,}000$$

Contribution	=	Rs. 12,000
Less: Fixed Cost (bal.fig.)	=	Rs. 4,500
Profit	=	Rs. 7,500

$$\text{BES} = \frac{\text{Fixed Cost}}{\text{P V Ratio}} \times 100 = \frac{4{,}500}{40} \times 100 = \text{Rs.}11{,}250$$

Problem 26:

An analysis of Modern Manufacturing Co. Ltd, led to the following information;

Cost Element	*Variable Cost % of sales*	*Fixed Cost (Rs.)*
Direct material	32.8	—
Direct labour	28.4	—
Factory overheads	12.6	1,89,900
Distribution overheads	4.1	58,400
General administration		
Overheads	1.1	66,700

Budgeted sales are Rs. 18,50,000. you are required to determine:

(i) The break even sales volume

(ii) The profit at the budgeted sales volume

(iii) The profit if actual sales drop by 10%

The profit if actual sales increase by 5% from budgeted sales.

Solution:

Percentage of variable cost of sales is 79 calculated follows:

Direct Material	32.8%
Direct labour	28.4%
Factory overheads	12.6%

Distribution overheads	4.1%
Administrative overheats	1.1%
	79.0% of sales

Percentage of contribution of sales = 100 – 79 = 21

$$\text{P V Ratio} = \frac{C}{S} \times 100$$

$$= \frac{21}{100} \times 100 = 21\%$$

(i) BES

$$= \frac{\text{Fixed Costs}}{\text{P V Ratio}}$$

$$= \frac{\text{Rs.}1,89,900 + \text{Rs.}58,400 + \text{Rs.}66,700}{21\%}$$

$$= 3,15,000 \times \frac{100}{21} = \text{Rs. } 15,00,000$$

(ii) Profit at the budgeted sales volume

Profit = Contribution – Fixed Costs

Contribution = Sales × PVR

$$\text{Contribution} = 18,50,000 \times \frac{21}{100} = \text{Rs.}3,88,500$$

Profit = Rs. 3,88,500 – Rs. 3,15,000 = Rs. 73,500

(iii) The profit if actual sales drop by 10%

		Rs.
Budgeted Sales	=	18,50,000
Less: 10% drop	=	1,85,000
Net Sales	=	16,65,000

$$\text{Contribution} = 16,65,000 \times \frac{21}{100} = \text{Rs.}3,49,650$$

Profit = Rs. 3,49,650 – Rs. 3,15,000 = Rs. 34,650.

(iv) The profit if actual sales increase by 5% from budgeted sales

		Rs.
Budgeted sales	=	18,50,000
Add: 5% increase	=	92,500
Net sales	=	19,42,500

Contribution $= 19{,}42{,}500 \times \frac{21}{100} =$ Rs. 4,07,925

Profit = Rs. 4,07,925 – 3,15,000 = Rs. 92,925

Problem 27:

The statement of cost of a Radio is as follows:

Material	Rs. 225	Fixed Expenses	Rs. 100
Labour	Rs. 125	Profit	Rs. 150
Variable expenses	Rs. 100	Selling Price	Rs. 700

The number of Radios made and sold are 10,000 units

Find out:

(i) Break even point (in units)

(ii) How may radios (in units) must be produced and sold if the selling price is reduced by Rs. 20 and the same profit is maintained.

Solution:

(i) $\text{BEP (in units)} = \frac{\text{Fixed Expenses}}{\text{Contribution per unit}}$

Contribution p.u = Selling price p.u – Variable Cost p.u.

= 700 – 450 = Rs. 250.

Fixed expenses for 10,000 radios = 10,000 × 100 = Rs.10,00,000.

$\text{BEP (in unit)} = \frac{10{,}00{,}000}{250} = 4{,}000 \text{ units}$

(iii) Present profit for 10,000 units at Rs.150 per unit.

= 10,000 × 150 = Rs.15,00,000.

Present selling price per unit = Rs. 700

Less: Reduction in selling price to be made = Rs. 20

Revised selling price per unit = Rs. 680

Number of units to be produced to earn the present profit of Rs.15,00,000 is:

$$= \frac{\text{Fixed Expenses} + \text{Desired Profit}}{\text{Contribution per unit}}$$

Contribution Per Unit = 680 – 450 = Rs. 230.

$$\frac{10,00,000 + 15,00,000}{230} = 10,870 \text{ units}$$

Problem 28:

From the following data, calculate:

(1) Number of units to be sold to earn a profit of Rs. 1,20,000.

(2) Sales to earn a profit of Rs. 1,20,000.

Selling price per unit Rs. 40.

Variable selling cost per unit Rs.3

Variable manufacturing cost per unit per Rs. 22

Fixed factory overhead Rs. 1,60,000

Fixed selling cost Rs. 20,000.

Solution:

(i) Number **of units** to be sold to earn a profit of Rs. 1,20,000.

$$= \frac{\text{Fixed Expenses} + \text{Desired Profit}}{\text{Contribution per unit}}$$

$$= \frac{1,80,000 + 1,20,000}{40-25}$$

$$= \frac{3,00,000}{15} = 20,000 \text{ units}$$

(ii) Sales to earn a profit of Rs.1,20,000

$$= \frac{\text{Fixed Expenses} + \text{Desired Profit}}{\text{Contribution per unit}} \times \text{Selling Price Per Unit}$$

$$= \frac{3,00,000}{15} \times 40 = \text{Rs. } 8,00,000$$

Problem 29:

You are given:

Margin of safety Rs. 15,000 which represents 30% of sales.

PV/Ratio 40%

Calculate

(a) Sales, (b) Break even sales, (c) Fixed cost, and (d) profit.

Solution:

(a) Sales:

Margin of safety is 30% of sales.

If margin of safety is Rs. 30, sales = Rs. 100.

If margin of safety is Rs. 15,000

$$\text{Sales} = \frac{15,000}{30} \times 100 = \text{Rs. } 50,000$$

(b) Break Even Sales:

BES = Sales – Margin of Safety

= 50,000 – 15,000 = Rs. 35,000

(c) Fixed Cost:

PV Ratio = 40%

:- Contribution is Rs. 40 when sales are Rs. 100.

:- Contribution at break even sales = BES × PV Ratio

$$= 35,000 \times \frac{40}{100} \text{ Rs.}14,000$$

	Rs.
Contribution	14,000
Less: Fixed Cost (bal.fig.)	14,000
Profit at BES	0

(d) Profit:

Contribution = Sales × PV Ratio

$$= 50{,}000 \times \frac{40}{100} = \text{Rs. } 20{,}000$$

Profit = Contribution – Fixed Cost

= 20,000 – 7,500

= 12,500.

Problem 30:

Your are required to calculate

(a) PV Ratio, (b) Margin of Safety, (c) Sales, and (d) Variable Cost from the following figures.

Fixed Cost Rs. 15,000; Profit Rs. 2,000; Break even sales Rs. 75,000

Solution:

(a) PV Ratio:

$$\text{BES} = \frac{\text{Fixed Cost}}{\text{PV Ratio}}$$

$$75{,}000 = \frac{15{,}000}{\text{PV Ratio}}$$

75,000 × PV Ratio = Rs. 15,000.

$$\text{Therefore, PV Ratio} = \frac{15{,}000}{75{,}000} \times 100 = 20\%$$

$$\textbf{(b) Margin of Safety} = \frac{\text{Profit}}{\text{PV Ratio}}$$

$$= \frac{2{,}000}{20\%}$$

$$= \frac{2{,}000}{20} \times 100 = \text{Rs.}10{,}000$$

(c) Sales = BES + Margin of Safety

= 75,000 + 10,000 = Rs. 85,000

(d) Variable Cost = Sales – Contribution

Contribution = Fixed Cost + Profit

$= 15,000 + 2,000 = \text{Rs. } 17,000$

Variable Cost $= 85,000 - 17,000 = \text{Rs. } 68,000.$

Problem 31:

The PV ratio of a firm dealing in precision instrument is 50% and margin of safety is 40%. You are required to workout the BEP and net profit if sales volume is Rs. 5,00,000.

Solution:

Profit = Contribution – Fixed Expenses.

(i) Contribution:

$$\text{PV Ratio} = \frac{\text{Contribution}}{\text{Sales}} \times 100$$

$$50\% = \frac{\text{Contribution}}{5,00,000}$$

$$\text{Contribution} = 5,00,000 \times \frac{50}{100} = \text{Rs. } 2,50,000$$

(ii) Break Even Sales:

	Rs.
Sales	5,00,000
Less : Margin of Safety	2,00,000
(40% of Sales)	
BES	3,00,000

(iii) Fixed Cost:

$$\text{BES} = \frac{\text{Fixed Expenses}}{\text{PV Ratio}}$$

$$3,00,000 = \frac{\text{Fixed Expenses}}{50\%}$$

$$\text{Fixed Expenses} = 3,00,000 \times \frac{50}{100} = \text{Rs.}1,50,000$$

(iv) Profit:

	Rs.
Contribution	2,50,000
Less: Fixed Expenses	1,50,000
Profit	1,00,000

Problem 32:

The competing companies Sun Ltd., and Moon Ltd., produce and sell the same type of product in the same market. For the year ended 31st March, 2002 their forecasted profit and loss accounts are as follows:

Particulars	***Sun Ltd.,*** ***Rs.***	***Rs.***	***Moon Ltd.,*** ***Rs.***	***Rs.***
Sales		5,00,000		5,00,000
Less: Variable Cost	2,75,000		2,50,000	
Fixed Cost	75,000	3,50,000	1,00,000	3,50,000
Estimated Profit		1,50,000		1,50,000

You are required to calculate:

(a) Profit volume ratio, break even point and margin of safety of each business.

(b) State sales volume at which each business will earn a profit of Rs. 75,000

(c) Explain giving reasons which business is likely to earn great profits in the condition of

(i) Heavy demand for the product

(ii) Low demand for the product

Solution:

Particulars	***Sun Ltd.,*** ***Rs.***	***Moon Ltd.,*** ***Rs.***
(a) PV Ratio $= \frac{c}{s} \times 100$	$= \frac{5,00,000 - 2,75,000}{5,00,000} \times 100$ $= \frac{2,25,000}{5,00,000} \times 100$ $= 45\%$	$\frac{5,00,000 - 2,50,000}{5,00,000} \times 100$ $= \frac{2,50,000}{5,00,000} \times 100$ $= 50\%$
BES (in Rs.) $= \frac{\text{Fixed Expenses}}{\text{PV Ratio}}$	$= \frac{75,000}{45} \times 100$	$= \frac{1,00,000}{50} \times 100$

	= Rs. 1,66,667	= Rs. 2,00,000
MOS = Present Sales - BES	= Rs. 5,00,000 – 1,66,667	= Rs. 5,00,000 – 2,00,000
	= Rs. 3,33,333	= Rs. 3,00,000
(b) Sales volume to earn a profit of Rs. 75,000.		
Desired Profit =	$= \frac{75,000 + 75,000}{45} \times 100$	$= \frac{1,75,000}{50} \times 100$
$\frac{\text{Fixed Cost + Desired Profit}}{\text{PV Ratio}}$	= Rs. 3,33,333	= Rs. 3,50,000

(c) **(i) Heavy demand for the product:**

In conditions of heavy demand for the product a company with a higher PV Ratio can earn greater profit. Hence, Moon Ltd., is likely to earn greater profits.

(ii) Low demand for the product:

In conditions of low demand for the product a company with lower BES can earn more profits. In this case Sun Ltd., is likely to earn greater profits.

Problem 33:

The following information relates to production and sale of an article for November and December, 2009.

Particulars	November Rs.	December Rs.
Sales	55,000	80,000
Profit	—	5,000
Loss	2,000	—

Calculate:

(i) Break even sales volume.

(ii) Profit or loss at Rs, 60,000 sales.

(iii) Sales to earn a profit of Rs. 10,000

Solution:

$$\text{PV Ratio} = \frac{\text{Changesin profit}}{\text{Changesin sales}} \times 100$$

$$= \frac{7,000}{25,000} \times 100 = 28\%$$

Fixed Cost:

Fixed Cost = Contribution – Profit

Contribution = Sales × PV Ratio

$$\text{Contribution} = 80{,}000 \times \frac{28}{100} = \text{Rs. } 22{,}400$$

Fixed Cost = 22,400 – 5,000 = Rs. 17,400

(i) $\text{BES} = \dfrac{\text{Fixed Cost}}{\text{PV Ratio}}$

$$= \frac{17{,}400}{28} \times 100$$

= Rs. 62, 143.

(ii) Profit/Loss at Rs. 60,000 sales

Profit = Contribution – Fixed Expenses

Contribution = Sales × PV Ratio

$$= 60{,}000 \times \frac{28}{100} = \text{Rs. } 16{,}800$$

	Rs.
Contribution	16,800
Less: Fixed Expenses	17,400
Loss	(-) 600

(iii) Sales to earn a profit Rs. 10,000

$$= \frac{\text{Fixed Expenses} + \text{Desired Profit}}{\text{PV Ratio}}$$

$$= \frac{17{,}400 + 10{,}000}{28} \times 100$$

$$= \frac{27{,}400}{28} \times 100$$

= Rs. 97,857.

Problem 34:

Vasu Ltd., furnishes you the following information relating to the half-year ended 30th June, 2009.

Fixed Expenses	Rs. 50,000
Sales Value	Rs. 1,50,000
Profit	Rs. 25,000

During the second half of the year, the company has a projected loss of Rs. 20,000.

Calculate:

(i) The break even sales and margin of safety for six months ending 30th June, 2009,

(ii) Expected sales volume for second half of the year assuming that the PV ratio and fixed expenses remain constant in the second half of the year also.

(iii) The break even sales and margin of safety for the whole year 2009.

Solution:

(i) BES and margin of safety for six months ending 30th June, 2009:

$$BES = \frac{\text{Fixed Expenses}}{\text{PV Ratio}}$$

$$\text{PV Ratio} = \frac{C}{S} \times 100$$

Contribution = Fixed Expenses + Profit

Contribution = 50,000 + 25,000 = Rs. 75,000

$$\text{PV Ratio} = \frac{75{,}000}{1{,}50{,}000} \times 100 = 50\%$$

$$BES = \frac{50{,}000}{50} \times 100 = Rs. 1{,}00{,}000$$

Margin of safety = Present Sales – BES

= 1,50,000 – 1,00,000 = Rs. 50,000

(ii) Expected sales for the second half of the year:

Contribution = Fixed Expenses – Loss

= 50,000 – 20,000 = Rs. 30,000

$$\text{Sales} = \frac{\text{Contribution}}{\text{PV Ratio}}$$

$$= \frac{30,000}{50} \times 100$$

Therefore, sales for the second half of the year = Rs. 60,000.

(iii) BES and margin of safety for the whole year:

Fixed expenses for half year Rs. 50,000

Fixed expenses for whole year Rs. 1,00,000

$$\text{BES} = \frac{\text{Fixed Expenses}}{\text{PV Ratio}}$$

$$= \frac{1,50,000}{50} \times 100 = \text{Rs. } 2,00,000$$

Margin of Safety = Present Sales – BES

= 2,10,000 (i.e., 1,50,000 + 60,000) – 2,00,00 = Rs. 10,000.

Problem 35:

From the following data relating to a company, calculate:

(i) The break even sales; and

(ii) Sales required to earn a profit of Rs. 65,000 per period.

Period	*Total Sales Rs.*	*Total Cost Rs.*
I	4,00,000	3,60,000
II	3,50,000	3,25,000

Solution:

$$\text{PV Ratio} = \frac{\text{Changes in Profit}}{\text{Changes in Sales}} \times 100$$

$$= \frac{40,000 - 25,000}{4,00,000 - 3,50,000} \times 100$$

$$= \frac{15,000}{50,000} \times 100 = 30\%$$

Fixed Cost = Contribution – Profit

Contribution = Sales × PV Ratio

$$\text{Contribution} = 4,00,000 \times \frac{30}{100} = \text{Rs.}1,20,000$$

	Rs.
Contribution	1,20,000
Less: Profit	40,000
Fixed Cost	**80,000**

(i) BES (in Rs.) $= \frac{\text{Fixed Cost}}{\text{PV Ratio}}$

$$= \frac{80,000}{30} \times 100$$

= Rs. 2,66,667.

(ii) Sales required to earn a profit of Rs. 65,000

$$= \frac{\text{Fixed Cost} + \text{Desired Profit}}{\text{PV Ratio}}$$

$$= \frac{80,000 + 65,000}{30\%}$$

$$= \frac{1,45,000}{30} \times 100$$

= Rs. 4,83,333.

Problem 36:

Rakshaa Ltd., a multi-product company, furnishes you the following data relating to the year 2005.

	First half of the year	*Second half of the year*
Sales	Rs. 50,000	Rs. 55,000
Total Cost	Rs. 45,000	Rs. 49,000

Assuming that there is no change in prices and variable costs and that the fixed expenses are incurred equally in the two half-year periods. Calculate for the year 2005.

(i) The profit volume ratio

(ii) Fixed expenses

(iii) Break even sales

(iv) Percentage of margin of safety.

Solution:

Profit for first half = Sales – Total Cost

= 50,000 – 45,000 = Rs. 5,000

Profit for second half = 55,000 – 49,000 = Rs. 6,000

(i) PV Ratio $= \frac{\text{Change in Profit}}{\text{Change in Sale}} \times 100$

$$= \frac{6{,}000 - 5{,}000}{55{,}000 - 50{,}000} \times 100$$

$$= \frac{1{,}000}{5{,}000} \times 100 = 20\%$$

(ii) Fixed Expenses = Contribution – Profit

Contribution = Sales × PV Ratio

$$\text{Contribution} = 50{,}000 \times \frac{20}{100} = \text{Rs.}10{,}000$$

Fixed Expenses = 10,000 – 5,000 = Rs. 5,000

Fixed expenses for half-year = Rs. 5,000

@ Fixed Expenses for whole year = Rs. 5,000 × 2 = Rs. 10,000

(iii) BES $= \frac{\text{Fixed Expenses}}{\text{PV Ratio}}$

$$= \frac{10{,}000}{20} \times 100 = \text{Rs.}50{,}000$$

(v) Percentage of Margin of Safety

MOS = Present Sales – BES

= 1,05,000, i.e., (50,000 + 55,000) – 50,000 = Rs. 55,000

$$\text{Percentage of Margin of Safety} = \frac{55,000}{1,05,000} \times 100$$

= 52.38%

Problem 37:

Assuming that the cost structure and selling prices remain the same in periods I[st] and IInd find out:

(i) PV ratio

(ii) BE Sales

(iii) Profit when sales are Rs. 1,00,000

(iv) Sales required to earn a profit of Rs. 25,000; and

(v) Margin of safety in I[st] period

Period	*Sales (in Rs.)*	*Profit (in Rs.)*
I	1,20,000	9,000
II	1,40,000	14,000

Solution:

i) PV Ratio $= \dfrac{\text{Changes in Profit}}{\text{Changes in Sales}} \times 100$

$$= \frac{14,000 - 9,000}{1,40,000 - 1,20,000} \times 100 = \frac{5,000}{20,000} \times 100 = 25\%$$

(ii) BE Sales $= \dfrac{\text{Fixed Expenses}}{\text{PV Ratio}}$

Fixed Expenses = Contribution – Profit

Contribution = Sales × PV Ratio

$$\text{Contribution} = 1,40,000 \times \frac{25}{100} = \text{Rs.}\,35,000$$

Fixed Expenses = 35,000 – 14,000 = Rs. 21,000

$$\text{BES} = \frac{21,000}{25} \times 100 = \text{Rs.}\,84,000$$

(iii) Profit when sales are Rs. 1,00,000

Profit = Contribution – Fixed Expenses

Contribution = Sales × PV Ratio

$$\text{Contribution} = 1{,}00{,}000 \times \frac{25}{100} = \text{Rs. } 25{,}000$$

Profit = 25,000 – 21,000 = Rs. 4,000

(iv) Sales required to earn a profit of Rs. 25,000

$$= \frac{\text{Fixed Expenses + Desired Profit}}{\text{PV Ratio}} = \frac{21{,}000 + 25{,}000}{25} \times 100$$

$$= \frac{46{,}000}{25} \times 100 = \text{Rs. } 1{,}84{,}000.$$

(v) Margin of Safety in first period = Present Sales – BES

= 1,20,000 – 84,000 = Rs. 36,000

Problem 38:

The following relates to production and sale of an article for January and February 2002.

Particulars	***November Rs.***	***December Rs.***
Sales	38,000	65,000
Profit	—	3,000
Loss	2,400	—

Calculate:

(i) PVR

(ii) Fixed Cost

(iii) Break even sales volume.

Solution:

(i) **PV Ratio** $= \frac{\text{Change in Profit}}{\text{Change in Sales}} \times 100$

$$= \frac{5{,}400}{27{,}000} \times 100 = 20\%$$

(ii) **Fixed Cost:**

Fixed Cost = Contribution – Profit

Contribution = Sales × PV Ratio

$$\text{Contribution} = 65{,}000 \times \frac{20}{100} = \text{Rs. } 13{,}000$$

Fixed Cost = 13,000 –35,000 = Rs. 10,000

$$\text{(i) BES} = \frac{\text{Fixed Cost}}{\text{PV Ratio}}$$

$$= \frac{10{,}000}{20} \times 100$$

= Rs. 50,000.

Formula

$$\text{(1) PVR} = \frac{\text{Contribution}}{\text{Sales}} \times 100$$

$$\text{(2) PVR} = \frac{\text{Changes in Profit}}{\text{Changes in Sales}} \times 100$$

$$\text{(3) BEP (in Unit)} = \frac{\text{Fixed Expenses}}{\text{Contribution Per Unit}}$$

$$\text{(4) BEP (in Unit)} = \frac{\text{Fixed Expenses}}{\text{Contribution Per Unit}} \times \text{Selling Price Per Unit}$$

(or)

$$\text{BEP (in Unit)} = \frac{\text{Fixed Expenses}}{\text{Contribution}} \times \text{Sales}$$

$$\text{BEP (in Unit)} = \frac{\text{Fixed Expenses}}{\text{PVR}}$$

(5) Margin of Safety $= \dfrac{\text{Profit}}{\text{PVR}}$ (or) Actual Sales – Break Even Sales

(6) Number of units to be sold to earn a profit of Rs. ....

$$= \frac{\text{Fixed Expenses} + \text{Desired Profit}}{\text{Contribution Per Unit}}$$

(7) Sales required to earn a profit of Rs.———

$$= \frac{\text{Fixed Expenses} + \text{Desired Profit}}{\text{Contribution Per Unit}}$$

(or)

$$= \frac{\text{Fixed Expenses} + \text{Desired Profit}}{\text{Contribution}}$$

(or)

$$= \frac{\text{Fixed Expenses} + \text{Desired Profit}}{\text{PVR}}$$

MODEL QUESTIONS

OBJECTIVE TYPE

Choose the best answer from the given alternatives:

(i) Contribution margin is also known as —

(a) Marginal Income (b) Net Profit;

(c) Gross Profit (d) All of the above

Ans. a

(ii) In which costing method the fixed overheads are also considered along with the valuation of stock?

(a) Marginal Costing; (b) Direct Costing

(c) Absorption Costing (d) None of the above

Ans. c

(iii) When fixed cost is Rs. 20,000 and PV ratio is 40%, the break even point will be-

(a) Rs. 28,000 (b) Rs. 40,000

(c) Rs. 50,000 (d) Rs. 75,000

Ans. c

(iv) When margin safety is 25% and PV ratio is 50%, the profit will be-

(a) 12.5% (b) 25%

(c) 7.5% (d) 15%

Ans. a

(v) When sales are Rs. 3 lakh, fixed costs, Rs. 40,000, PV ratio 40% the amount of profit will be-

(a) Rs. 80,000 (b) Rs. 60,000

(c) Rs. 1,20,000 (d) Rs. 75,000

Ans. a

(vi) Break even analysis is also called-

(a) Cost Volume Profit analysis (b) Abnormal Cost Analysis

(c) Fixed Cost Analysis (d) All of the above

Ans. a

(vii) Marginal Cost means

(a) Additional Cost (b) Variable Cost

(c) Indirect cost (d) Fixed Cost

Ans. b

(viii) PV Ratio is 60%, Marginal cost of the product is Rs. 20, selling price is —

(a) Rs. 30 (b) Rs. 40

(c) Rs. 50 (d) Rs. 45

Ans. c

(ix) A large margin of safety indicates-

(a) Over production (b) Over capitalisation

(c) The soundness of the business (d) None of the above

Ans. c

(x) Fixed Cost means-

(a) Sunk Cost (b) Uncontrollable

(c) Flexible Cost (d) All of the above

Ans. a

(xi) Period cost means-

(a) Variable Cost (b) Prime Cost

(c) Fixed Cost (d) All of the above

Ans. c

(xii) The formula for calculating break even point in rupees is-

(a) $\frac{S - V}{S} \times 100$ (b) $\frac{F}{\text{PV Ratio}}$

(c) $\frac{P}{\text{PV Ratio}}$ (d) $\frac{F + P}{\text{PV Ratio}}$

Ans. b

State True or False:

1. Break even chart depicts cost-volume-profit relationship. **(True)**
2. The technique of marginal costing can be used in conjunction with standard costing or budgetary control. **(False)**
3. Contribution is the difference between the sales and the fixed cost. **(False)**
4. Semi-variable costs form a part of product cost in marginal costing. **(False)**
5. The fixed costs are included in the valuation of work-in-progress and finished goods stocks in the case of marginal costing. **(False)**
6. At break even level, the company earns only a minimum profit. **(False)**
7. Margin of safety $= \frac{\text{Profit}}{\text{PV Ratio}}$ **(True)**
8. PV Ratio indicates the relationship between profit and sales. **(False)**
9. The differential cost analysis can be made in the case of both absorption costing as well as marginal costing. **(True)**
10. The technique of marginal costing helps in making decisions involving alternative choices **(True)**

11. The absorption costing technique is also termed as traditional or full cost method. **(True)**
12. Contribution is also known as gross margin. **(True)**

Fill in the Blanks:

1. _________ is the difference between sales and marginal cost of sales. **(Contribution)**
2. Sales over and above break even sales are known as _____________ **(Margin of safety)**
3. ___________ is a technique where only the variable costs are considered while computing the cost of a product. **(Marginal Costing)**
4. Absorption costing technique is also termed as ___________ **(Traditional or full cost method)**
5. In marginal costing stock of finished goods is valued at ________ cost. **(Marginal)**
6. Both fixed and variable costs are charged to products in the case of _______ costing. **(Absorption)**
7. Profit-volume ratio shows the relationship between _______ and ______ **(Contribution, Sales)**
8. At break even point, total cost is equal to___________ **(Total sales)**
9. The intersection of ____ line and ______ line makes the angle of incidence **(Sales, Total cost)**
10. The break even point _______ when selling price is increased. **(Decreases)**

Short Answer Type Questions:

1. Define Marginal Cost and Marginal Costing.
2. What do you mean by PV Ratio?
3. What is break even point?
4. Define angle of incidence.
5. What is cash break even point?
6. What do you mean by composite break even point?
7. Distinguish between absorption costing and marginal costing.
8. Briefly explain the cost-volume-profit analysis.
9. Explain the concept of 'Margin of safety'.
10. What is meant by differential cost?

Essay Type Questions:

1. Explain the concept of 'Marginal Costing'. What are the characteristics and assumptions of marginal costing?
2. What is meant by break even analysis? Discuss the assumptions and limitations of this technique.
3. "The technique of marginal costing can be a valuable aid to management." Discuss.

4. Briefly explain the importance of cost-volume-profit relationship in business management.
5. What benefits are gained from marginal costing? Are there any pitfalls in the application of marginal costing? Discuss these matters critically.
6. Explain the advantages and limitations of marginal costing.
7. What do you understand by contribution? How does it help management in solving various problems?
8. "The effect of a price reduction is always to reduce the PV ratio, to raise break even point, and to shorten the margin of safety." Explain and illustrate the above by numerical examples.

EXERCISES

1. Calculate the PV ratio and Break even point from the following particulars:

	Rs.
Sales	5,00,000
Fixed cost	1,00,000
Profit	1,50,000

(Ans: PVR = 50%, BEP = Rs. 2,00,000.)

2. Calculate break even point from the following particulars

	Rs.
Fixed expenses	1,50,000
Variable cost per unit	10
Selling price per unit	15

(Ans: BEP (in units) 30,000 in Rs. 4,50,000.)

3. From the following information find out the amount of profit earned during the year using the marginal costing technique:

Fixed cost	Rs. 5,00,000
Variable cost	Rs. 10 per unit
Selling price	Rs. 15 per unit
Output level	1,50,000 unit

(Ans: Profit Rs. 2,50,000.)

4. Calculate break even point

Selling price	Rs. 50/unit
Variable cost	Rs. 30/unit
Fixed cost	Rs. 2,000

(Ans: BEP in units – 100, BEP in Rs. 5,000)

5. From the followings calculate:
   (i) PVR
   (ii) BES
   (iii) MOS
   (iv) How many additional units should be sold to earn the same amount of profit if the selling price is reduced to Rs. 20.?

	Rs.
Sales (Rs. 25 per unit)	1,00,000
Variable cost	72,000
Fixed cost	16,800

(Ans: i) 28% ii) Rs. 60,000 iii) Rs. 40,000 iv) 10,000 units)

6. The statements of cost of a cycle is as follows:

	Rs
Material	200
Labour	100
Variable expenses	25
Fixed expenses	75
Profit	125
Selling price	525

The number of cycles made and sold are 10,000 units.

Find out —
   (i) Break even point
   (ii) How many cycles must be produced and sold if the selling price is reduced by Rs. 25 and the same profit is maintained?

(Ans: (i) 3,750 units, (ii) 11,428 units)

7. The PV ratio of a firm dealing in precision instrument is 50% and the margin of safety is 40%. You are required to workout the BEP and the net profit if sales volume is Rs. 50,00,000.

(Ans: BES Rs. 30,00,000, Net profit Rs. 10,00,000)

8. You are given the following:

Budgeted output	80,000 units
Fixed expenses	Rs. 4,00,000

Variable expenses per unit Rs. 10

Selling price per unit Rs. 20

Find out —

(i) Break even point.

(ii) What will be the new BEP if the selling price is reduced to Rs. 15 per unit?

(iii) Also find out the break even point if selling price is Rs. 25.

(Ans: (i) BEP(units) : 40,000; BEP(Rs.) 8,00,000;

(ii) BEP(units) : 80,000; BEP(Rs.) 12,00,000;

(iii) BEP(units) : 26,667; BEP(Rs.) . 6,66,675)

9. From the following figures calculate:

(i) BEP; (ii) Margin of safety; and (iii) Sales to earn a profit of Rs. 1,20,000

	Rs.
Sales	6,00,000
Variable cost	3,75,000
Fixed cost	1,80,000

(Ans: Rs. 4,80,000; (ii) Rs. 1,20,000, and (iii) Rs. 8,00,000)

10. From the following data, calculate —

(i) PV ratio

(ii) Profit when sales are Rs. 20,000

(iii) New break even point if selling price is reduced by 20%

Fixed expenses Rs. 4,000 Break even point Rs.10,000.

(Ans: (i) P/V ratio 40% (ii) profit Rs.4,000 (iii) New BEP Rs. 16,000)

11. Raja Corporation Ltd., has prepared the following budget estimates for the year 2008 – 09. Sales units 15,000; Fixed Expenses Rs. 34,000; sales value Rs. 1,50,000; variable costs Rs. 6 per unit. You are required to —

(i) Find the PV ratio, break even point and margin of safety.

(ii) calculate the revised PV ratio, break even point and margin of safety in each following:

(1) Decreasing of 10% in selling price, and

(2) Increase of 10% variable costs.

(Ans):

	Q.No.	PVR(%)	BEP(UNITS)	BEP(Rs.)	MOS(Rs.)
(i)		40	8,500	85,000	65,000
(ii)	1	33.33	11,333	1,01,997	33,033
(ii)	2	34	10,000	1,00,000	50,000

12. The sales turnover and profit during two periods were as follows:

	Sales	Profit
	Rs.	Rs.
Period I	20,00,000	2,00,000
Period II	30,00,000	4,00,000

Calculate:

a. PV Ratio

b. Fixed Cost

c. Break even point

d. Profit when sales are Rs. 10,00,000

e. Sales required to earn a profit of Rs. 5,00,000

(Ans: (a) 20% (b) Rs. 2,00,000 (c) Rs. 10,00,000 (d) NIL (e) Rs. 35,00,000)

13. Following information has been made available from the cost records of United Automobiles Ltd., manufacturing spare parts:

	Per unit
Direct Materials	
X	Rs. 8
Y	Rs. 6
Direct wages	
X	24 hours @ 25 paise per hour
Y	16 hours @ 25 paise per hour
Variable overheads	150% of Direct wages
Fixed overheads (total)	Rs. 750
Selling price	
X	Rs. 25
Y	Rs. 20

The directors want to be acquainted with the desirability of adopting any one of the following alternative sale mixes in the budget for the next period:

(i) 250 units of X 250 units of Y

(ii) 400 units of Y only

(iii) 400 units of X and 100 units of Y

(iv) 150 units of X and 350 units of Y

State which of the alternative sales mixes you would recommend to the management.

(Ans: The alternative (iv) is most profitable since it gives the maximum profit of Rs. 950)

14. The cost per unit of three product are given below:

	A	*B*	*C*
Direct materials	20	16	18
Direct labour	12	14	12
Variable expenses	8	10	6
Fixed expenses	6	6	4
Total cost	46	46	40
Selling price	64	60	52
Number of units produced	10,000	5,000	8,000

Production arrangements are such that if one product is given up, the others can be raised by 50%. Director proposed to drop product C. Present suitable analyses of the data indicating whether the proposal should be accepted.

(Ans: The proposal to give up product C is not advisable.)

15. From the following data, calculate the break even point at this point:

	Rs.
Selling price per unit	25
Direct material cost per unit	8
Direct labour cost per unit	5
Fixed overheads	24,000

Variable overheads @ 60% on direct labour trade discount 4%

If sales are 15% and 20% above the break even volume, determine the net profit.

(Ans : BEP (units)3,000: BEP (Rs.) 72,000

Net profit if sales are 15% above the BEP Rs. 3,600

Net profit if sales are 20% above the BEPRs. 4,800)

16. Two competing companies ABC Ltd., and XYZ Ltd., produce and sell same type of products in the same market. For the year ended March 2003, their forecasted profit and loss accounts are as follows:

	ABC Ltd.		XYZ Ltd	
	Rs.	Rs.	Rs.	Rs.
Sales		3,00,000		3,00,000
Less: Variable Cost	2,00,000		1,50,000	
Fixed Costs	25,000	2,25,000	75,000	2,25,000
Forecasted net profit before tax		75,000		75,000

(i) PV Ratio

(ii) Break even sales volume

You are also required to state which company is likely to earn greater profits in conditions of:

(a) How Demand, and

(b) High Demand

(Ans: PV Ratio ABC Ltd. 33.33%, XYZ Ltd. 50%
BES: ABC Ltd. Rs. 75,000, XYZ Ltd. Rs. 1,50,000
Low Demand: ABC Ltd. High Demand: XYZ Ltd.)

17. From the following data, which product would you recommend to be manufactured in a factory, time being the key factor?

Particulars	*Per unit of Product A Rs.*	*Per unit of Product B Rs.*
Direct material	24	14
Direct labour @ Re. 1 per hour	2	3
Variable overhead @ 2 per hour	4	6
Selling price	100	110
Standard time to produce	2 hours	1 hours

(Ans: Product A more profitable and is recommended to be manufactured.)

18. A factory engaged in manufacturing plastic buckets is working at 40% capacity and produces 10,000 buckets per annum.

The present cost break-up for bucket is as under:

Material	Rs. 10
Labour	Rs. 3
Overheads	Rs. 5 (60% fixed)

The selling price is Rs. 20 per bucket

If it is decided to work the factory at 50% capacity, the selling price falls by 3%. At 90% capacity the selling price falls by 5% accompanied by a similar fall in the prices of material.

You are required to calculate the profit at 50% and 90% capacities and also calculate the break even point for the same capacity productions.

(Ans:	**50%**	**90%)**
Profit	**Rs. 25,000**	**Rs. 71,250**
BEP (in units)	**6,818**	**6,667**
BEP (in Rs.)	**Rs. 1,32,270**	**Rs. 1,26,673**

19. Following information has been made available from the cost records of SAMY Ltd., manufacturing spare parts.

Direct Materials	**Per Unit**
V1	Rs. 5.40
V2	Rs. 3.90
Direct Wages	
V1	24 hours at 40 palse per hour
V2	24 hours at 40 paise per hour
Variable Overheads	100% of Wages
Fixed Expenses Rs. 1,000	
Selling Price	
V1	Rs. 26
V2	Rs. 26

The directors want to be acquainted with the desirability of adopting any one of the following alternative sales mixes in the budget for the next period:

(a) 300 units of V1and 300 units of V2.

(b) 600 units of V2 only

(c) 400 units of V1 and 200 units of V2

(d) 250 units of V1 and 250 units of V2

State which of the alternative sales mixes you would recommend to the management?

20. From the following data calculate:

(i) Number of units to be sold to earn a profit of Rs. 2,40,000.

(ii) Sales to earn a profit of Rs. 2,40,000.

Selling price per unit Rs. 60.

Variable selling cost per unit Rs. 4

Variable manufacturing cost per unit per Rs. 26

Fixed factory overhead Rs. 1,80,000

Fixed selling cost Rs. 40,000.

21. From the following data relating to a company calculate:

(i) The break even sales; and

(ii) Sales required to earn a profit of Rs, 50,000 per period.

Period	***Total Sales Rs.***	***Total Cost Rs.***
I	4,00,000	3,50,000
II	3,60,000	3,35,000

22. JC Co., furnishes you the followings:

Particulars	***First year Rs.***	***Second Year Rs.***
Sales	8,10,000	10,26,000
Profit	21,600	64,800

From the above, compute the followings assuming that the fixed cost remains the same in both the periods :

(i) PVR

(ii) Fixed cost

(iii) BES

(iv) Profit or loss when sales are Rs. 6,48,000

(v) Sales required to earn a profit of Rs. 1,08,000

(Ans: (i) 20% (ii) Rs. 1,40,400 (iii) Rs. 7,02,000

(iv) Loss Rs. 10,800 (v) Rs. 12,42,000)

23. Rakesh Ltd., manufactures and sells four types of products under the brand names A,B,C and D. The sales mix in value comprises 33 1/3%, 41 2/3%, 16 2/3% and 8 1/3% of A,B,C and D respectively. The total budgeted sales (100%) is Rs. 60,000 per month. Operating costs are (percentage of selling price)

A	60%
B	68%
C	80%
D	40%

Fixed Costs = Rs. 14,700 per month.

Calculate the break even point for the products on an overall basis.

(Ans: A Rs. 14,000 B Rs. 17,500 C Rs. 7,000 D Rs. 3,500)

☆☆☆

CHAPTER 5

BUDGETING AND BUDGETARY CONTROL

- Budgeting and Budgetary Control
    - Definition
    - Importance
    - Essentials
- Classifications of Budget
- Master Budget
- Preparation of Different Budget

Steps in Budgetary Control.

BUDGET

Meaning

The word 'budget' is derived from the French word "BOUGETTE" which means a small leather bag in which funds are appropriated for meeting anticipated expenses.

Budget is a blue print of a plan expressed in quantitative terms. It is prepared for a definite period well in advance. A budget is the monetary and/or quantitative expression of business plans and policies to be pursued in the future period of time.

Definition

According to Wheldon "A budget is a standard with which to measure the actual achievements of people, department, etc."

BUDGETARY CONTROL

Meaning

Budgetary control has become an essential tool of the management for controlling costs and maximising profits. Budgetary control is the process of determining various budgeted figures for the enterprises for the future period and then comparing the budgeted figures with the actual performance.

Definition

According to Scoot J.A. "It is the system of management control and accounting in which all operations are forecasted and so far as possible planned ahead and the actual results compared with the forecasted and planned ones".

Budget, Budgeting and Budgetary Control

A budget is a blue print of a plan expressed in quantitative terms. On the other hand, budgeting is a technique for formulating budgets.

Budgetary control refers to the principles, procedures and practices of achieving given objectives through budgets.

Objective of Budgetary Control

The objectives are summarised as follows:

- To reduce wastages
- To predict the capital expenditures
- To increase profitability
- To record the actual performance
- To correct deviations from established standards

Advantages of Budgetary Control

- It is very helpful for getting bank credit
- It helps the management to control the various activities
- It helps in predicting the financial needs
- It defines the policies of the business
- It is an important tool for measuring performance
- It also enables the introduction of incentive schemes

- It helps the management to reduce the costs

Limitations of Budgetary Control

- There may be lack of co-operation and teamwork among different departments
- It discourage the efficient employees by fixing the targets
- It is only a tool for management but not a substitute for decisions-making
- It fully depends upon the support from the top management failing which it will collapse
- Every department tries to get the maximum funds under budgets which is bound to create conflicts among them

Steps in Implementation of a Budgetary Control System

(1) **Organisation Chart:** There should be well defined organisation chart for budgetary control. The chief executive should be the overall incharge of the budgetary system.

(2) **Budget Manual:** It is a document which spells out the duties and responsibilities of each employee.

Some important matters covered in this are

Objectives of budgetary control	:	Duties and powers of the budget officer;
Functions of budget committee	:	Time table for all stages of budgeting;
Procedure to be followed in the entire system	:	Length of various budget periods;

(3) **Budget Centres:** A budget centre is that part of the organisation for which the budget is prepared. A budget centre may be a department, or a section of the department. The establishment of budget centre is essential for covering all parts of the organisation. The budget centres are also necessary for cost control purpose.

(4) **Budget Committee:** The budget committee will consists of heads of the various departments such as production, sales, finance, etc; with the budget controller as its chairman. It will be the duty of the budget committee to submit, discuss and finally approve of the budget figures.

(5) **Budget Period:** A budget period is the length of time for which a budget is prepared. The budget period depends upon a number of factors. The budget period depends upon the following considerations:

(a) The type of budget, i.e., sales budget, production budget, raw materials purchase budget, capital expenditure budget, etc. A capital expenditure budget may be for a longer period, i.e., three to five years while the purchase, sale budgets may be for one year.

(b) The nature of demand for the products.

(c) The timings for the availability of finances.

(d) The economic situation of the cycles.

(e) The length of trade cycles.

(6) Key Factor: It is also known as limiting factor or governing factor or principal budget factor. A key factor is one which restricts the volume of production. It may arise due to the shortage of material, labour, capital, plant capacity or sales.

Classification of Budget

These budgets are also known as functional budgets. These budgets relate to the different activities of the firm. Their number depends upon the size and nature of the business. The following are the various classification of functional budgets.

- Production budget
- Production cost budget
- Selling and distribution overhead budget
- Sales budget
- Master budget

Raw materials budget

Labour budget

Capital expenditure budget

Cash budget

(1) **Production Budget:** The preparation of production budget is dependent on the sales budget. Production budget is an estimate of quantity of goods that must be produced during the budget period. Production may be calculated as follows:

Estimated Production = Estimated Sales + Desired Closing Stock – Opening Stock

Problem 1:

Prepare a production budget for three months ending 31.3.2009 for a factory producing four products.

Type of product	*Opening stock (units)*	*Sales (units)*	*Closing stock (units)*
J1	3,000	15,000	7,500
J2	4,500	22,500	6,000
J3	6,000	19,500	4,500
J4	7,500	18,000	3,000

Solution:

Production budget for three months ending 31.3.2009

Particulars	***J1***	***J2***	***J3***	***J4***
Estimated Sales	15,000	22,500	19,500	18,000
Add: Desired closing stock	7,500	6,000	4,500	3,000
	22,500	**28,500**	**24,000**	**21,000**

Less: Opening stock	3,000	4,500	6,000	7,500
Estimated production	19,500	24,000	18,000	13,500

Problem 2:

Rakshaa Limited has prepared the following sales budget for the first five months of 2009:

Month	*Sales Budget (in units)*
January	10,800
February	15,600
March	12,200
April	10,400
May	9,800

The inventory of finished products at the end of every month is to be equal to 25% of the sales estimate for the next month. On January 1, 2009 there were 2,700 units of product on hand. There is no work-in-process at the end of any month.

Prepare a production budget for the first quarter of 2009.

Solution:

Production Budget (Units)

Particulars	*Jan.*	*Feb.*	*Mar.*
Estimated sales	10,800	15,600	12,200
Add: Desired closing stock	3,900	3,050	2,600
	14,700	18,650	14,800
Less: Opening stock	2,700	3,900	3,050
Estimated production	12,000	14,750	11,750

Problem 3:

Prepare a production budget for three months ending 30.6.2009

Month	**Estimated sales**
April	1,40,000
May	1,60,000
June	1,30,000
July	1,20,000

It is the policy of the company to maintain 50% of the month's sales as opening stock.

Solution:

Production Budget (Units)

Particulars	*April*	*May*	*June*
Estimated Sales	1,40,000	1,60,000	1,30,000
Add: Desired closing stock	80,000	65,000	60,000
	2,20,000	2,25,000	1,90,000
Less: Opening stock	70,000	80,000	65,000
Estimated production	**1,50,000**	**1,45,000**	**1,25,000**

Problem 4:

JJ Ltd., plans to sell 1,10,000 units of a certain product-line in the first fiscal quarter, 1,20,000 units in the second quarter, 1,30,000 units in the third quarter and 1,50,000 units in the fourth quarter and 1,40,000 units in the first quarter of the following year. At the beginning of the first quarter, there are 14,000 units of product in stock. At the end of each quarter, the company plans to have an inventory equal to one-fifth of the sales for the next fiscal quarter.

How many units must be manufactured in each quarter of the current year?

Solution:

Production Budget (Units)

Particulars	*I Quarter Units*	*II Quarter Units*	*III Quarter Units*	*VI Quarter Units*
Estimated Sales	1,10,000	1,20,000	1,30,000	1,50,000
Add: Desired closing stock	24,000	26,000	30,000	28,000
	1,34,000	1,46,000	1,60,000	1,78,000
Less: Opening stock	14,000	24,000	26,000	30,000
Estimated production	1,20,000	1,22,000	1,34,000	1,48,000

Problem 5:

The sales director of a manufacturing company reports that next year he expects to sell 60,000units of a particular product. The production department gives the following figures:

Two kinds of raw materials A and B are required for manufacturing the product. Each product requires three units of material A and four units of material B. The estimated opening balances next year will be:

Finished product – 13,000 units, material A – 10,000 units, material B – 17,000 units.

The desirable closing balances at the end of the year are:

Finished product – 18,000 units, Material A – 15,000 units, Material B – 20,000 units.

Draw up a materials purchase budget.

Solution:

Production Budget (in units)

Particulars	*Units*
Estimated Sales	60,000
Add: Desired closing stock	18,000
	78,000
Less: Opening stock	13,000
Estimated production	**65,000**

Materials Purchase Budget

Particulars	*Material 'A'*	*Material 'B'*
Estimated Sales A 65,000 × 3 B 65,000 × 4	1,95,000	2,60,000
Add: Desired closing stock	15,000	20,000
	2,10,000	2,80,000
Less: Opening stock	10,000	17,000
Estimated production	2,00,000	2,63,000

Problem 6:

Your company manufactures two products A and B. A forecast of the number of units to be sold in the first seven months of the year is given below:

	January	*February*	*March*	*April*	*May*	*June*	*July*
Product A	1,000	1,200	1,600	2,000	2,400	2,400	2,000
Product B	2,800	2,800	2,400	2,000	1,600	1,600	1,800

It is anticipated that,

(i) There will be no work-in-progress at the end of any month;

(ii) Finished units equal to half the sales for the next month will be in stock at the end of each month (including the previous December)

Budgeted production and production costs for the whole year are as follows:

	Product A	*Product B*
Production (units)	22,000	24,000
Per unit :		
Direct material	Rs. 10	Rs. 15
Direct labour	Rs. 5	Rs. 10
Total factory overhead apportioned	Rs. 88,000	Rs. 72,000

Prepare for the six months ending 30th June, a production budget for each month and summarised production cost budget.

Solution:

Production Budget

PRODUCT A

(For Six months ending 30th June)

Particulars	*January*	*February*	*March*	*April*	*May*	*June*
Estimated Sales	1,000	1,200	1,600	2,000	2,400	2,400
Add: Desired closing stock	600	800	1,000	1,200	1,200	1,000
	1,600	**2,000**	**2,600**	**3,200**	**3,600**	**3,400**
Less: Opening stock	500	600	800	1,000	1,200	1,200
Estimated Production	**1,100**	**1,400**	**1,800**	**2,200**	**2,400**	**2,200**

Total budgeted production for six months:

1,100 + 1,400 + 1,800 + 2,200 + 2,400 + 2,200 = 11,100 units.

PRODUCT B

(For Six months ending 30th June)

Particulars	*January*	*February*	*March*	*April*	*May*	*June*
Estimated Sales	2,800	2,800	2,400	2,000	1,600	1,600
Add: Desired closing stock	1,400	1,200	1,000	800	800	900
	4,200	**4,000**	**3,400**	**2,800**	**2,400**	**2,500**
Less: Opening stock	1,400	1,400	1,200	1,000	800	800
Estimated production	**2,800**	**2,600**	**2,200**	**1,800**	**1,600**	**1,700**

Total budgeted production:

2800 + 2,600 + 2,200 + 1,800 + 1,600 + 1,700 = 12,700 Units.

Summarised Production Cost Budget

Particulars	*Product A (Output 11,100 units)*		*Product B (Output 12,700 units)*		*Total Rs.*
	Per Unit Rs.	*Amount Rs.*	*Per Unit Rs.*	*Amount Rs.*	
Direct Material	10.00	1,11,000	15.00	1,90,500	3,01,500
Direct Labour	5.00	55,500	10.00	1,27,000	1,82,500
Overheads	4.00	44,400	3.00	38,100	82,500
Cost of Production	**19.00**	**2,10,900**	**28.00**	**3,55,600**	**5,66,500**

Working:

$$\text{Factory Overheads Per Unit} = \frac{\text{Total Annual Factory Overheads}}{\text{Total Annual Output}}$$

$$\text{Product A} = \frac{88,000}{22,000} = \text{Rs. } 4$$

$$\text{Product B} = \frac{72,000}{24,000} = \text{Rs. } 3$$

Problem 7:

From the following figures prepare raw materials purchase budget for Jan. 2010.

Materials (Units)

	A	*B*	*C*	*D*	*E*	*F*
Estimated stock on January 1	16,000	6,000	24,000	2,000	14,000	28,000
Estimated stock on January 31	20,000	8,000	28,000	4,000	16,000	32,000
Estimated consumption	1,20,000	44,000	1,32,000	36,000	88,000	1,72,000
Standard Price Per Unit	25 p	5 p	15 p	10 p	20 p	30 p

Solution:

Raw Materials Purchase Budget for January, 2010.

Particulars	**A**	**B**	**C**	**D**	**E**	**F**
Estimated consumption	1,20,000	44,000	1,32,000	36,000	88,000	1,72,000
Add : Estimated stock on Jan-31 (units)	20,000	8,000	28,000	4,000	16,000	32,000
	1,40,000	52,000	1,60,000	40,000	1,04,000	2,04,000
Less : Estimated stock on Jan.1	16,000	6,000	24,000	2,000	14,000	28,000

Estimated Purchase (units)	1,24,000	46,000	1,36,000	38,000	90,000	1,76,000
Rate per unit (Rs.)	0.25	0.05	0.15	0.10	0.20	0.30
Estimated purchase (Rs.)	31,000	2,300	20,400	3,800	18,000	52,800

Problem 8:

Prepare a selling overhead budget of Rakesh Ltd., from the estimates given below:

Advertisement	Rs. 10,000
Salaries of the sales department	Rs. 15,000
Expenses of sales department (Fixed)	Rs. 5,000
Salesmen's salaries and dearness allowance	Rs. 20,000

Commission at 2% on sales effected

Carriage outwards: Estimated at 3% on sales

Agents Commission: 10% on Sales

The sales during the period were estimated as follows:

Rs. 5,00,000 including agent's sales	Rs. 50,000
Rs. 6,00,000 including agent's sales	Rs. 60,000
Rs. 6,50,000 including agent's sales	Rs. 75,000

Solution:

Rakesh Ltd.,

Selling Overheads Budget for the period....

Particulars	*Rs.*	*Rs.*	*Rs.*
Estimated Sales (including agent's sales)	5,00,000	6,00,000	6,50,000
Fixed overheads:			
Advertisement	10,000	10,000	10,000
Salaries of the sales department	15,000	15,000	15,000
Expenses of sales department	5,000	5,000	5,000
Salesmen's salaries and DA	20,000	20,000	20,000
	50,000	50,000	50,000
Variable overheads:			
Salesmen's commission	9,000	10,800	11,500
Carriage outward 3% on sales	15,000	18,000	19,500
Agent's commission	5,000	6,000	7,500
Total selling overheads	**79,000**	**84,800**	**88,500**

Problem 9:

From the following particulars prepare a sales overhead budget for the months of June, July and August:

	Rs.
Advertisement	7,500
Salaries of the sales department	10,000
Expenses of the sales department	3,000
Counter salesmen's salaries	10,000

Commission to counter salesmen at 2% on their sales.

Travelling salesman's commission at 5% on their sales and expenses at 5% on their sales.

The sales during the period were estimated as follows:

Month	*Counter Sales Rs.*	*Travelling Salesman's Sales Rs.*
June	2,00,000	20,000
July	2,50,000	30,000
August	3,00,000	25,000

Solution:

Selling Overheads Budget for the period June to August

Particulars	*June (Rs.)*	*July (Rs.)*	*August (Rs.)*
Counter sales	2,00,000	2,50,000	3,00,000
Travelling salesman's sales	20,000	30,000	25,000
Total Sales	**2.20,000**	**2,80,000**	**3,25,000**
Sales Overheads:			
Advertisement	7,500	7,500	7,500
Salaries of the sales dept	10,000	10,000	10,000
Expenses of the sales dept	3,000	3,000	3,000
Counter salesmen's salaries	10,000	10,000	10,000
Commission to counter salesmen at 2%	4,000	5,000	6,000
Commission to travelling salesman at 5%	1,000	1,500	1,250
Travelling expenses at 5%	1,000	1,500	1,250
Total Sales Overheads	**36,500**	**38,500**	**39,000**

Problem 10:

JJ Ltd., manufactures two brands of pen Hero and Zero. The sales division of the company has three departments in different areas of the country.

The sales budget for year ending 31st December, 2009 were:

Hero – Department I – 3,00,000; Department II – 5,62,500; Department III – 1,80,000 and Zero – Department I – 4,00,000; Department II – 6,00,000; and Department III – 20,000. Sales prices are Rs. 3 and Rs. 1.20 in all departments.

It is estimated that by forced sales promotion the sale of 'Zero' in Department I will increase by 1,75,000. It is also expected that by increasing production and arranging extensive advertisement, Department III will be enabled to increase the sale of 'Zero' by 50,000.

It is recognised that the estimated sales by department II represent an unsatisfactory target. It is agreed to increase both estimates by 20%.

Prepare a sales budget for the year 2010.

Solution:

Sales Budget for 2010

Department	*Hero* SP P/U Rs. 3		*Zero* SP P/U Rs. 1.20		*Total*
	Units	*Rs.*	*Units*	*Rs.*	*Rs.*
Department I	3,00,000	9,00,000	5,75,000	6,90,000	5,90,000
Department II	6,75,000	20,25,000	7,20,000	8,64,000	8,89,000
Department III	1,80,000	5,40,000	70,000	84,000	6,24,000
Total	**11,55,000**	**34,65,000**	**13,65,000**	**16,38,000**	**21,03,000**

Problem 11:

According to the sales of your company, the sales of the company's product is slacking and the budgeted sales of 1,50,000 units per year can only be met if the trade discount is raised from 25% to 30%. If the discount is raised to 35%, the sales will increase by 20% over the budget, for which the production capacity exists.

Indicate which of the two alternatives is more profitable. The retail price of the product is Rs. 10 each. The cost of production is Rs. 6 of which Rs. 4 is variable.

Solution:

Comparativestatement

Particulars	*30% Discount (1,50,000 Units)*	*35% Discount (1,80,000 Units)*
Gross sales	15,00,000	18,00,000
Less: Discount	4,50,000	6,30,000
Net sales (A)	10,50,000	11,70,000
Variable cost (Units × 4)	6,00,000	7,20,000
Fixed cost(1,50,000 × 2)	3,00,000	3,00,000
Total costs (B)	9,00,000	10,20,000
Profit (A–B)	**1,50,000**	**1,50,000**

(**Note***:* It is clear from the above statement that both alternatives are earning the same amount of profit. Hence, it is advisable that the company must go for other sales promotion policies.)

Problem 12:

Summarised below are the income and expenditure forecasts for the months of March to July 2009.

Month	*Sales Rs.*	*Purchases Rs.*	*Wages Rs.*
March	60,000	36,000	9,000
April	62,000	38,000	8,000
May	64,000	33,000	10,000
June	58,000	39,000	8,500
July	56,000	39,000	9,500

Prepare cash budget for three months ending on 31st July, 2009.

(i) Cash balance on 1st May, 2009 Rs. 8,000.

(ii) Advance tax Rs. 8,000 payable in March and June each.

(iii) Credit allowed by suppliers is two months and allowed to customer is one month.

(iv) Lag in payment of wages is one month.

Solution:

Cash Budget for Three Months Ending on 31st July, 2009

Particulars	May (Rs.)	June (Rs.)	July (Rs.)
Opening cash balance	8,000	26,000	34,000
Add: Receipts			
Collection from debtors	62,000	64,000	58,000
Total	70,000	90,000	92,000
Less: Payments			
Payment to creditors	36,000	38,000	33,000
Wages	8,000	10,000	8,500
Advance Tax	--------	8,000	---------
Total	**44,000**	**56,000**	**41,500**
Closing Balance	**26,000**	**34,000**	**50,500**

Problem 13:

Prepare a cash budget for three months ending December 2009

Month	Sales Rs.	Materials Rs.	Labour Rs.	Overheads Rs.
August	10,000	6,000	1,000	1,100
September	12,000	6,600	1,200	1,230
October	14,000	6,400	1,400	1,450
November	16,000	7,200	1,600	1,600
December	18,000	7,600	1,800	1,750

Credit terms are:

(a) Sales – 20% of sales are on cash

50% credit sales is received in the same month and remaining 50% in the next month.

(b) Materials – 1 month credit.

(c) Wages and overheads – ½ month credit.

Cash and bank balance on 1st October is Rs. 5,500.

Other information's are:

(i) Income tax paid in December 2009 in Rs. 3,500 and

(ii) Sale of old car Rs. 20,000 received in November 2009.

Solution:

Cash Budget for Three Months Ending 31.12.2009

Particulars	*Oct. (Rs.)*	*Nov. (Rs.)*	*Dec. (Rs.)*
Opening cash balance	5,500	9,460	35,235
Add: Receipts:			
Cash sales	2,800	3,200	3,600
Collection from debtors	4,800	5,600	6,400
	5,600	6,400	7,200
Sale of old car	———	20,000	———
Total	**18,700**	**44,660**	**52,435**
Less: Payments:			
Payment to creditors	6,600	6,400	7,200
Labour	600	700	800
	700	800	900
Overheads	615	725	800
	725	800	875
Income tax paid	———	———	3,500
Total	**9,240**	**9,425**	**14,075**
Closing balance	**9,460**	**35,235**	**38,360**

Problem 14:

Samy Ltd., wishes to arrange overdraft facilities with their bankers during the period April to June 2009. Prepare a cash budget for the above period, from the following data, indicating the extent of the bank facilities, the company will require at the end of each month.

(i)

Month	Credit Sales Rs.	Purchases Rs.	Wages Rs.
Feb. – 2009.	1,80,000	1,24,800	12,000
March	1,92,000	1,44,000	14,000
April	1,08,000	2,43,000	11,000
May	1,74,000	2,46,000	10,000
June	1,26,000	2,68,000	15,000

(ii) 50% of the credit sales are realised in the month following the sales and the remaining in the second month following.

(iii) Creditors and wages are paid in the next month.

(iv) Cash at bank on 1.4. 2009. (Estimated) Rs. 25,000.

Solution:

SAMY Ltd.,

Cash Budget for 3 Months Ending June 2009.

Particulars	April (Rs.)	May (Rs.)	June (Rs.)
Opening cash balance	25,000	53,000	--------
Add: Receipts:			
Collection from debtors	90,000	96,000	54,000
	96,000	54,000	87,000
Total: Receipts:	2,11,000	2,03,000	1,41,000
Less: Payments:			
Payment to creditors	1,44,000	2,43,000	2,46,000
Labour	14,000	11,000	10,000
Total: Payments:	1,58,000	2,54,000	2,56,000
Surplus or (Deficit)	53,000	-51,000	-1,15,000
Estimated O/D (assumed)	------	51,000	1,15,000
Closing balance	**53,000**	------	------

Problem 15:

Summarised are the income and expenditure forecasts for the months of March to August 2009:

Month	*Sales (credit) Rs.*	*Purchases (credit) Rs.*	*Wages Rs.*	*Mfg. expenses Rs.*	*Office expenses Rs.*	*Selling expenses Rs.*
March	60,000	36,000	9,000	4,000	2,000	4,000
April	62,000	38,000	8,000	3,000	1,500	5,000
May	64,000	33,000	10,000	4,500	2,500	4,500
June	58,000	35,000	8,500	3,500	2,000	3,500
July	56,000	39,000	9,500	4,000	1,000	4,500
August	60,000	34,000	8,000	3,000	1,500	4,500

You are given the following further information:

(a) Plant costing Rs. 16,000 is due for delivery in July payable 10% on delivery and the balance after two months.

(b) Advance tax of Rs. 8,000 is payable in March and June each.

(c) Period of credit allowed (i) by suppliers two months, and (ii) to customers one month.

(d) Lag in payment of manufacturing expenses half month.

(e) Lag in payment of all other expenses one month.

Prepare a cash budget for three months starting on 1st May, 2009, when there was a cash balance of Rs. 8,000.

Solution:

Cash Budget for the quarter ended 31 July, 2009

Particulars	*May (Rs.)*	*Jun (Rs.)*	*July (Rs.)*
Opening cash balance	8,000	15,750	12,750
Add: Receipts:			
Collection from debtors	62,000	64,000	58,000
Total	**70,000**	**79,750**	**70,750**
Less: Payments:			
Payment to creditors	36,000	38,000	33,000
Wages	8,000	10,000	8,500
Manufacturing expenses	3,750	4,000	3,750
Office expenses	1,500	2,500	2,000
Selling expenses	5,000	4,500	3,500
Advance tax	-----	8,000	-----
Purchase of plant (10% on delivery)	-----	-----	1,600
Total	**54,250**	**67,000**	**52,350**
Closing balance	**15,750**	**12,750**	**18,400**

Problem 16:

From the following, prepare a cash budget for the months March to June 2009:

Month	*Sales (credit) Rs.*	*Purchases (credit) Rs.*	*Wages Rs.*	*Factory expenses Rs.*	*Office expenses Rs.*	*Distribution expenses Rs.*
Jan 2009	50,000	25,000	4,000	2,000	1,500	1,000
Feb.	60,000	26,000	4,000	2,200	1,550	1,100
Mar.	75,000	25,000	4,500	2,000	1,600	1,200
Apr.	80,000	27,000	4,500	2,100	1,700	1,250
May	1,00,000	27,500	4,750	2,200	1,750	1,200
June	1,05,000	29,000	5,000	2,500	1,800	1,400

Additional information is as follows:

(1) Balance of cash in hand on 1st March, 2009 is Rs. 20,000.

(2) The customers are allowed a credit period of two months.

(3) The creditors are allowing a credit of one month.

(4) A dividend of Rs. 25,000 is payable in June.

(5) Capital expenditure to be incurred:Machinery purchased 20th April for Rs. 10,000; a land has been purchased on 1st March and the payments are to be made in monthly instalments of Rs. 5,000 each.

(6) Interest on investment of Rs. 25,000 is receivable in May.

(7) Wages are paid on the 1st week of the next month.

(8) Lag in payment of other expenses is one month.

Solution:

Cash Budget for four months ending 30th June, 2009

Particulars	*March* *Rs.*	*April* *Rs.*	*May* *Rs.*	*June* *Rs.*
Opening cash in hand	20,000	30,150	40,850	99,300
Add : Receipts				
Collection from debtors	50,000	60,000	75,000	80,000
Interest on investment	—	—	25,000	—
Total Receipts	**70,000**	**90,150**	**1,40,850**	**1,79,300**
Less: Payments				
Purchases of machinery	—	10,000	—	—
Purchase of building	5,000	5,000	5,000	5,000
Payment of dividend	—	—	—	25,000
Payment to creditors	26,000	25,000	27,000	27,500
Wages	4,000	4,500	4,500	4,750
Factory expenses	2,200	2,000	2,100	2,200
Office expenses	1,550	1,600	1,700	1,750
Distribution expenses	1,100	1,200	1,250	1,200
Total Payments	**39,850**	**49,300**	**41,550**	**67,400**
Closing Balance	**30,150**	**40,850**	**99,300**	**1,11,900**

Problme 17:

Prepare a Cash Budget of M/s. Raj & Sons, from the following information for the six months commencing April 2009:

(a) Cash sales are 10% of the total sales and balance 90% will be credit sales.

(b) 50% of credit sales are collected in the month following the sales, balance 25% and 25%in the two following months thereafter. All debts are good.

(c) Gross profit margin 20%.

(d) Sales forecasts are:

Jan	Rs. 2,00,000	April	Rs. 8,00,000	July	Rs. 12,00,000
Feb.	Rs. 4,00,000	May	Rs. 10,00,000	Aug.	Rs. 12,00,000
Mar.	Rs. 6,00,000	June	Rs. 10,00,000	Sept.	Rs. 10,00,000

(e) Anticipated Purchases:

April	Rs. 3,50,000	June	Rs. 6,50,000	Aug.	Rs. 9,00,000
May	Rs. 5,50,000	July	Rs. 7,00,000	Spet.	Rs. 8,00,000

(f) Salaries to be paid :

April	Rs. 75,000	June	Rs. 1,00,000	Aug.	Rs. 1,25,000
May	Rs. 75,000	July	Rs. 1,00,000	Sept.	Rs. 1,50,000

(g) Interest at 5% on Bonds of Rs. 5,00,000 is to paid in June every year.

(h) Excise deposit due in Aug. 2006 Rs. 50,000.

(i) Capital expenditure for land and building planned for Sept. Rs. 1,50,000.

(j) Company has a cash balance of Rs. 1,75,000 as at March, 31, 2009.

(k) Rent is Rs. 5,000 per months.

Solution:

Cash Budget of M/s. Raj & Sons., for Six Months commencing from April 2009

Particulars	*Apr. Rs.*	*May Rs.*	*June Rs.*	*July Rs.*	*Aug. Rs.*	*Sep. Rs.*
Opening Balance	1,75,000	2,30,000	2,85,000	3,70,000	5,40,000	5,70,000
Add: Receipts:						
Cash Sales	80,000	1,00,000	1,00,000	1,20,000	1,20,000	1,00,000

Collection from						
Debtors	2,70,000	3,60,000	4,50,000	4,50,000	5,40,000	5,40,000
	90,000	1,35,000	1,80,000	2,25,000	2,25,000	2,70,000
	45,000	90,000	1,35,000	1,80,000	2,25,000	2,25,000
Total Receipts	**6,60,000**	**9,15,000**	**11,50,000**	**13,45,000**	**16,50,000**	**17,05,000**
Less : Payments						
Purchases	3,50,000	5,50,000	6,50,000	7,00,000	9,00,000	8,00,000
Wages	75,000	75,000	1,00,000	1,00,000	1,25,000	1,50,000
Interest on bond	—	—	25,000	—	—	—
Excise deposit due	—	—	—	—	50,000	—
land and building	—	—	—	—	—	1,50,000
Rent	5,000	5,000	5,000	5,000	5,000	5,000
Total Payments	**4,30,000**	**6,30,000**	**7,80,000**	**8,05,000**	**10,80,000**	**11,05,000**
Closing balance	**2,30,000**	**2,85,000**	**3,70,000**	**5,40,000**	**5,70,000**	**6,00,000**

Problem 18:

From the following, prepare a cash budget for the months of January to April.

	Expected Purchases Rs.	***Expected Sales Rs***
January	48,000	60,000
February	80,000	40,000
March	81,000	45,000
April	90,000	40,000

Wages to be paid to workers Rs. 5,000 each month. Balance at bank on 1st January Rs. 8,000. It has been decided by the management that:

(i) In case deficit of funds within the limit of Rs. 10,000, an arrangement can be made with the bank.

(ii) In case deficit of fund exceeding Rs. 10,000 but within the limit of Rs. 42,000, issue of debentures is to preferred.

(iii) In case deficit of fund exceeding Rs, 42,000, issue of share is preferred (considering the fact it is within the limit of authorised capital).

Solution:

Cash Budget

(For the Months from January to April)

Particulars	*Jan. (Rs.)*	*Feb. (Rs.)*	*March (Rs.)*	*April (Rs.)*
Opening Balance	8,000	1,41,000	96,000	55,000
Add: Receipts				
Cash sales	60,000	40,000	45,000	40,000
Issue of shares	1,26,000			
Total receipts	**1,94,000**	**1,81,000**	**1,41,000**	**95,000**
Less: Payments				
Purchases	48,000	80,000	81,000	90,000
Wages	5,000	5,000	5,000	5,000
Total payments	**53,000**	**85,000**	**86,000**	**95,000**
Closing balance c/f	1,41,000	96,000	55,000	---------

Note:

Calculation of issue of shares	***Rs.***
Total payments during four months	3,19,000
Total receipts during four months	1,93,000
Total deficiency	1,26,000

Flexible Budget

According to the C.I.M.A. London, a flexible budget is "a budget designed to change in accordance with the level of activity actually attained". Thus, a budget prepared in a manner so as to give the budgeted cost for any level of activity is known as a flexible budget. Such a budget is prepared after considering the fixed and variable elements of cost and the changes that may be expected for each item at various levels of operations.

Problem 19:

Prepare a flexible budget for overheads on the basis of following data. Ascertain overhead rates at 50%, 60%, and 70% capacity.

	At 60% capacity
	Rs.
Variable overheads	
Indirect material	6,000
Indirect Labour	18,000
Semi-variable overheads	
Electricity (40% fixed, 60% variable)	30,000
Repairs (80% fixed, 20% variable)	3,000
Fixed overhead	
Depreciation	16,500
Insurance	4,500
Salaries	15,000
Total overheads	93,000
Estimated direct labour hours	1,86,000

Solution:

Flexible Budget

Particulars	*50%*	*60%*	*70%*
	Rs.	*Rs.*	*Rs.*
Variable overheads			
Indirect material	5,000	6,000	7,000
Indirect labour	15,000	18,000	21,000
Semi-variable overheads			
Electricity			
Fixed: 30000 × 40 %	12,000	12,000	12,000
Variable: 30000 × 60%	15,000	18,000	21,000
Repairs			
Fixed: 3000 × 80%	2,400	2,400	2,400
Variable: 3000 × 20%	500	600	700
Fixed overheads			
Depreciation	16,500	16,500	16,500
Insurance	4,500	4,500	4,500

Salaries	15,000	15,000	15,000
Total overheads	**85,900**	**93,000**	**1,00,100**
Estimated direct labour hours	1,55,000	1,86,000	2,17,000
Overhead rates	Re. 0.55	Re. 0.50	Re. 0.46

Workings:

$$\text{Overhead rates} = \frac{\text{Total overheads}}{\text{Estimated direct labour hours}}$$

Problem 20:

Draw up a flexible budget for overhead expenses on the basis of the following data and determine overhead rates at 70%, 80% and 90% plant capacity.

Particulars	*At 70% Capacity Rs.*	*At 80% Capacity Rs.*	*At 90% Capacity Rs.*
Variable Overheads:			
Indirect labour	——	12,000	——
Stores including spares	——	4,000	——
Semi-variable Overheads:			
Power		20,000	
(30% fixed, 70% variable)	——		
Repairs and maintenance		2,000	——
(60% fixed, 40% variable)	——		
Fixed Overheads:			
Depreciation	——	11,000	——
Insurance	——	3,000	——
Salaries	——	10,000	——
Total Overheads	——	**62,000**	——
Estimated direct labour hours		1,24,000 hrs.	

Solution:

Flexible Budget for the period

Particulars	*At 70% Capacity Rs.*	*At 80% Capacity Rs.*	*At 90% Capacity Rs.*
Variable Overheads			
Indirect labour	10,500	12,000	13,500
Stores including spares	3,500	4,000	4,500
Semi-variable Overheads			
Power – Fixed 20000 × 30%	6,000	6,000	6,000
Variable 20000 × 70%	12,250	14,000	15,750
Repairs and Maintenance			
Fixed 2000 × 60%	1,200	1,200	1,200
Variable 2000 × 40%	700	800	900
Fixed Overheads			
Depreciation	11,000	11,000	11,000
Insurance	3,000	3,000	3,000
Salaries	10,000	10,000	10,000
Total Overheads	**58,150**	**62,000**	**65,850**
Estimated direct labour hours	1,08,500	1,24,000	1,39,500
Direct labour hour rate	Re. 0.54	Re. 0.50	Re. 0.47

Working:

Direct labour rates have been computed as follows:

$$\text{Overhead rates} = \frac{\text{Total overheads}}{\text{Estimated direct labour hours}}$$

Problem 21:

The expenses for the budgeted production of 10,000 units in a factory are given below:

Particulars	*Per Unit (Rs.)*
Materials	70
Labour	25
Variable overheads	20
Fixed overheads (Rs. 1,00,000)	10

Variable expenses (Direct)	5
Selling expenses (10% fixed)	13
Distribution expenses (20% fixed)	7
Administrative expenses (Rs. 50,000)	5
Total cost	**155**

Prepare a flexible budget for the production of (i) 8,000 units, and (ii) 6.000 units.

Solution:

Flexible Budget

Particulars	*6,000 units*		*8,000 units*		*10,000 units*	
	Per Unit Rs.	*Total Rs.*	*Per Unit Rs.*	*Total Rs.*	*Per Unit Rs.*	*Total Rs.*
Variable Expenses:						
Materials	70.00	4,20,000	70.00	5,60,000	70.00	7,00,000
Labour	25.00	1,50,000	25.00	2,00,000	25.00	2,50,000
Overheads	20.00	1,20,000	20.00	1,60,000	20.00	2,00,000
Direct expenses	5.00	30,000	5.00	40,000	5.00	50,000
Semi-variable Expenses:						
Selling expenses:						
Fixed	2.17	13,000	1.63	13,000	1.30	13,000
Variable	11.70	70,000	11.70	93,600	11.70	1,17,000
Distribution Expenses:						
Fixed	2.33	14,000	1.75	14,000	1.40	14,000
Variable	5.60	33,600	5.60	44,800	5.60	56,000
Fixed Expenses:						
Fixed overheads:	16.67	1,00,000	10.00	1,00,000	12.50	1,00,000
Administration expenses	8.33	50,000	5.00	50,000	6.25	50,000
Total overheads	**166.80**	**10,00,600**	**160.68**	**12,62,400**	**155.00**	**15,50,000**

Problem 22:

With the following data for a 50% activity, prepare a budget for production at 75% and 90% capacity.

Production at 50% capacity	1000 units
Direct materials	Rs. 50 per unit
Direct wages	Rs. 25 per unit
Direct expenses	Rs. 15 per unit
Factory overheads	Rs. 25,000 (70% variable)
Administration overheads	Rs. 20,000 (25% variable)

Solution:

Flexible Budget

Particulars	*50% 1000 Units*		*75% 1500 Units*		*90% 1800 Units*	
	Per Unit	*Total*	*Per Unit*	*Total*	*Per Unit*	*Total*
Variable Expenses:						
Direct materials	50.00	50,000	50.00	75,000	50.00	90,000
Direct wages	25.00	25,000	25.00	37,500	25.00	45,000
Direct expenses	15.00	15,000	15.00	22,500	15.00	27,000
Semi-variable Expenses:						
Factory overheads:						
Variable	17.50	17,500	17.50	26,250	17.50	31,500
Fixed	7.50	7,500	5.00	7,500	4.166	7,500
Administration Overheads:						
Variable	5.00	5,000	5.00	7,500	5.00	9,000
Fixed	15.00	15,000	10.00	15,000	8.333	15,000
Total Cost	**135.00**	**1,35,000**	**127.50**	**1,91,250**	**124.999**	**2,25,000**

Problem 23:

Alagappan Ltd., manufacturing a single product is facing a severe competition in selling it at Rs.75/- per unit. The company is operating at 50% level of activity at which the sales are Rs. 15,00,000. Variable cost is Rs. 40 per unit. Semi-variable cost may be considered as fixed at Rs. 1,00,000 when the output is nil and variable element is Rs. 300 for each additional 1% level of activity. Fixed cost are Rs. 2,00,000 at the present level of activity but if a level of activity is 75% or above is reached these costs are expected to increase by Rs. 75,000.

The management of the company is considering a proposal to reduce the selling price by 10%. You are required to prepare a statement showing the operating profit at the levels of activity of 50%, 75%, 90% assuming that:

(a) The selling price remains at Rs. 75

(b) The reduction in selling price by 10%

(a) Selling price remains at Rs. 75

Solution:

Statement of Profitability

Particulars	*50% (20,000 Units) Rs.*	*75% (30,000 Units) Rs.*	*90% (36,000 Units) Rs.*
Sales (A)	**15,00,000**	**22,50,000**	**27,00,000**
Variable cost	8,00,000	12,00,000	14,40,000
Semi-variable cost:			
Fixed	1,00,000	1,00,000	1,00,000
Variable	15,000	22,500	27,000
Fixed cost	2,00,000	2,75,000	2,75,000
Total cost (B)	**11,15,000**	**15,97,500**	**18,42,000**
Profit (A-B)	**3,85,000**	**6,52,500**	**8,58,000**

(b) Reduction in selling price by 10%

	Rs.	***Rs.***	***Rs.***
Sales	13,50,000	20,25,000	24,30,000
Less: Total cost	11,15,000	15,97,500	18,42,000
Profit	**2,35,000**	**4,27,500**	**5,88,000**

Problem 24:

Vasanthi Ltd., is currently working at 60% capacity and produces 15,000 units. Estimate the profits of the company when it works at 75% and 90% capacity.

At 75% capacity, the raw material cost increases by 5% and the selling price falls by 5%.

At 90% capacity, the raw material cost increases by 5% and selling price falls by 10%.

At 60% capacity working, the product costs Rs. 150 per unit and is sold at Rs. 190 per unit. The unit cost of Rs. 150 is made up as follows:

Direct material	Rs. 75
Direct wages	Rs. 25
Factory overheads	Rs. 30 (60% fixed)
Office and administration overheads	Rs. 20 (30% variable)

Solution:

Statement of Profitability

Particulars	*75% Capacity (Output – 18,750 Units)*		*90% Capacity (Output – 22,500 Units)*	
	Per unit Rs.	*Total Rs.*	*Per unit Rs.*	*Total Rs.*
Variable overheads:				
Direct material	77.25	14,48,437.50	78.75	17,71,875
Direct wages	25.00	4,68,750.00	25.00	5,62,500
Semi-variable overheads:				
Factory overheads:				
Fixed	14.40	2,70,000.00	12.00	2,70,000
Variable	12.00	2,25,000.00	12.00	2,70,000
Office and administration overheads:				
Fixed	11.20	2,10,000.00	9.3333	2,10,000
Variable	6.00	1,12,500.00	6.00	1,35,000
Total cost	**145.85**	**27,34,687.50**	**143.0833**	**32,19,375**
Profit (bal. fig)	34.65	6,49,687.50	27.9167	6,28,125
Sales	180.50	33,84,375.00	171.0000	38,47,500

Problem 25:

The following information at 50% capacity is given. Prepare a flexible budget and forecast the profit or loss at 70%, 80% and 100% capacity.

Particulars	*Expenses at 50% capacity Rs.*
Fixed Expenses:	
Salaries	1,25,000
Rent and rates	1,00,000
Depreciation on plant	80,000
Administrative expenses	90,000
Variable Expenses:	
Materials	5,00,000
Labour	4,50,000

Other variable expenses	1,60,000
Semi-variable Expenses:	
Repairs and maintenance	2,30,000
Indirect labour	3,00,000
Sales department salaries	2,10,000

It is estimated that fixed expenses will remain constant at all capacities. Semi-variable expenses will not change between 45% and 60% capacity, will rise by 20% between 60% and 75% capacity, a further increase of 15% when capacity crosses 75%.

Estimated sales at various levels of capacity are:

Capacity	50%	70%	80%	100%
Sales (in Rs.)	24,00,000	30,00,000	32,00,000	37,00,000

Solution:

Flexible Budget

Particulars	*50%*	*70%*	*80%*	*100%*
	Rs.	*Rs.*	*Rs.*	*Rs.*
Variable Expenses:				
Materials	5,00,000	7,00,000	8,00,000	10,00,000
Labour	4,50,000	6,30,000	7,20,000	9,00,000
Other variable expenses	1,60,000	2,24,000	2,56,000	3,20,000
Semi-variable Expenses:				
Repairs and maintenance	2,30,000	2,76,000	2,64,500	2,64,500
Indirect labour	3,00,000	3,60,000	3,45,000	3,45,000
Sales department salaries	2,10,000	2,52,000	2,41,500	2,41,500
Fixed Expenses:				
Salaries	1,25,000	1,25,000	1,25,000	1,25,000
Rent and rates	1,00,000	1,00,000	1,00,000	1,00,000
Depreciation on plant	80,000	80,000	80,000	80,000
Administrative expenses	90,000	90,000	90,000	90,000
Total cost	22,45,000	28,37,000	30,22,000	34,66,000
Sales	24,00,000	30,00,000	32,00,000	37,00,000
Less: Total cost	22,45,000	28,37,000	30,22,000	34,66,000
Profit	**1,55,000**	**1,63,000**	**1,78,000**	**2,34,000**

Problem 26:

The following information at 50% capacity is given. Prepare a flexible budget and forecast the profit or loss at 60%, 70% and 90% capacity.

	Expenses at 50% capacity *Rs.*
Fixed Expenses:	
Salaries	50,000
Rent and taxes	40,000
Depreciation	60,000
Administrative expenses	70,000
Variable Expenses:	
Material	2,00,000
Labour	2,50,000
Others	40,000
Semi-variable Expenses:	
Repairs	1,00,000
Indirect labour	1,50,000
Others	90,000
	10,50,000

It is estimated that fixed expenses will remain constant at all level of capacities. Semi-variable expenses will not change between 45% and 60% capacity, will rise by 10% between 60% and 75% capacity, a further increase of 5% when capacity crosses 75%. Estimated sales at various level of capacity are

Capacity	60%	70%	90%
Sales (Rs.)	11,00,000	13,00,000	15,00,000

Solution:

Flexible Budget

Particulars	Capacities			
	50%	*60%*	*70%*	*90%*
Fixed Expenses:	*Rs.*	*Rs.*	*Rs.*	*Rs.*
Salaries	50,000	50,000	50,000	50,000
Rent and taxes	40,000	40,000	40,000	40,000
Depreciation	60,000	60,000	60,000	60,000
Administrative expenses	70,000	70,000	70,000	70,000
Variable Expenses:				
Materials	2,00,000	2,40,000	2,80,000	3,60,000
Labour	2,50,000	3,00,000	3,50,000	4,50,000
Others	40,000	48,000	56,000	72,000
Semi-variable Expenses:				
Repairs	1,00,000	1,00,000	1,10,000	1,15,000
Indirect labour	1,50,000	1,50,000	1,65,000	1,72,500
Others	90,000	90,000	99,000	1,03,500
Total Cost	**10,50,000**	**11,48,000**	**12,80,000**	**14,93,000**
Profit (+) or Loss (–)	—	48,000	+20,000	+7,000
Estimated sales		11,00,000	13,00,000	15,00,000

Master Budget

A master budget is defined as, "the summary budget incorporating the functional budgets which is finally approved, adopted and employed". The budget may take the form of budgeted profit and loss account and Balance Sheet. It contains sales, production cost, cash position, debtor, fixed assets, bills payable, etc.

Problem 27:

A Star Manufacturing Company requires you to present the master budget from the following information:

Sales

Toughened Glass	Rs. 8,00,000
Bent Toughened Glass	Rs. 10,00,000

Direct Material Cost	50% of Sales
Direct Wages	25 workers @ Rs. 250 per month
Factory Overheads	
Works Manager Salary	Rs. 2000 per month
Foremen Salary	Rs. 1000 per month
Stores and Spares	5% on sales
Depreciation Plant	Rs. 15,500
Light and Power	Rs. 7,500
Miscellaneous Expenses	Rs. 8,000
Administration and Selling Expenses	Rs. 33,000 per annum
Repairs and Maintenance	Rs. 15,000

Solution:

Master Budget for the period ending ....

Particulars			*Rs.*
Sales:			
Toughened glass			8,00,000
Bent toughened glass			10,00,000
Less: Cost of Production:			18,00,000
Direct material cost		9,00,000	
Direct Wages		75,000	
(25 × 250 × 12)			
Prime cost		9,75,000	
Factory Overheads:			
Variables:			
Stores and spares	90,000		
Light and power	7,500		
Repairs and maintenance	15,000	1,12,500	
Fixed:			
Works Manager salary	24,000		
Foremen's Salary	12,000		

Depreciation on plant	15,500		
Miscellaneous expenses	8,000	59,500	
Work Cost:			11,47,000
Gross profit			6,53,000
Less: Administration and selling expenses			33,000
Net profit			**6,20,000**

ZERO BASE BUDGETING (ZBB)

Meaning

Zero Base Budgeting was introduced by the U.S. in 1961. Peter A. Phyrr designed its basic frame-work in 1970 and popularised its wider use in the private sector. In 1979, President Jimmy Carter issued a mandate asking for the use of ZBB throughout the Federal Government Agencies for controlling state expenditure.

The traditional technique of budgeting is to take previous year's cost levels as a base for preparing this year's budget. This type of budgeting assumes that allocation of funds in the past was correct. In most cases, an addition is made to the previous year's figure to allow for an increase in cost. Because of this budgets (particularly government budgets) take an upward direction in spite of declining efficiency year after year. Thus, the inefficiencies of a previous year are carried forward in formulating the subsequent year's budget. Managers tend to inflate their budget requests resulting in more demand for funds.

On the other hand, ZBB is simply starting from scratch. Every year is taken as a new year and the previous year is not at all taken as the base, in the preparation of budgets. Rather zero is taken as the base. Something will not be allowed simply because it was allowed in the past. ZBB proceeds on the assumption that nothing is to be allowed. A manager has to justify why he wants to spend. The manager proposing an expenditure or activity has to prove that it is essential and the amounts asked for are reasonable.

Definition

In the words of Peter A. Phyrr, "A planning and budgeting process which requires each manager to justify his entire budget request in detail from scratch (Hence, Zero Base) and shifts the burden of proof to each manager to justify why he should spend money at all. The approach requires that all activities be analysed in 'decision packages' which are evaluated by systematic analysis and ranked in order of importance".

Steps or Process Involved in ZBB

While preparing a ZBB, one should take into account the following steps:

- The objective of budgeting should be clearly determined because the objectives differ from concern to concern.
- Whether it should be adopted in all operational areas or only in specific areas should be decided.
- Proper decision packages must be identified.
- Cost benefit analysis is undertaken, which will help in fixing priority for various projects.
- Last step is to finalise the budget.

Merits of ZBB

ZBB has got the following advantages:

- It helps the management to allocate the funds, according to benefits.
- It will be very helpful for the management to improve the efficiency.
- It helps in identifying and controlling the wasteful areas.
- It will allow, only those activities which will help in the achievement of organisational goals.
- It will be helpful in determining the utility of each and every activity of the business.
- It is an important tool in integrating the managerial activities of planning and control.

Demerits of ZBB

- The limitations of ZBB are:
- Flexible budgeting is not possible under ZBB.
- It is a time-consuming one.
- The cost of operating it is highly expensive.
- It is not suitable for non-financial matters.

MODEL QUESTIONS

Objective type questions:

Choose the best answer from the given alternatives:

(1) A summary budget for the entire enterprise is:

(a) Master budget (b) Cash budget

(c) Working capital budget (d) Production budget

(2) A budget which changes with the level of activity is —

(a) Fixed budget (b) Flexible budget

(c) Cash budget (d) None

(3) The budgetary control is a system of controlling ________.

(a) Costs (b) Purchases and sales

(c) Profit (d) None of the above

(4) A flexible budget requires a careful study and classification of expenses into:

(a) Past and current expenses (b) Variable, semi-variable and fixed expenses

(c) Overheads (d) None of the above

(5) Which one of the following is usually a long-term budget?

(a) Sales "B" (b) Cash "B"

(c) Capital expenditure "B" (d) Fixed "B"

(6) The first step in preparing a budget is —

(a) Cash "B" (b) Production "B"

(c) Sales "B" (d) Materials "B"

(7) Zero based budgeting is —

(a) Preparation of budget (b) Taking into account only quantitative values

(c) Containing future estimates only (d) None of the above

(8) The master budget is the summary budget incorporating its component-

(a) Production budget only (b) Sales budget only

(c) Flexible budget (d) Functional budget

(9) The budget that is always prepared first is-

(a) Cash budget (b) Master budget

(c) Budget for the key factor (d) None

(10) A budget is generally evolved from-

(a) Forecast (b) Plan

(c) Policies and procedures (d) None

(11) Rolling budget is otherwise known as —

(a) Current budget (b) Sales budget

(c) Progressive budget (d) None

(12) Who is the father of zero base budgeting?

(a) A. Phyrr (b) Mr. Himmy Corter

(c) Malcomn (d) None

(13) Zero base budget originated in the soil of

(a) USSR (b) UK

(c) USA (d) None

(Ans: 1 a 2 b 3 a 4 b 5 c 6 c 7 a

8 d 9 c 10 b 11 c 12 a 13 c.)

State True or False:

(1) There is no difference between a forecast and a budget

(2) Flexible budgets change with the level of activity

(3) Fixed budget is a dynamic one

(4) Master budget is also known as summary budget.

(5) Calendar ratio calculates the ratio between actual and budgeted days.

(Ans: True 2,4,5 False 1,3.)

Fill in the Blanks:

(1) Budgetary control helps management to ____________

(2) ____________ is a summary of all functional budgets in a capsule form.

(3) A fixed budget is also called as ____________

(4) Cash budget is a ____________

(5) Key factor is also known as ____________factor.

(6) Zero base budgeting was first used by ____________

(7) Budgetary control is a system of ____________

(Ans:

(1) Plan and Control (2) Master Budget (3) Static Budget

(4) Short term Budget (5) Limiting or governing or principal budget

(6) US Department of Agriculture (7) Controlling Cost.)

Short Answer Questions:

(1) Distinguish between fixed and flexible budget.

(2) What is a cash budget? What are its advantages? How is it prepared?

(3) Explain the features of flexible budget.

(4) Why is budgetary control needed?

(5) Compare budget, budgeting and budgetary control.

(6) What is budget manual and budget committee?

(7) Explain the term, "Key factor".

Essay Type Questions:

(1) Explain the objectives and essentials of budgetary control. Distinguish between fixed and flexible budget.

(2) Explain the different types of budgets.

(3) What are the stages involved in the preparation of zero base budgeting?

(4) What is a master budget? How is it prepared?

(5) What do you mean by budgetary control? What are its advantages and limitations?

(6) "The sales budget is the pivot of budgetary control". Discuss this statement.

(7) How budgets are helpful in decision-making of a company?

(8) Write short notes on:

(a) Budgetary control

(b) Master budget

(9) Distinction between budgeting and forecasting.

(10) How far is a budgetary control a tool in the hand of management. Explain.

EXERCISE:

(1) Prepare a production budget for three months ending 31.3.2009 for a factory producing four products.

Type of product	*Opening stock (Units)*	*Sales (Units)*	*Closing stock (Units)*
P	1,000	5,000	2,500
Q	1,500	7,500	2,000
R	2,000	6,500	1,500
S	2,500	6,000	1,000

(**Ans:** Estimated production (Units) 6,500, 8,000, 6,000, 4,500.)

(2) Prepare a production budget for three months ending March 2009 for a factory producing four products:

Type of Products	*Estimated Stock (1.1.09)* Rs.	*Estimated Sales during Jan–Mar 09* Rs.	*Desired Closing Stock (31.3.09)* Rs.
A	2,000	10,000	5,000
B	3,000	15,000	4,000
C	4,000	13,000	3,000
D	5,000	12,000	2,000

Ans: (13,000 16,000 12,000 9,000.)

(3) A company is manufacturing two products X and Y. A forecast about the number of units to be sold in the first seven months is given below. Prepare production budget for the two products X and Y for the first six months ending June (in units)

Month	**January**	**February**	**March**	**April**	**May**	**June**	**July**
Product X	10,000	12,000	16,000	20,000	24,000	24,000	20,000
Product Y	28,000	28,000	24,000	20,000	16,000	16,000	18,000

It is anticipated that

(a) There will be no work- in -progress at the end of any month.

(b) Finished units equal to half the sales of the next month will be in stock at the end of each month. (including December of previous year).

(**Ans:** Product X: 11,000 14,000 18,000 22,000 24,000 22,000

Product Y: 28,000 26,000 22,000 18,000 16,000 17,000.)

(4) The sales director of a manufacturing company reports that next year he expect to sell 50,000 units of a particular product.

The production manager consults the storekeeper and casts his figures as follows:

Two kinds of raw materials A and B, are required for manufacturing the product. Each unit of the product requires two units of A and three units of B. The estimated opening balances at the commencement of the next year are:

Finished Product: 10,000 units

Raw Materials A: 12,000 units

Raw Materials B: 15,000 units

The desirable closing balances at the end of the next year are:

Finished product 14,000 units

Raw Materials A: 13,000 units

Raw Materials B: 16,000 units

Prepare production budget and materials purchase budget for the next year.

(Ans: Estimated Production 54,000

Estimated purchases A 1,09,000 B 1,63,000.)

(5) The following information has been made available from the accounting records of Karthi Ltd., for the last six months of 2008 (and of only the sales for January 2009) in respect of Fishplate X produced by it:

(i) The unit to be sold in different months are:

July	2,200	November	5,000
August	2,200	December	4,600
September	3,400	January, 09	4,000
October	3,800		

(ii) There will be no work-in-progress at the end of any month.

(iii) Finished units equal to half the sales for the next month will be in stock in the end of every month (including June, 08).

(iv) Budgeted production and production costs for the year ending Dec., 08 are as follows:

Production (units)	44,000
Direct materials per unit	Rs. 10.00
Direct wages per unit	Rs. 4.00
Total factory overheads	
Apportioned to product	Rs. 88,000

Prepare:

(a) Production budget for the last six months of 2009; and

(b) Production cost budget for the same period.

(Ans: 22,100 units; Rs. 3,53,600.)

(6) You are required to prepare the selling overhead budget from the following:

	Rs.
Advertisement	1,000
Salaries	1,000
Expenses of the sales dept. (fixed)	750
Dearness allowance	3,000
Commission 1% on sales effected	
Carriage outwards – estimated at 5% on sales	
Agents Commission – 6½% on sales	

The sales during the period were estimated as follows:

Period I - Rs. 80,000 including agent's sales —	Rs. 8,000
Period II - Rs. 90,000 including agent's sales —	Rs. 10,000
Period III - Rs. 1,00,000 including agent's sales —	Rs. 10,500

(Ans: Selling overheads 10,990 11,700 12,328.)

(7) Following information is given about a Limited Company You are required to prepare a

Selling overheads budget:	*Rs.*
Advertisement	2,000
Salaries of sales department	2,000
Expenses of sales department fixed	950
Salesmen's remuneration:	
Salaries	6,000
Commission @ 1% on sales effected	
Carriage outwards: Estimated @ 5% on sales	
Agent's Commission 6% on sales	

Sales during the period were estimated as follows:

Rs. 1,00,000 including agent's sales Rs. 10,000

Rs. 1,50,000 including agent's sales Rs. 20,000.

Rs. 2,00,000 including agent's sales Rs. 20,000.

(Ans: Rs. 17,450; Rs. 20,950; Rs. 23,950.)

(8) Samsung Ltd., wishes to arrange overdraft facilities with its bankers during the period July to September 2007 when it will be manufacturing mostly for stock. Prepare a cash budget for the above period from the following data, indicating the extent of the bank facilities the company will require at the end of each month.

(a)

Month	*Credit Sales* *Rs.*	*Purchases* *Rs.*	*Wages* *Rs.*
May	2,50,000	2,00,000	22,000
June	2,75,000	2,60,000	25,500
July	1,72,000	2,40,000	31,000
August	2,25,000	2,30,000	29,000
September	1,85,000	2,55,000	30,500

(b) 50% of credit sales are realised in the month following the sales and the remaining 50% in the second month following.

(c) Period of credit allowed by suppliers two months.

(d) Lag in payment of wages one month.

(e) Cash at bank on 1.7.2007 (estimated) Rs. 15,000.

(Ans:			
Surplus (or) Deficit	52,000	- 15,500	- 70,500
Estimated Overdraft	——	15,500	70,500
Closing Balance	52,000	——	——)

(9) From the particulars given below, prepare a cash budget for three months from June 2009:

(i) **Expected Sales**

April 2009 – Rs. 2,00,000;

May 2009 – Rs. 2,20,000;

June 2009 – Rs. 1,90,000;

50% of sales of every month is on cash basis. Credit allowed to customers – two months.

(ii) Estimated Purchases:

May 2009 – Rs. 1,20,000;

June 2009 – Rs. 1,10,000;

40% of the purchase of every month is on cash basis and the balance is payable next month.

(iii) Rs. 2,000 is payable as rent every month.

(iv) Time lag in payment of overhead is half month. Overhead for May – Rs. 12,000; for June – Rs. 11,000.

(v) Depreciation for the year is Rs. 12,000.

(vi) Interest receivable on investment during June and Dec. Rs. 3,000 each.

(vii) Tax payable during April 2009 – Rs. 10,000.

(viii) Estimated cash balance as on 1.6.09 is Rs. 42,500.

Ans : [Closing balance Rs. 1,11,000.]

(10) From the following information draw out cash budget for three months ending 31st May

(i) Cash balance on 1st March Rs. 1,00,000.

(ii) Actual and budgeted sales

Month	Rs.	
January	5,50,000	(Actual)
February	6,00,000	(Actual)
March	6,40,000	(Budgeted)
April	6,60,000	(Budgeted)
May	7,00,000	(Budgeted)

(iii) Purchases – Actual and budgeted figures are:

Month	Rs.	
January	4,50,000	(Actual)
February	4,30,000	(Actual)
March	4,60,000	(Budgeted)
April	4,80,000	(Budgeted)
May	4,50,000	(Budgeted)

(iv) Wages and expenses – Actual and budgeted:

Month	Wages (in Rs.)	Expenses (in Rs.)
January (Actual)	75,000	40,000
February (Actual)	90,000	40,000
March (Budgeted)	1,00,000	50,000
April (Budgeted)	1,20,000	50,000
May (Budgeted)	1,20,000	60,000

(v) Special Items:

(a) Payment of income tax in April Rs. 25,000

(b) Plant acquired and price paid in May Rs. 50,000

(vi) 25% purchases and sales are on cash basis.

(vii) Period of credit:

Credit Sales	: 1 month
Credit Purchases	: 2 months
Wages	: 1 month
Expenses	: half-month

(**Ans:** Closing balance Rs. 1,22,500 Rs. 1,50,000 Rs. 1,37,500.)

(11) Prepare a cash budget for the three months ending 30th June from the following information:

(a)

Month	Sales Rs.	Materials Rs.	Wages Rs.	Overheads Rs.
February	14,000	9,600	3,000	1,700
March	15,000	9,000	3,000	1,900
April	16,000	9,200	3,200	2,000
May	17,000	10,000	3,600	2,200
June	18,000	10,400	4,000	2,300

(b) Credit terms are:

Sales/Debtors – 10% sales are on cash, 50% of the credit sales are collected next month and the balance in the following month.

(c) Creditors: Materials, two months.

Wages, quartel month.

Overheads, half month.

(d) Cash and bank balance on 1st April expected to be Rs. 6,000.

(e) Other relevant information are:

(1) Plant and machinery will be installed in February at a cost of Rs. 96,000. the monthly instalments of Rs. 2,000 are payable from April onwards.

(2) Divided @ 5% on preference share capital of Rs. 2,00,000 will be paid on 2nd June.

(3) Advance to be received for sale for vehicles Rs. 9,000 in June.

(4) Dividends from investments amounting to Rs. 1,000 are expected to be received in June

(5) Income tax (advance) to be paid in June is Rs. 2,000.

(Ans: [Rs. 3,950 Rs. 3,000 Rs. 300.)]

(12) From the following forecasts of income and expenditure prepare a cash budget for the three months commencing 1st June, when the bank balance was Rs. 1,00,000:

Month	Sales Rs.	Purchases Rs.	Wages Rs.	Factory expenses Rs.	Admn. and selling expenses Rs.
April	80,000	41,000	5,600	3,900	10,000
May	76,500	40,500	5,400	4,200	14,000
June	78,500	38,500	5,400	5,100	15,000
July	90,000	37,000	4,800	5,100	17,000
August	95,000	35,000	4,700	6,000	13,000

A sales commission of 5% on sales, due two months after sales, is payable in addition to selling expenses. Plant valued at Rs. 65,000 will be purchased and paid for in August, and the dividend for the last financial year of Rs. 15,000 will be paid in July. There is a two months credit period allowed to customers and also received from suppliers. Wages and other expenses are payable in the following month.

(Ans: [Closing Balance Rs. 1,11,400 Rs. 1,03,075 Rs. 47,250.)]

(13) The expenses for the production of 5,000 units in a factory are given below:

Particulars	Per Unit Rs.
Materials	50
Labour	20
Variable expenses	15
Fixed overheads (Rs. 50,000)	10
Administrative expenses (5% variable)	10
Selling expenses (20% fixed)	6
Distribution expenses (10% fixed)	5
Total cost of sales	**116**

You are required to prepare a budget for the production of 7,000 units.

(Ans: Total cost of sales for 5,000 units Rs. 116, 5,80,000, for 7,000 units Rs.109.94, Rs.7,69,600)

(14) With the following data for 60% activity, prepare a budget for 50% activity.

Production at 60% activity — 600 units

Material Rs. 100 per unit, labour Rs. 40 per unit, direct expenses Rs. 10 per unit.

Factory expenses Rs. 40,000 (40% fixed)

Office expenses Rs. 30,000 (60% fixed)

(Ans: Total Cost For 500 units Rs. 278, Rs. 1,39,000, For 600 units Rs. 266.67 Rs. 1,60,000.)

(15) You are required to prepare a sales overhead budget from the estimates given below:

	Rs.
Advertisement	2,500
Salaries of the sales department	5,000
Expenses of sales department	1,500
Counter salesmen salaries and DA	6,000

Travelling salesmen commission at 10% on their sales and expenses at 5% on their sales. Commission to counter salesmen at 1% on their sales.

Sales during the period were estimated as follows:

Counter Sales	Travelling Salesmen
Rs.	**Rs.**
80,000	10,000
1,20,000	15,000
1,40,000	20,000

(**Ans:** January February March
17,300 18,450 19,400)

(16) From the following particulars of Ram Ltd., prepare a cash budget for the month December 2003

(i) Expected sales:

November 2003 Rs. 3,75,000; December Rs. 4,00,000

Credit allowed to customers is one month and 25% of the sales of every month is on cash basis.

(ii) Estimated purchases:

October 2003 Rs. 1,75,000; November Rs. 1,50,000; December Rs. 2,00,000 50% of the purchase of every month is on cash basis and credit allowed by creditors is two months.

(iii) Rs. 3,500 is payable as rent every month.

(iv) Lag in payment of overhead is half month.

Overhead: For November Rs. 20,000; for December Rs. 18,000

(v) Depreciation for the year is Rs. 10,000

(vi) Dividend receivable during June and December Rs. 5,000 each.

(vii) Tax payable during December 2003 Rs. 25,000

(viii) Estimated cash balance as on 1.12.2003 is Rs. 25,000

(**Ans:** 1,76,250)

17. From the following prepare a cash budget of LG Ltd., for six months commencing from 1st March, 2002 when the bank balance is estimated to be Rs. 1,50,000

Month	Sales	Wages	Purchases	Overheads			
				Selling	Factory	Office	Research and Development
	Rs.	Rs.	Rs.	Rs.	Rs.	Rs.	Rs.
January	1,00,000	4,000	40,000	5,000	6,000	2,000	3,000
February	1,02,000	4,000	42,000	5,200	6,200	2,200	3,200
March	1,05,000	4,000	44,000	5,500	6,300	2,100	3,000
April	1,00,000	5,000	45,000	5,500	6,400	2,300	3,200
May	1,05,000	5,000	44,000	6,000	6,500	2,500	3,400
June	1,10,000	5,000	46,000	6,200	6,500	2,600	3,400
July	1,12,000	6,000	48,000	6,400	6,400	2,600	3,500
August	1,15,000	6,000	48,000	6,500	6,500	2,500	3,500

Lag in payment of wages — half month

Lag in payment of all overheads — one month

Period of credit allowed by Creditors — two months

Period of credit allowed to Debtors — one month

Other information relevant to the preparation of cash budget is as follows:

(i) A sales commission of 5% on sales, and due one month after sales, is payable in addition to selling overheads.

(ii) Capital expenditure planned is:

(a) Furniture purchased in July 2002 for Rs. 50,000 payable on delivery; and

(b) Building purchased in June 2002 for Rs. 4,00,000 payable in four half-yearly instalments, the first being payable in June 2002.

(iii) Interest on investment amounting to Rs. 40,000 each is to be received in April and August 2002.

(iv) Cash sales are estimate at Rs. 10,000 per month.

(v) A dividend of Rs. 5,000 is to be paid in July 2002.

(vi) Tax amounting to Rs. 20,000 is to be paid on 1st May, 2002.

(vii) A call of Rs. 3 per share on equity share capital of Rs. 7,50,000 divided into 75,000 share of Rs. 10 each is to be received on 1st May, 2002.

(Ans: Closing Balance 61,100 1,37,450 3,71,050 3,02,400 2,83,700 3,59,200.)

(18) The following data are available in a manufacturing company for the year 2002

	Rs. lakhs
Fixed Expenses	
Wages and salaries	12.21
Rent, rates and taxes	7.53
Depreciation on machinery	5.48
Sundry office expenses	6.32
Semi-variable expenses(At 50% of Capacity):	
Repairs and maintenance	4.00
Indirect labour	8.40
Sales department salaries	4.20
Sundry administration expenses	3.20
Variable expenses (At 50% of capacity)	
Direct materials	24.00
Direct labour	22.00
Other variable expenses	9.00
Total	**106.34**

Assume that the fixed expenses remain constant for all levels of production; semi-variable expenses remain constant between 40 per cent and 65 per cent of capacity, increasing by 15 per cent between 65 per cent and 90 per cent capacity and by 20 per cent between 90 per cent and 100 per cent capacity.

Sales at various levels are:	Rs. lakh
50% Capacity	108.00
60% Capacity	129.60
70% Capacity	151.20
85% Capacity	183.60
100% Capacity	216.00

Prepare a flexible budget for the year 2009 and forecast the profit at 60 per cent, 70 per cent 85 per cent and 100 per cent capacity.

(Ans	50%	60%	70%	85%	100%
Total cost	106.34	117.34	131.31	147.81	165.30
Profit	1.66	12.26	19.89	35.79	50.70)

☆☆☆